Course Design for TESOL

A GUIDE TO INTEGRATING CURRICULUM AND TEACHING

Florin M. Mihai

University of Central Florida

and

Kerry Purmensky

University of Central Florida

Ann Arbor
University of Michigan Press

The pages marked as reproducible in the book may be reproduced for individual classroom use, but may not be distributed in any other way.

ISBN-13: 978-0-472-03554-0

2019   2018   2017   2016   4   3   2   1

Acknowledgments

Thank you to Arrow Studio for creating images for this book, including the beginning-level needs analysis form.

A very special thanks to:

> Hoyoung Lee, a former MA TESOL student at UCF, for sharing his insights on EFL in South Korea.
>
> Mafe Olivera, MA TESOL student, for creating the False Friends activity.
>
> Maria Spelleri, UCF MA TESOL graduate
>
> Rachel Wilkinson, UCF MA TESOL graduate
>
> Ting Yang, a PhD in TESOL student at UCF, for sharing her insights regarding English teaching in China.

We are also very grateful to Kelly Sippell at the University of Michigan Press for her support and guidance through this process.

Photos courtesy of Thinkstock.com.

Contents

Why This Book

Many textbooks on English language curriculum design tend to separate curriculum design components from teaching activities. As a result, textbooks either focus exclusively on the teaching of language skills without considering the specific teaching environment or they detail curriculum design but do not emphasize application of these principles in varied teaching situations. With this book, we propose a deliberate integration of the TESOL curriculum and teaching activities that allows L2 educators to utilize our textbook in a way that takes them from needs analysis to course design and application to teaching and assessment. This approach covers curricular and instructional elements that make a language course successful, including but not limited to theoretical knowledge, goal setting, syllabus writing, lesson planning, instructional techniques, activity creation, and inclusive assessment. It also offers a current perspective of knowledge that is needed to address the challenges and opportunities of the contemporary L2 classroom. Throughout the book, important terms and concepts appear in running text in boldface with definitions. Readers should note, however, that boldface is also used for design and display purposes.

Audience

This book has been designed to reach English language teachers at all levels, from beginning teachers who want to teach or are teaching overseas to practicing English language instructors who want to know more about TESOL course design and implementation in depth, to pre-service teachers pursuing a master's in TESOL. This book assumes readers have a basic knowledge of English grammar to understand grammar concepts such as parts of speech or tense. All theoretical or pedagogical concepts and principles presented in this book are accompanied by enough detail to make them comprehensible for students who have not yet taken Applied Linguistics or Second Language Acquisition classes. The book may also be used in Methods courses or combined Curriculum Design/Methods courses (Principles and Practices).

Principal Features/Structure

Following an introductory chapter presenting the framework of the book, Part 1 discusses the primary language acquisition theories and their influence on teaching practices.

Building on these theories and their influence on L2 teaching practices, Part II focuses on establishing a needs analysis plan, setting goals in the classroom, creating a syllabus, putting together a lesson plan, and choosing a textbook.

Part III focuses on teaching and assessing language skills, including listening, speaking, reading, writing, grammar, and culture. All skills are discussed in terms of important theories and concepts, followed by specific teaching and assessment activities for the L2 classroom.

The final section of the book discusses global trends in language course design. Covering programs from Europe to Asia, this section discusses the drive toward standards in North America and Europe, current teaching practices in Asia, and the influence of technology in contemporary L2 courses.

How to Use the Instructional Activities

Chapters 7–12 feature activities that reflect the theoretical perspectives presented. These activities are designed to be used by students in teacher preparation programs as a way to connect theory to teaching practice through role-playing or modeling during class time. The activities are directly linked to the theory and pedagogy of language teaching explored in each chapter and organized around sound curricular components: the rationale and objectives, pre-planning, methodology/procedures, evaluation, and follow-up practice. The activities are also included so that practicing teachers can use or adapt them for their own classrooms.

The activities follow a consistent pattern for ease of use. For each activity, readers will first find the **Objectives** listed, which is followed by: a **Pre-Planning** section, which details the student knowledge necessary to engage in the activity, the materials needed, and the level/age for which the activity is designed; the **Procedures** section, which explains exactly how to implement the activity in the classroom; and the **Evaluation** piece, which provides information to ensure effective evaluation of the activity and what the students have learned. The **Homework** piece of the Evaluation section offers ideas for student work outside the classroom.

For each activity used as a role-play in class, we recommend that pre-service teachers read the chapters and role play the activity. Then, they should discuss how the activity relates to the concepts in the chapters and how it can be adapted to other levels and age groups.

Summarizing Statements/Reflection and Application

Each chapter concludes with **Summarizing Statements** and **Reflection and Application** questions. The summarizing statements serve as a quick review of the larger themes and issues. The reflection questions are designed for the reader to reflect on what was presented in the chapter and apply it to real-life teaching situations. The reflection questions are often geared toward pairs and groups, so the class can share their experiences and pool their collective knowledge about the chapter and its application to the L2 classroom.

Our hope for this book is that we present teachers with not only a valuable course text but an effective pedagogical resource that can be used in current or future classroom situations. We hope that the material has immediate applicability for those who are currently teaching and offers inspiration for future teachers. We hope this books helps to answer the question, "What do I do on Monday in my class?" with practices that can be adapted to a variety of language teaching situations.

Chapter 1 ▲

An Introduction to the Integrated Nature of Teaching and Curriculum Design in TESOL

This first chapter provides an introduction to a **TESOL** (Teaching English to Speakers of Other Languages) course design model, which integrates teaching with curriculum design. This chapter begins by defining what the TESOL profession is, how someone becomes a TESOL professional, and who the second language learners we teach are. Then our focus turns to this textbook and how it pertains to programs of study for TESOL students and teachers. In addition, the text explains how to integrate teaching with language curriculum design. **Curriculum design,** a critical aspect of teaching at any level, involves planning and creating the purposes, objectives, content, and timeline of what students will learn over a period of time. Chapter 1 includes four scenarios related to TESOL curriculum and teaching to highlight the textbook chapters where information on curriculum design and teaching is located.

The TESOL Profession

TESOL is the general name of the field encompassing teaching English in various circumstances and environments. When English is taught to young adults and adults in a post-secondary setting, the discipline identifies this teaching environment as English as a Second Language (**ESL**) (even if the language is actually a third or fourth language). In the case of learners of all ages learning English as a Foreign Language in a foreign country, the acronym **EFL** applies. For young learners in the K–12 schools in the United States, the field has assigned the English to Speakers of Other Languages (**ESOL**) identifier and often refers to students as English language learners (**ELLs**) or English learners (**ELs**). In this textbook, we use the terms **L2 learner** and

language learner to refer to any student in an ESL/EFL/ESOL environment who is studying English, which is not their first, or native, language.

Graduate, undergraduate, and private TESOL programs across the world are housed in different departments and colleges. For example, at the University of Central Florida (UCF), the Master's of Arts in TESOL is located in the Department of Modern Languages and Literatures in the College of Arts and Humanities. Additionally, the College of Education and Human Performance has an ESOL program within the School of Teaching, Learning, and Leadership and employs faculty that primarily focus on ensuring that pre-service teachers are prepared to work with English learners in K–12 schools in the United States. As a result of the successful collaboration between the TESOL and the ESOL programs, UCF has started a TESOL track within the existing PhD in Education offered by the College of Education and Human Performance.

The TESOL profession encompasses many types of teaching around the world. Many TESOL programs prepare students for one of four general job markets:

1. teaching English to young English learners who are non-native English speakers in the public or private school systems
2. teaching English to non-native adult English learners in community colleges; adult education centers; English Language Institutes (**ELIs**), where students take English for Academic Purposes (**EAP**) courses focused on preparing learners for higher education classes; Intensive English Programs (**IEPs**) focused on developing critical language skills for different purposes, including college courses; or English for Specific Purposes (**ESP**) programs focused on very specific types of English including legal, medical, or business
3. teaching English in a country where English is not the native language used
4. teaching TESOL-specific courses such as Applied Linguistics, Curriculum Development, or Assessment

Some of the courses in these TESOL programs often include Grammar, Applied Linguistics, Assessment, Second Language Acquisition, Materials and Methodology, and Curriculum and Instructional Development. Our book is designed to be used in courses with a focus on integrating curriculum design with teaching activities. How does our language course design integrate the two? To better understand the benefits of using this book and the language course design it proposes, let's look at four possible scenarios that a TESOL professional may face.

Four Scenarios in TESOL

Scenario 1: EFL in Turkey

After graduating from the university with a master's degree in TESOL, Emily has moved to Turkey to take the position of EFL instructor in a university English language program. The English program is brand new so there is no formal curriculum in place. The director of the program has asked Emily to develop and design the English language curriculum for the entire program.

In this scenario, Emily has to create an entire language course curriculum. A language course curriculum is defined as all subject matter to be studied within that area. Curriculum design activities include needs analysis, goals and objectives, materials, teaching, and assessment (Brown, 1995). This book defines all of these concepts of design, discusses them in detail, and integrates concrete examples. To learn how to conduct a student-based needs analysis, Emily can read Chapter 5, which discusses how to conduct a needs analysis (a process of determining the goals and content of a course) (Macalister, 2012) for all levels of students. Chapter 5 provides Emily with a well-defined blueprint to conduct her student-based needs analysis. The chapter identifies three types of needs for language students, as well as provides needs analysis instruments for different proficiency levels. She can also turn to Chapter 12, which provides activities on culture, because she knows it will be critical for her to understand the place of the target language and culture on the Turkish culture before she designs activities and chooses material appropriate for her audience.

Scenario 2: ESL in the United States

José is teaching English at a language school affiliated with a state college in the United States. His institution has received a technology grant to upgrade the language lab. José has been asked to review and revise the language school's existing curriculum to ensure that technology will be utilized consistently throughout the curriculum.

One of his first steps will be to use the needs analysis format from Chapter 5 to determine what technologies teachers and students view as important to the educational process. The chapter presents different types of needs analysis formats and also advises how the analysis can be adapted for varying levels of English learners. The information presented can be used to determine the needs of a school, of teachers, and particularly of L2 learners. José can utilize Chapter 15, Technology-Transformed Language Learning, to assist him in choosing technology that is appropriate for his particular school. This chapter uses the SAMR (Substitution, Augmentation, Modification, Redefinition) Model to show how various types of technology can be adapted effectively into the language classroom. José can use some of the specific language activities listed in the chapter to help him determine what technologies would best meet the school needs as determined by his needs analysis survey.

Scenario 3: ESOL in the United States

Lindsey is a lead teacher for ESOL at her middle school, which is adapting new ESOL standards required by the state. Lindsey's responsibility is to create a new syllabus for the ESOL classes offered to English learners as well as to choose the accompanying textbook and supplementary materials. She also has to update every lesson plan to integrate the new standards.

In this scenario, Lindsey needs to design a new syllabus for all the ESOL classes her middle school offers to ESOL learners. This book helps Lindsey understand what a syllabus is and provides her with several options. Chapter 6 is dedicated entirely to syllabus design and gives examples for the different approaches. We define a syllabus as a document that describes the order and the selection and progression of what will be studied in the language classroom. Syllabi are also a reflection of language acquisition theories, which are the organizing principle and focus of syllabi and teaching activities. Chapter 13 also provides Lindsey with essential information that will make her syllabi effective. According to this chapter, one of the global trends in language teaching that is also reflected in the United States is communicative language teaching, defined as an approach that focuses on language that occurs while communicating in real-life situations. Therefore, her design choices may include syllabi associated with communicative language teaching: situational-topical, notional-functional, skills-based, or task-based approaches. Chapter 6 gives Lindsey definitions and examples of these syllabi, so that she can select the one that best addresses the needs of her students and is aligned to the new language standards.

Scenario 4: EFL in South Korea

At his South Korean university, Hoyoung has been asked to teach a Listening class for one of his colleagues who had to leave suddenly. He has never taught a Listening class before, and the class starts in two days. He not only has to prepare a lesson plan but also has to lead two teaching and assessment activities for that day.

The first thing Hoyoung needs to do is to prepare a lesson plan for that day. If Hoyoung is a teacher with a great deal of experience, he probably knows what a lesson plan looks like and what it should contain. For teachers with little or no experience regarding lesson plan creation, they can use the information presented in Chapter 6, which offers an opportunity to learn about the components of a lesson plan. The same chapter also provides an actual example of a lesson plan.

In addition to creating a lesson plan, Hoyoung has to have two teaching and assessment activities for a class he has never taught before. Chapter 7 provides Hoyoung with a framework for creating two listening activities where teaching and assessment components are embedded. The chapter also provides Hoyoung with concrete examples of activities based on that framework so he could either adopt or adapt those existing activities for his class.

Now, let's compare a typical language course design sequence with the approach used in this book.

Integrating Teaching with Curriculum Design

TESOL professionals often find themselves at the forefront of language curriculum design for their own classrooms, which can include selecting textbooks, writing lesson plans, setting objectives, and creating assessments. Many curriculum design projects or language teaching course books have followed a four-step process of design for language curriculum (Nation & Macalister, 2010). Taking into account learners' aims for studying English, the first step of the process is represented by identifying the goals and objectives for each lesson in the course. Next, language curriculum designers decide on the content as well as the sequence of the language content to be covered in the course. The next step involves format and presentation and covers instructional activities, materials, and lesson plans. The final step is assessment, where assessment instruments for goals and objectives are designed and implemented. This cascading process of language book course design is illustrated in Figure 1.1.

This book takes a different approach to English language course design by putting teaching at the forefront and integrating it more with curriculum design. We believe this approach is more effective for TESOL professionals because it includes teaching strategies at the early stages of

Figure 1.1:   A Cascading Model of Curriculum Design

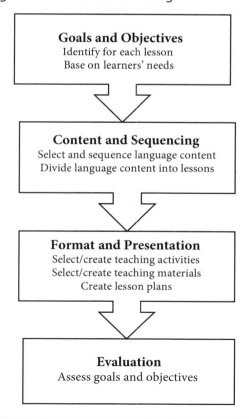

Figure 1.2:   An Integrated Model of Language Course Design

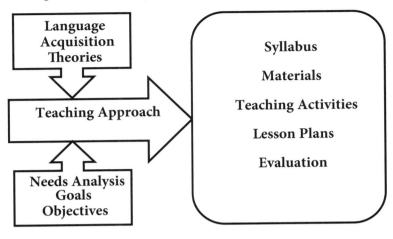

curriculum planning, thus making the end product more effective. In this approach, instructors and curriculum designers start with language acquisition theories to provide an essential understanding regarding how languages are learned. Language teaching is based on language acquisition theory so instructors and curriculum designers need to know it to select the best teaching approach that addresses the needs of their learners, which can be determined by a needs analysis, a process of determining the goals and content of a course. The information gathered through needs analysis is filtered through language acquisition theories. For the direction in language course design proposed in this textbook, the teaching approach based on goals and objectives stemming from learners' needs and on language acquisition theory is central. It determines the goals and syllabus design of the language course as well as the selection and creation of teaching and assessment materials and activities. This integrated approach is shown in Figure 1.2.

Organization of This Textbook

This textbook deliberately promotes the understanding of the interconnectedness of language, curriculum, and instruction (Wette, 2009) in the L2 classroom. Part I, Chapters 2–4, begins by concentrating on second language acquisition theories and pedagogy. The second chapter emphasizes behaviorism and the audiolingual method (ALM), the third chapter addresses input theory and communicative language teaching, and the fourth chapter discusses sociocultural theory and task-based learning. These three theories are not the only second language acquisition theories in the field, but they are the ones with the most prevalent influence in language teaching (Lightbown & Spada, 2013). These chapters will help you understand the language-related foundation of the TESOL curriculum and instructional design resources presented in Parts II and III of the book.

In Part II, Chapter 5 defines a needs analysis for the English language classroom, explains the importance of this instrument in curriculum design, and shares various examples of needs analysis documents that you can adapt to your own language classroom. Special attention is paid to setting goals and objectives. Chapter 6 offers examples of various approaches to syllabus design, another critical component in the language curriculum development, as well as a template for lesson plans. The ability to design an effective syllabus and lesson plans for various levels and ages of learners is a vital skill that every TESOL professional needs, as this provides the framework for how to conduct and deliver content in the classroom. Chapter 6 will help readers understand the most effective approaches to syllabus and lesson plan design based on sound pedagogical theory.

The teaching of language skills presented in Part III, Chapters 7–12, is based on the research and theory in language acquisition presented in Part I. This theoretical groundwork provides the background for presenting sound pedagogical suggestions to teaching listening, speaking, reading, writing, grammar, and culture in the ESL/EFL classroom. Each of these chapters defines the targeted language skill, discusses varying approaches to teaching the language skill, shares model activities based on sound theory and pedagogy, and presents important information on assessment techniques. The connections among language acquisition theory, curriculum, teaching, and assessment will be evident throughout the chapters. The goal is for readers to understand the essential language skills for L2 learners and have some tools and strategies so that they feel more comfortable teaching those skills for various ages and language levels.

Part IV, Chapters 13–15, takes a global approach to discussing the TESOL profession. Chapter 13 provides a comprehensive look at TESOL from around the world, including a discussion of two curricular instruments utilized in Europe and the United States: the Common European Framework of Reference for Languages (CEFR) and the TESOL PreK–12 English Language Proficiency Standards. Chapter 14 continues this global focus by presenting the history and current state of EFL in two countries with extensive TEFL programs, China and South Korea. Chapter 15 details how technology has transformed the teaching of ESL and EFL in the modern classroom. While these three chapters have very distinct emphases, the overarching goal is to help readers see the global nature of TESOL and how technology has impacted all forms of education.

Summarizing Statements

1. The field of **TESOL** encompasses various teaching environments, such as teaching English abroad (**EFL**), teaching English to adult learners in countries where English is the primary language (**ESL**), or teaching English in K–12 (**ESOL**).

2. Typical TESOL preparation programs include courses in Grammar, Applied Linguistics, Second Language Acquisition, Materials and Methodology, Assessment, and Curriculum and Instructional Development.

3. For Curriculum and Instructional Development courses, we recommend the use of the integrative approach exemplified in this book with teaching at the forefront, instead of a cascading model that considers teaching later in the process.

REFLECTION AND APPLICATION

1. Review the four different job markets listed for TESOL professionals. Does one of the markets describe your current job or one you hope to obtain? Describe your current job or the job you would like to have after studying TESOL. What qualifications do you need for the job that you want?

2. Review Figure 1.2 (see page 6). How important are each of these components in English language curriculum design? Share your own experiences with each of these topics as either a teacher or a student in the classroom. Is any one of them more important than the other?

3. Re-read the four scenarios used to exemplify activities a TESOL professional may engage in while working in this field. Write about what you hope to learn about the profession after reading this book. Share your ideas on how you can gain confidence in teaching through knowledge and practice with your peers in the course.

REFERENCES

Brown, J. D. (1995). *The elements of language curriculum: A systematic approach to program development.* Boston: Heinle & Heinle.

Lightbown, P. M., & Spada, N. (2013). *How languages are learned* (4th ed.). Oxford, U.K.: Oxford University Press.

Macalister, J. (2012). Narrative frames and needs analysis. *System, 40*(1), 120–128.

Nation, I. S. P., & Macalister, J. (2010). *Language curriculum design.* New York: Routledge.

Wette, R. (2009). Making the instructional curriculum as an interactive, contextualized process: Case studies of seven ESOL teachers. *Language Teaching Research, 13*(4), 337–365.

PART I ————————————————————————

Language Acquisition Theories and Their Influence on Teaching Practices

To understand the teaching of a second language, we first need to have some understanding of the primary second language acquisition (SLA) theories that influence teaching in the 21st century. Toward this end, Chapters 2–4 focus on three important theories and how they may be reflected in ESL/EFL classrooms. The theories covered are behaviorism and its influence on the audiolingual method (Chapter 2), input theory and the communicative language teaching movement (Chapter 3), and sociocultural theory and its role in task-based learning (Chapter 4).

Chapter 2
▲

Behaviorism and the Audiolingual Method

This chapter addresses the basic principles of **behaviorism** and explores its impact on teaching a second or foreign language through the audiolingual method (ALM).

Behaviorism in Language Acquisition

The behaviorists were early 19th century psychological theorists who believed that learning occurs when behaviors are taught through a process of conditioning. Ivan Pavlov was a Russian scientist whose work training dogs to react to a bell signal when rewarded with food is credited with this theoretical shift in the field of psychology (Pavlov & Gantt, 1928). Rather than a focus on the unconscious mind, as most psychologists did at that time, scientists such as Pavlov, John B. Watson, and Burrhus Frederic Skinner focused on conditioned and observable behaviors (Skinner, 1938; Watson & Raynor, 1920). Behaviorism is considered an environment-based learning theory because people must interact with their environment in some manner in order for learning to take place. According to the behaviorists, learning occurs through a process of conditioning whereby behaviors are either rewarded, and therefore promoted and repeated, or punished, and therefore avoided. From a **second language acquisition (SLA)** perspective, behaviorists believe that language development can be encouraged or discouraged in a systematic and observable manner with no consideration of internal processes, such as those occurring in the brain, which are unobservable.

Because the behaviorists view language as a systematic process of developed habits, learning takes place through positive and negative reinforcements, through stimulus and response. When a behavior is positively reinforced, that behavior increases and becomes a habit over time. If a behavior is negatively reinforced, that behavior is discouraged and discarded through this process. Behaviorists believe that L2 students learn through a process of imitating language to which they have been exposed, and that if they are rewarded for that behavior, they will repeat it and learn a language over time. This perspective found its way into the language learning classroom through the grammar translation approach and the audiolingual method, both of which are still seen in various forms in the language classroom today. We will begin by discussing grammar translation approach in the language classroom, followed by ALM, giving examples of how these methodologies are represented in the current language classroom.

Grammar Translation

Because students focus on learning grammar rules in English and translating them to their native language, the development of reading and writing skills was considered to be of utmost importance. The underlying reason for this emphasis was likely that grammar translation was employed in the teaching of Latin and classical Greek centuries ago, and these two languages no longer have an oral component.

Typically **grammar translation** relies heavily on grammar knowledge of the target language as well as the ability to accurately translate texts from and into the target language. The native language of the L2 learner is used extensively and is not seen as a barrier, but as a facilitator, of development of the target language. An example of a grammar translation activity for a Czech student who is learning English as a beginner in the current language classroom might look something like this:

První osoba jednotného čísla slovesa *to be* je v angličtině *am*. Přeložte tyto české věty do angličtiny se slovesem *to be* v první osobě jednotného čisla: (The first-person singular of the verb *to be* in English is always *am*. Translate these Czech sentences into English using first person.)	
Ja jsem vysoký.	*(I am tall.)*
Ja jsem nízký.	*(I am short.)*
Ja jsem rychlý.	*(I am fast.)*
Ja jsem pomalý.	*(I am slow.)*

Because behaviorist theorists felt that language was developed through a process of memorization of specific vocabulary, grammar, and texts, the focus of grammar translation is usually on reading. Language instructors who teach using this methodology use the language itself, not ways the language works, so rules are learned through a process of deduction based on the material at hand. L2 learners spend their time on focused drills, with language development being a crucial component. **Language drills**, which are focused on correct habit formation, are classroom activities in which language learners repeat set phrases in the target language over and over, with the intent of leading to mastery of the language. Because learners are expected to be able to translate from their first language into the target language, there is an expectation that they attain native fluency in the language based on memorization of specific language texts. Another type of exercise that L2 learners using grammar translation might complete is called **Vanishing Dialogues,** where they are presented with whole dialogues to memorize, utilizing both their native and target languages. Words or phrases are slowly removed until the learners re-create those dialogues by heart. Here is an example of a Vanishing Dialogue for a native German speaker who is a beginning learner of English. The goal is for language learners to practice this dialogue repeatedly until they have memorized the phrases and can use them spontaneously.

Teacher:	**Write this dialogue on the board and ask students to read it individually. Then ask students to divide into pairs and role play the two parts. Gradually erase words, choosing one word randomly from each line of the dialogue at a time, so that students continue practicing, each time needing to remember more of the Vanishing Dialogue until they have memorized the entire dialogue.**
Student 1:	Good morning, Frederick.
Student 2:	Good morning Claus.
Student 1:	How was the meeting last night?
Student 2:	It went very well. We started at 6 PM and finished at 9 PM.
Student 1:	When is the next meeting?
Student 2:	We will meet again on September 12.

These are just two examples of grammar translation drills and dialogues that have been developed under the influence of behaviorism. Although the traditional forms of these language activities are not seen in the classrooms today, drills and dialogues have been adapted, updated, and are widely utilized in current language acquisition activities.

The Audiolingual Method

In contrast to the more traditional method of grammar translation with its focus on reading and translation skills, the **audiolingual method (ALM)** approach to language learning is focused on developing oral language skills. ALM adopted some aspects of behaviorism, such as a focus on habit formation, but it also featured a more focused approach on form and production (Castagnaro, 2006). ALM provides a sequential, structured approach for oral language skill development, and ALM-focused activities include oral drills that consist of potential dialogues for L2 learners to practice in pairs or groups. For lower level–proficiency language learners, dialogues are used to help them memorize patterns of language, enhance pronunciation, and accurately respond to prompts. Tone, stress, and pronunciation are all emphasized. At more advanced levels, learners are expected to respond rapidly, adapt to changing language patterns, and demonstrate great proficiency in oral production, including the ability to accurately respond to oral prompts.

In ALM, the teacher's role is to be a language modeler and drill leader. The teacher is expected to provide rich examples of language so learners can accurately imitate what they have heard. The L2 learners must then practice this model language repeatedly until it becomes a habit to use the language, which reflects the behaviorist point of view for optimal language development. Ideally, the language learner develops a robust habit in using the language so that there is ultimately no delay in speaking or responding in the target language.

Contemporary research has pinpointed some of the drawbacks of ALM, which is why traditional ALM drills are rarely found in the current language classroom. When language learners find themselves participating in real conversations that don't match the patterns they have learned in class, a complex and difficult situation is created. Without specific preparation for the interaction, they are obliged to draw on whatever general linguistic resources are at their disposal—words, rules, and some formulaic patterns learned for similar but not identical contexts—and they have to hope this will work for them. At times, it might work, but in other cases, there may be a communication breakdown. They also have to be able to navigate the type of interaction that may not be familiar to them within the cultural norms of the exchange (Fitzpatrick & Wray, 2006). Spontaneity of language and cultural understanding are problematic in a strictly ALM approach.

Another defining characteristic of ALM is the importance assigned to the spoken form. For audiolingualists, the listening and speaking skills are the foundation for the development of all other language skills. In the early stages, the focus is on oral skills and proficiency, which is seen as accurate pronunciation, as well as the ability to respond quickly and accurately to various situations in which the speaking skills are paramount. When reading and writing skills are taught, they rely heavily on previously developed oral skills. For example, in a lesson based on ALM, language learners will be introduced to new vocabulary using oral drills or dialogues. After they show proficiency with pronunciation and understanding, learners will then interact with the new language through further readings and writing assignments.

Because ALM emphasizes the idea of creating good language habits, audiolingualists have repeatedly attempted to identify the source of target language errors that might prevent the creation of error-free language production. A result of their endeavor, **contrastive analysis** attempts to identify differences between the first language and the target language, particularly those which might cause error in target language production. One of the most preeminent audiolingualists, Robert Lado (1957), told us that "we can predict and describe the patterns that will cause difficulty in learning, and those that will not cause difficultly, by comparing systematically the language and the culture to be learned with the native language and culture of the student" (p. vii). A practical result of this theoretical analysis was reflected in the content of ALM materials, which were routinely organized around differences and similarities between the L1 and the target language.

In the teaching activities employed in audiolingual environments, dialogues and drills occupied an important segment of classroom practice. Dialogues were repeated and memorized, and a very strong emphasis is placed on ensuring that language learners generate the correct pronunciation, stress, and intonation. After the dialogues have been repeated and memorized, specific grammatical aspects are selected to become the focus of various drills and pattern-practice exercises. A few examples of various types of drills are shown in Table 2.1.

Because of the importance assigned to listening and speaking, audio recordings have a central role in the audiolingual classroom. Language labs commonly provided learners with additional drill work. The procedures that are to be found in a typical audiolingual lesson are outlined in Table 2.2.

Table 2.1:   Types of ALM Drills

Type	Example
Repetition	*Teacher*: Today is Monday. *Student*: Today is Monday.
Substitution	*Teacher*: John is a good student. *Student*: He is a good student.
Restatement	*Teacher*: Tell her to give you her pen. *Student*: Give me your pen.
Completion	*Teacher*: John is a boy and Mary is ___ _____. *Student*: John is a boy and Mary is a girl.
Transformation	*Teacher*: He likes football. *Student*: He doesn't like football. Does he like football?
Contraction	*Teacher*: Write your name on the board. *Student*: Write your name there.

Table 2.2:   A Typical Instructional Sequence in an ALM Class

Step	Description
Dialogue memorization	Students listen and then repeat a dialogue containing the structures that are the focus of the lesson. When errors occur, they are corrected immediately and directly. The dialogue is then memorized by the students.
Drill practice	Drills based on the structures introduced in the dialogue are practiced in chorus and then individually. There may be some grammar explanations, but they are not extensive.
Additional reading/writing/ vocabulary activities	Additional reading, writing, and vocabulary activities based on the practiced dialogue and drills may be introduced. If a language laboratory is available, students may complete additional drill and dialogue exercises.

ALM and Error Correction

What happens when a L2 learner makes mistakes in oral production? Typically, the language teacher would provide **error correction**—correct the mistake and prompt the learner to repeat the phrase or sentence correctly (Lyster & Ranta, 1997). However, this strategy of providing corrective feedback is not the only strategy available. Other strategies directly address errors following the principles of behaviorism and emphasizing the creation of accurate language production. Table 2.3 defines and presents six possible error correction strategies that are available to language teachers. These error correction strategies are focused on promoting accuracy and fluency in language (discussed in more detail in Chapter 8) by giving L2 learners prompt feedback and allowing learners time to correct themselves.

Table 2.3: Error Correction Strategies

Type	Definition	Example
Explicit correction	The teacher provides the correct form to indicate that the student's utterance was incorrect.	*Student*: He goed to Orlando yesterday. *Teacher*: No, you say, he **went** to Orlando yesterday.
Recast	The teacher implicitly restates the student's utterance without indicating that the student's utterance was incorrect.	*Student*: He goed to Orlando yesterday. *Teacher*: So he went to Orlando yesterday.
Clarification requests	The teacher uses phrases such as *Excuse me* or *Sorry* to indicate that the student's utterance contained an error.	*Student*: He goed to Orlando yesterday. *Teacher*: Excuse me?
Metalinguistic hints	The teacher asks questions or provides comments or information related to the student's utterance.	*Student*: He goed to Orlando yesterday. *Teacher*: Now think about the verb here. What tense are you trying to use? Is this a regular or irregular verb?
Elicitation	The teacher directly elicits the correct form from the student by asking questions (*How do we say that in English?*), by pausing to allow the student to complete the teacher's utterance (*It's a....*) or by asking students to reformulate the utterance (*Say that again*).	*Student*: He goed to Orlando yesterday. *Teacher*: Say that again please.
Repetition	The teacher repeats the student's error and adjusts intonation to draw the student's attention to it.	*Student*: He goed to Orlando yesterday. *Teacher*: Goed?

While pure ALM principles are not widely utilized in the contemporary language classroom, many types of activities reflect the pedagogy of ALM to a certain extent. Oral language skill development is considered a principal component of many language teaching methodologies such as communicative language teaching (see Chapter 3). Current teaching practices incorporate characteristics of ALM drills.

This chapter detailed the principles of behaviorism and how those principles reflected in the pedagogy of ALM and grammar translation. Future and current L2 instructors do not need to discard methodologies related to ALM and grammar translation altogether simply because they were developed decades ago. Some of their guiding principles can be incorporated in the language classroom of today, especially in foreign language settings.

Summarizing Statements

1. L2 instructors should have a basic understanding of some of the language acquisition theories that influence current teaching practices. Certain principles of behaviorism have inspired language learning practices, including ALM and grammar translation.

2. ALM and grammar translation activities continue to be used, although drills now take into account modern ideas on communication in language.

3. L2 instructors should adapt elements of ALM, such as grammar drills and pronunciation exercises, when necessary.

4. Different error correction strategies can be utilized to facilitate language accuracy and fluency in oral skills.

REFLECTION AND APPLICATION

1. Table 2.1 shows six different types of ALM drills. Choose three, write a brief definition of each of them, and then create a drill that represents that particular style. Be sure to include information about the age and level of the student and the type of class in which this drill would work. Share it with other students and reflect with the class on the place of drills in the modern English language classroom.

2. Re-read this quote from the chapter: "Spontaneity of language and cultural understanding are problematic in a strictly ALM approach." In pairs or small groups, discuss this statement and its possible implications for the language classroom. Pool your knowledge of language learning, either as a teacher or a student, and talk about how spontaneous language or cultural understanding was utilized in your classroom.

3. How to provide effective oral error correction in the ESL/EFL classroom is a question that every teacher must address. Review the types of error correction listed in Table 2.3. For each scenario presented, write which type of error correction, if any, you would use. Compare and share your thoughts with a small group or the class.

   a. A student answers a question about a reading in class. The answer is correct, but the student makes a language error in phrasing the answer, such as, *The main character name is Sally*.

   b. A student asks you a question about the homework for tomorrow in front of the class. She makes a pronunciation error in her question.

   c. You ask the class to provide an answer to this question: "What is the first-person singular form of the *be* verb?" One student answers *is*.

   d. You ask students what they do for fun. One student answers, *I like to running every day*.

REFERENCES

Castagnaro, P. J. (2006). Audiolingual method and behaviorism: From misunderstanding to myth. *Applied Linguistics*, *27*(3), 519–526.

Fitzpatrick, T., & Wray, A. (2006). Breaking up is not so hard to do: Individual differences in L2 memorization. *Canadian Modern Language Review*, *63*(1), 35–57.

Lado, R. (1957). *Linguistics across cultures: Applied linguistics for language teachers*. Ann Arbor: University of Michigan Press.

Lyster, R., & Ranta, L. (1997). Corrective feedback and learner uptake. *Studies in Second Language Acquisition*, *19*(1), 37–66.

Pavlov, I. P., & Gantt, W. H. (1928). *Lectures on conditioned reflexes*. New York: Liveright.

Skinner, B. F. (1938). *The behavior of organisms: An experimental analysis*. New York: Appleton-Century-Crofts. (1960 reprint.)

Watson, J. B., & Rayner, R. (1920). Conditioned emotional reactions. *Journal of Experimental Psychology*, *3*(1), 1–14.

Chapter 3
▲

Input Theories and
Communicative Language Teaching

This chapter discusses an approach that gives center stage to communication and fluency. The tension between accuracy and fluency is perhaps one of the most important topics of discussion in the field of L2 language teaching. Can we find balance between accuracy and fluency, or are they mutually exclusive? To answer this very important question, readers must be familiar with the theory and practice of both. After touching on how Noam Chomsky influenced beliefs about the innate nature of language, this chapter will detail Stephen Krashen's theories of SLA and the interactionists' theories of modified interaction. In addition, special attention will be paid to communicative language teaching, which is based on the theoretical principles of Krashen and the interactionists.

Input Theories

Input theories stand in contrast to behaviorism's focus on forms and output. The term *input theories* is really a catch-all term to refer to the hypotheses that focus on level-specific instruction and emphasize meaningful input in the classroom. By *input,* we mean any reading or listening materials, or teacher- and L2 learner–generated communication.

Krashen's Theory of Second Language Acquisition

Noam Chomsky (see www.chomsky.info for more information), a professor of Linguistics at the Massachusetts Institute of Technology, has had a tremendous influence in the field of language acquisition. Because he believed that all people are born with the ability to learn a language, he proposed the **universal grammar** theory, which suggests the existence of a set of basic grammatical elements that are common to all natural human languages (Chomsky, 1965). According to this theory, everyone is born with the grammar principles of all languages, but each brain will select the principles it needs based on the language each person hears. As a result of this universal grammar, Chomsky believes that there is no need to teach grammar explicitly because we are already born with it.

From an L2 perspective, this theory is quite controversial because of the de-emphasis on grammar instruction, an important part of behaviorism, the grammar translation approach, and the audiolingual method. Although Chomsky did not directly address second language acquisition, his theory has had a profound influence on SLA researchers; one researcher is Stephen Krashen, whose theory says that the processes for acquiring a first and a second language are similar. In Krashen's model, grammar is no longer at center stage. Rather, meaningful language communication necessary to activate existing grammar principles is paramount. **Krashen's** theory (1987) consists of **five hypotheses** as part of a comprehensive explanation of the SLA process: the Acquisition-Learning Hypothesis, the Natural Order Hypothesis, the Monitor Hypothesis, the Input Hypothesis, and the Affective Filter Hypothesis.

The **Acquisition-Learning Hypothesis** explains what Krashen believed are two independent systems for developing knowledge of a second language: (1) the **acquired system,** which is subconscious and does not really address grammar rules and (2) the **learning system,** which is concerned with the grammar rules and being aware of them. Each system has different functions: The acquired system is used to produce language, and the learning system acts as an evaluator of the acquired system to make sure that what the acquired system is producing is correct.

The **Natural Order Hypothesis** supports the idea that the rules of language are acquired in a predictable order. For example, in English, learners acquire the progressive *–ing (I'm waiting)*, plural *–s (books)*, and active voice *(I washed my car yesterday)* before they acquire the third person *–s (She takes the bus to work)* or passive voice *(The car was washed by me yesterday)*. The order is the same regardless of whether the language is learned through instruction or not. The natural order is part of the acquired system, which is not influenced by the learned system (Krashen, 1987). This is an important departure from a grammar approach that followed an "easy to difficult structure" curriculum sequence. Present tense simple is introduced early because it is easier to explain to students, as they only need to add an *–s* to the third person, the rest of verb conjugations remaining unchanged. Because of the Natural Order Hypothesis, curriculum designers and classroom teachers have taken a different approach when it comes to introducing grammar structures. Their decisions are now based on research detailing a sequence of acquisition for grammatical structures, instead of the perceived level of difficulty of that structure from a form or usage perspective.

The **Monitor Hypothesis** is based on formal learning. The learned system is responsible for monitoring language output when certain conditions make it possible. To use the Monitor Hypothesis, L2 learners need time to consciously think about and utilize the appropriate rule, and they should know the rule they want to apply. Additionally, L2 learners should be able to pay attention to what is being said and should focus on form. Therefore, the Monitor Hypothesis, a result of formal learning, cannot be employed by L2 learners in all situations, with probable consequences on accuracy when focus on form is not possible. An important pedagogical consequence of this hypothesis is reflected in communicative language teaching (CLT), which will be discussed later in the chapter. CLT recognizes that the formal learning of grammatical rules is not very productive as students cannot employ the Monitor Hypothesis in all situations. Consequently, fluency in meaningful interactions is promoted instead of decontextualized study of grammar. As a result, teachers teach for communicative proficiency, not just mastery of structures.

In the **Input Hypothesis,** Krashen (1987) theorized that learners need comprehensible input in order to move through the natural order of acquisition. Learners acquire a second language by receiving **comprehensible input,** described as a message that contains structures and vocabulary unknown to the L2 learner that can be made comprehensible through the additional support of non-verbal input. As the learner's L2 proficiency increases, less non-verbal input is needed. To advance L2 learner's current language proficiency, the target language used by the teachers has to include structures and vocabulary at one level higher than what the learner has already acquired. Let's suppose that an L2 learner knows all the words in this sentence: *Put the book on your desk.* A teacher could change the sentence to *Put the book on the floor* to add new vocabulary. By changing the known sentence, the teacher provides new material *(on the floor)* that builds off of the learner's prior knowledge. Thus, acquisition for learners with language knowledge "i" can only take place if they are exposed to comprehensible input at a slightly higher level, which Krashen describes as level **i + 1**. In the example, "i" represented by *Put the book on your desk* is the current acquired linguistic competence. Then L2 learners' progress from "i" to i+1 by comprehending input that contains i+1, as in *Put the book on the floor.* The +1 *(on the floor)* is symbolic of the new language structures and knowledge that the learners are ready to acquire.

The **Affective Filter Hypothesis** explains differences in individual learners that can be a potential barrier to SLA, particularly negative factors such as self-doubt, anxiety, or boredom. The theory states that obstacles to learning a second language can be reduced by providing a low-anxiety environment, sparking the learner's interest, and boosting self-esteem. In summary, learners should receive comprehensible input and need to have a low affective filter for acquisition to take place (Krashen & Terrell, 1983). Table 3.1 summarizes Krashen's hypotheses.

In summary, these five hypotheses work together to explain how to facilitate second language acquisition. The process starts with the Input Hypothesis, which provides the information that the learner needs in order to acquire the language. As the input becomes comprehensible to the learner, it makes its way into the developing system, which is the acquisition part of Krashen's hypothesis. The rules that L2 learners are taught about the language, called **metalinguistic knowledge,** constitute the Acquisition-Learning Hypothesis. In addition, the metalinguistic knowledge gained through formal learning becomes the Monitor, which corrects language that the learner produces. Differences that may exist between language learners can be explained through the Affective Filter Hypothesis. For input to be understood by the learner, the Affective Filter must be low. All of these hypotheses in concert provide a framework for promoting the second language acquisition of the learner, according to Krashen (1987).

Table 3.1:   Krashen's Theories of Second Language Acquisition

Hypothesis	Description
Acquisition-Learning	Acquisition is the product of subconscious processes similar to L1 acquisition, whereas learning is the process of conscious instruction resulting in metalinguistic knowledge about L2.
Natural Order	The rules of language are acquired in a predictable order.
Monitor	The monitor or "internal editor" is the product of conscious learning and is utilized when L2 learners know the grammatical rule, focus on form, and have time to do so.
Input	Comprehensible input (i+1), an essential condition for L2 acquisition, is input that is one level above the actual language abilities of L2 learners.
Affective Filter	Affective factors influence L2 acquisition positively (the Affective Filter is down) or negatively (the Affective Filter is up).

Interactionism

Like Krashen (1987), interactionists, of whom the most prominent has been Michael Long, also believe in the importance of comprehensive input. They believe that because unchanged input is not enough, it is necessary to modify interaction to make language comprehensible. According to Long (1983, 1996), **modified interaction** includes but is not limited to linguistic simplification. It may also include conversational modifications such as comprehension checks (efforts made by native speakers to make sure that an L2 learner understands the meaning of their utterances), clarification requests (efforts made by the L2 learner asking the native speaker to clarify an aspect of the conversation that has not been understood), and self-repetition or paraphrasing (efforts made by the native speaker to repeat or paraphrase aspects of the conversation either partially or entirely).

Interactionists are interested in the ways that speakers engaged in conversations negotiate meaning. Negotiation of meaning leads to modified interaction, which consists of various modifications (i.e., linguistic simplification). Long (1983) states that negotiation for meaning that triggers interactional modifications between the native speaker and the L2 speaker facilitates acquisition because it connects **input,** such as internal learner capacities (particularly selective attention), and **output** in productive ways. In other words, interactional modifications make input comprehensible, and comprehensible input promotes second language acquisition.

In addition to the modification of speech to ensure comprehension, native English speakers often engage in **foreigner talk.** Ferguson (1971), another interactionist, defines foreigner talk as a speech variety used by a native speaker when he or she communicates with a non-native speaker (NNS) in an attempt to simplify and improve communication. Table 3.2 illustrates some

Table 3.2: Native Speaker Strategies to Help Non-Native Speakers Understand

Feature	Description
Slower rate of delivery	Native speakers use clear and slower speech, where each word is enunciated in a more deliberate manner. Native speakers pause more frequently.
Basic and stylistically neutral vocabulary	Native speakers use high-frequency words and avoid idioms, colloquialisms, and slang expressions.
Short and simple sentences	Native speakers avoid compound sentences and use active verbs instead of passive verbs.
Repetition and restatement	Native speakers repeat and rephrase, especially when they contain difficult lexical terms.
Checking comprehension and asking for confirmation	Native speakers ask non-native speakers to convey to native speakers their understanding of what has been discussed.
Non-verbal tools	Native speakers use gestures, visuals, and simulations to describe events.

of the main strategies used by native speakers when they engage in foreigner talk with the purpose of facilitating the comprehension of non-native speakers (Wooldridge, 2001).

A reflection of the theoretical concept proposed by Krashen and Long is called **communicative language teaching (CLT)** and its pedagogy is significantly different from the structural approaches in that grammar is not the driving force of the curriculum. Instead, in CLT, L2 learners acquire the target language through meaningful communication.

The Principal Emphases of Communicative Language Teaching

CLT focuses on language that occurs while communicating in real-life situations. Unlike the ALM, which relies on repetition and drills and little or no context, CLT allows L2 learners to be creative with the language. As a result, the outcome of classroom activities will vary according to L2 learners' reactions and responses. L2 learners are motivated to learn because communicative activities encourage them to communicate in meaningful ways and on meaningful topics and contexts. According to Berns (1984), "Language is interaction; it is an interpersonal activity and has a clear relationship with society. In this light, language study has to look at the use (function) of language in context, both its linguistic context (what is uttered before and after a given piece of discourse) and its social, or situational, context (who is speaking, what their social roles are, why they have come together to speak)" (p. 5).

Central to an understanding of CLT is an understanding of the term **communicative competence.** It includes three components: grammatical competence, sociolinguistic competence, and strategic competence (Canale & Swain, 1980). **Grammatical competence** refers to the knowledge of grammatical rules, as well as vocabulary, phonetics, and phonology. **Sociolinguistic competence** includes knowledge of whether a particular language phrase or utterance is used appropriately in accordance with the social context. **Strategic competence** includes the strategies L2 learners utilize in difficult grammatical or sociolinguistic situations. To emphasize the idea that language is communication in a variety of contexts, Canale (1983) added a fourth competence called **discourse competence**, which focuses on understanding how ideas are connected. Discourse competence includes **coherence** (the logical connections perceived in a written or oral text) and **cohesion** (the use of repetition, transitional expressions, pronouns, etc., to guide and show how the parts of a written or oral text relate to one other). All four competencies are needed to communicate effectively in English.

Communicative competence has come to be used in language teaching contexts to refer to the ability to be language proficient, which is to successfully combine linguistic, sociolinguistic, and discourse rules in communicative interactions (Savignon, 1983). Communicative competence focuses on both written and oral communication and has inspired a broad range of classroom strategies and techniques. One example of how communicative competence is reflected in the speaking and writing classrooms is illustrated in Table 3.3.

Strategic competence is perhaps one of the most overlooked components of communicative competence, even though it has a great deal of influence in the flow of communication attempted by L2 leaners. Strategic competence needs to be taught and developed because it gives L2 learners

Table 3.3:   Communicative Competence in Speaking and Writing

Competence	Speaking	Writing
Grammatical	Learning the basic sounds of letters and syllables and the pronunciation of words including intonation and stress.	Learning the grammar, vocabulary, and mechanics of the language.
	Understanding and applying the rules of word formation and sentence formation.	
Sociolinguistic	Using appropriate language to apologize, praise, summarize, agree, disagree, and persuade.	Using language that is appropriate in terms of audience, purpose, genre, and topic.
	Adjusting speech according to context— for example, formal or informal.	
Strategic	Using a variety of speaking strategies such as paraphrasing, clarifying, stalling, or asking for assistance.	Creating text that fits the purpose and audience.
Discourse	Demonstrating connections of ideas such as time or cause and effect.	Using transitional devices (reference, conjunction) that connect one element in a text with another.

the ability to fill the gap between what they want to communicate and their available linguistic resources. Appealing or asking for assistance is a common communication strategy used by L2 learners. Faucette (2001) believes that this strategy is very useful for lower-proficiency L2 learners because it allows them to immediately participate in conversation. One way of developing this strategy is detailed in this exercise designed to equip L2 learners with the vocabulary needed when they do not know a word or phrase and want to ask for assistance. This exercise takes place in a communicative context, thus making the learning and application of the strategy in focus more relevant than memorizing a list of vocabulary items (Maleki, 2010):

1. Bring several printouts depicting animals or objects to class.

2. Divide the class into four teams.

3. Select one printout, and give it to Team 1. Team 1 holds up the selected printout.

4. Team 2 asks questions such as, "What's this/that?" "What are these/those?" "Who's this/that?" and "How do you say… in English?"

5. Teams 3 and 4 answer the questions in writing.

6. Ask representatives of Teams 3 and 4 to read out their answers.

7. Rotate teams.

In communicative classrooms, teachers will be talking less and listening more and acting as facilitators to their students' learning (Larsen-Freeman, 1986). Although the teacher guides and sets up classroom activities, the teacher's role is to observe and monitor, rather than be the primary speaker, because the goal is for L2 learners to use and produce language in the classroom. Students should be doing most of the talking because the communicative classroom is full of activity and generally focused on group and pair work to encourage interactive communication. Because of their increased level of participation, L2 learners gain confidence using the target language within the classroom, which transfers to real-world situations. As a result, L2 learners take a more active role in their own language learning (Larsen-Freeman, 1986).

In marked contrast to the ALM's focus on discrete-point grammar, more recent decades in language teaching in general, and CLT in particular, have focused on meaning. Researchers and teachers around the world have recognized the importance of meaningful language use at all stages of second or foreign language acquisition, and many curricular innovations have been developed in response. For example, one way to practice writing is to use blogs, thus taking advantage of familiarity with technology many students may possess. A blog is a form of a website where the most recent content published appears at the top of the front page of the site. Teachers can set up a class blog where students post their reactions to various topics and respond to what other students have posted (Gresswell & Simpson, 2012).

CLT has become a universal effort that has found inspiration and direction through intersecting initiatives both theoretical and applied in many contexts, with contributions from linguists, methodologists, and materials writers. When communicative competence is the goal for the classroom, the most common feature in daily activities is that they involve the whole learner in the language process, which is a confluence among people, topics, and interaction (Savignon, 1983).

To exemplify how pedagogical principles of CLT reflect the theoretical basis of input theories, Table 3.4 looks at each component of Krashen's SLA theory and shows how the theory is applied in actual language classroom practices.

Table 3.4:   Krashen's Theories in Practice

Input Hypotheses	Pedagogical Principles	Classroom Practices
Acquisition-Learning	In order for language acquisition to take place, L2 learners must engage in relevant and free communication.	Instead of using grammar textbooks, which typically teach deductively, with L2 learners studying one finite grammar point at a time in depth, L2 learners use authentic texts doing pre-reading activities such as guessing, theorizing, and picturing.
Natural Order	Language structure should be taught based on what is considered to be a natural progression of SLA.	Teachers follow a set syllabus of L2 acquired rules, which they introduce before the lesson begins. For example, based on the natural order of acquisition, the teacher should introduce the present progressive (-*ing*) before the past regular (-*ed*).
Monitor	The monitor acts in a planning, editing, and correcting function.	After evaluating L2 learner writing, the teacher compiles a list of frequent errors and discusses them directly with each L2 learner.
Input	Comprehensible input (i+1) is an essential condition for SLA.	The teacher monitors oral language communication in the classroom to ensure that it is comprehensible but challenging enough to encourage increased language acquisition.
Affective Filter	The classroom environment should minimize the potential negative influence of affective factors.	Open the class with a get-to-know-you activity so L2 learners feel comfortable with each other. For example, ask L2 learners to pair up and share information about themselves with each other and then with the class.

In this chapter, we introduced the input theories and looked at the importance of meaningful input for L2 learners. Through the four activities listed in the chapter, we emphasized how communicative language teaching activities focus on interaction in the classroom with a strong emphasis on real-life situations that benefit language students both inside and outside the classroom setting. Next, we'll examine the influence of sociocultural theory on L2 pedagogy.

Summarizing Statements

1. The input theories focus on meaningful input and interaction in the language classroom as a critical component of language acquisition.

2. Stephen Krashen's theories, which consist of five hypotheses (Acquisition-Learning, Natural Order, Monitor, Input, and Affective Filter), offer a wide-ranging explanation of the SLA process.

3. The interactionists state that modified interaction and language negotiation facilitate L2 acquisition because they connect language input and output in productive ways.

4. Communicative competence is defined as the L2 learner's ability to understand and use language appropriately in authentic environments and has four components: grammatical, sociolinguistic, strategic, and discourse.

5. A learner-centered approach, CLT emphasizes meaningful and authentic input, communicative competence, and language interaction.

REFLECTION AND APPLICATION

1. Record a conversation between at least one non-native English speaker and at least one native English speaker. Using the information presented in Table 3.2, create an inventory of the most common strategies used by the native speaker(s) in their interaction with the non-native English speaker(s). Do you hear others that do not appear on the table?

2. Do you agree or disagree with the principle and components of communicative competence? Do you assign equal importance to each of the components discussed in the chapter? Is communicative competence different in an ESL or EFL context?

3. The chapter has illustrated one activity that can help develop strategic competence, one of the most overlooked components of communicative competence. Develop two more activities in which the development of strategic competence is addressed in a language classroom.

REFERENCES

Berns, M. S. (1984). Functional approaches to language and language teaching: Another look. In S. Savignon & M. S. Berns (Eds.), *Initiatives in communicative language teaching: A book of readings* (pp. 3–21). Reading, PA: Addison-Wesley.

Canale, M. (1983). From communicative competence to communicative language pedagogy. In J.C. Richards & R.W. Schmidt (Eds.), *Language and Communication* (pp. 2–27). London: Longman.

Canale, M., & Swain, M. (1980). Theoretical bases of communicative approaches to second language teaching and testing. *Applied Linguistics, 1,* 1–47.

Chomsky, N. (1965). *Aspects of a theory of syntax.* Cambridge: MIT Press.

Faucette, P. (2001). A pedagogical perspective on communication strategies: Benefits of training and an analysis of English language teaching materials. *Second Language Studies, 19*(2), 1–40.

Ferguson, C.A. (1971). Absence of copola and the notion of simplicity: A study of normal speech, baby talk, foreigner talk, and pidgin. In D. Hymes (Ed.), *Pidginization and creolization of languages* (pp. 141–150). Cambridge, U.K.: Cambridge University Press.

Gresswell, R., & Simpson, J. (2012). Class blogging in ESOL. In D. Mallows (Ed.), *Innovations in English language teaching to migrants and refugee* (pp. 105–116). London: British Council.

Krashen, S. (1987). *Principles and practices in second language acquisition.* New York: Prentice-Hall.

Krashen, S., & Terrell, T. (1983). *The natural approach: Language acquisition in the classroom.* Oxford, U.K.: Pergamon Press.

Larsen-Freeman, D. (1986). *Techniques and principles in language teaching.* Oxford, U.K.: Oxford University Press.

Long, M.H. (1983). Native speaker/non-native speaker conversation and negotiation of comprehensible input. *Applied Linguistics, 4*(2), 126–141.

Long, M.H. (1996). The role of the linguistic environment in second language acquisition. In W. Ritchie & T. Bhatia (Eds.), *Handbook of second language acquisition* (pp. 413–468). San Diego: Academic Press.

Maleki, A. (2010). Techniques to teach communication strategies. *Journal of Language Teaching and Research, 1*(5), 640–646.

Savignon, S. J. (1983). *Communicative competence: Theory and classroom practice.* Reading, PA: Addison-Wesley.

Wooldridge, B. (2001). Foreigner talk: An important element in cross-cultural management education and training. *International Review of Administrative Sciences, 67*(4), 621–634.

Chapter 4
▲

Sociocultural Theory and
Task-Based Learning

This chapter concentrates on sociocultural theory and second language acquisition. In the previous chapter, we saw how theorists of CLT and interactionism viewed social interaction as the impetus for language development. Sociocultural theory, however, considers language as the cultural tool that stimulates social interaction, which is the key to learning. Socioculturalists emphasized the capability of the individual in the L2 classroom in collaborative situations. In the L2 classroom, task-based learning reflects sociocultural theory, which focuses on collaborative tasks that foster individual skills and capabilities.

This chapter begins with the research that psychologists Jean Piaget and Lev Vygotsky conducted on learning and development and how that work relates to sociocultural theory. Their research from the early 1900s still influences educational practices in the language classroom today. It then details Vygotsky's Zone of Proximal Development and its application in the language classroom, particularly scaffolding. The chapter concludes by connecting task-based learning to its sociocultural roots and the categories of task-based activities in the language classroom.

Theoretical Considerations

Sociocultural theory, which comes out of the field of psychology, stresses the importance of socialization on cognitive development—in particular, how interaction impacts learners' psychological and social development. Within the realm of language learning, sociocultural theory can apply to how we acquire and develop communication skills, either in the first language or second languages. Two major researchers from the 1920s whose work impacted the L2 classroom include Swiss psychologist Jean Piaget and Russian psychologist Lev Vygotsky.

Some similarities exist between the two theorists on how learning takes place, but there are also meaningful differences. With regard to the cognitive development of children, Piaget's theories focus on age and cognitive (mental) differences and how these differences impact the capability of the child to develop language. Vygotsky's theories hone in on the social and cultural tools that can enhance learning at the cognitive level and on the potential, rather than the capability, of the learner. The implications for the classroom are clear for both theorists. Piaget's research focused on the cognitive development of children at particular developmental (age) stages and how interactions within the educational environment can alter the path of that development. Vygotsky's research also emphasized the importance of the educational environment but with less emphasis on the age of the child and more emphasis on the potential of the child within the environment. Both theorists completed work with children that impacted sociocultural theory and its implications for the L2 classroom.

Vygotsky's view was in contrast to other theorists who tended to view development as an internal process and learning as an external process, such as Piaget (1953) posited in his cognitive development theories. Vygotsky believed learning and development were interconnected from the moment of the child's birth. Piaget and Vygotsky were both constructivists: They believed that human development is a process in which social interaction triggers the inner abilities that are in the process of perpetual construction. These inner abilities then influence social interaction. However, despite this shared belief, Piaget argued that cognitive development precedes learning.

Piaget (1953) proposed four biologically determined universal stages of cognitive development: 0–2 years, 2–7 years, 7–11 years, and 11–15 years. He stressed that children can't and/ or shouldn't be taught beyond their age capability. Some people have considered the relative artificiality of this division to hinder children's development and have questioned the stages. For example, from Piaget's perspective, children should not be introduced to literacy until age 6.2, the optimal age for literary learning; from a sociocultural perspective, theorists would not account for age but would instead focus on potential and interaction.

Lev Vygotsky (1896–1934) and the Zone of Proximal Development

In sociocultural theory, the central concept is represented by the **Zone of Proximal Development (ZPD)** and its influence on learning. To understand the ZPD, it is important to explore how Vygotsky (1978) viewed learning; he regarded learning as an internal developmental process that is stimulated when interacting in cooperation with peers. When interaction happens, it sets in motion a variety of developmental processes that would not occur in a noninteraction-based atmosphere. Thus, learning is a socially dependent process that fosters individual human functioning. In the context of the language classroom, we see how this theory is applied to L2 learning in a very concrete way. For example, when the L2 teacher forms pairs of students for activities where one learner is more advanced than the other, the expectation is that the more advanced peer will act as a model for the less advanced partner. Another example is when a more advanced L2 learner is chosen to model a dialogue with the teacher before less advanced students

Figure 4.1:   The Zone of Proximal Development

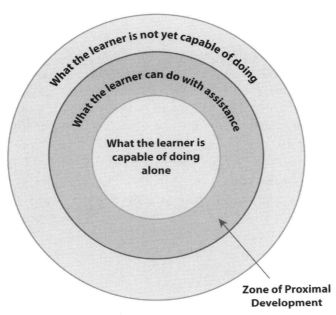

complete the dialogue on their own. This also exemplifies principles of the ZPD as the more capable peer demonstrates language to help the others in the class.

To explain how this social and participatory learning takes place, Vygotsky (1978) developed the concept of the ZPD, which he defined as the distance between the actual developmental level, determined through independent problem solving, and the level of potential development, determined through problem solving under adult guidance or in collaboration with more capable peers. Vygotsky applied his theory specifically to child development and learning. He believed that the sociocultural environment promoted learning and described the developmental level of a child as the "What I can do with help" area/zone as the critical stage of social learning. Figure 4.1 visually demonstrates the areas where the child is not yet capable, where the child is capable alone, and what the child is capable of with help.

Sociocultural Theories and Language Learning

Scaffolding

One critical strategy for moving L2 learners from what they know to what they are capable of learning is scaffolding. **Scaffolding** is a teaching technique that epitomizes Vygotsky's view that social learning leads to individual development because it refers to providing meaningful contextual supports to enhance understanding of new concepts through the use of varied techniques, which can include visuals, kinesthetic learning, simplified language, teacher/peer modeling, or group work. The teacher facilitates support in a deliberate manner, and as learners become more proficient, the scaffold is gradually removed. Students are now in a better position to become more responsible for their own learning, and teachers do less mediating of instruction (Diaz-Rico & Weed, 2002; Duffy & Roehler, 1986). Let's look at some concrete examples of the types of scaffolding that are effective in the English L2 classroom.

Types of Scaffolding

Because the ZPD is the difference between a student's current level of development and the potential level that can be obtained with support from the instructor or peers, scaffolding is designed to assist students gain conceptual understandings through support of the teacher. Scaffolding techniques represent a way for students to transition through their zones of proximal development to more independent understanding. Table 4.1 illustrates various scaffolding strategies that focus on the teacher-student interaction.

As students get better at these types of activities, the L2 learners can be increasingly responsible for the entire conversation around a lesson, using elaborated comments and questions that provide opportunities for ongoing knowledge connections. The language teacher should continue to solicit questions and comments but should allow the students to slowly take over leadership roles in any modeling behavior.

Some specific scaffolding techniques that can be used in the language classroom, in addition to those provided in Table 4.1, are:

1. **Simplifying the language:** The teacher simplifies language by shortening reading and writing selections, speaking in the present tense, and avoiding the use of idioms. This is a type of self-monitoring.

2. **Asking for completion, not generation:** The teacher asks students to choose answers from a list or complete a partially finished outline or paragraph. This is a type of leveling that is used when students do not yet have the language capability to generate complete answers and sentences.

3. **Using visuals:** The teacher presents information and asks students to respond through the use of graphic organizers, tables, charts, outlines, and graphs. This is effective for visual learners and provides schema where little or none may exist.

Task-Based Learning

A further application of sociocultural theory that is more specific to the language classroom is **task-based learning**. This methodology utilizes scaffolding techniques and social interaction as the primary vehicles to facilitate language acquisition. It emphasizes the importance of language production and social interaction in the acquisition of a second language. Task-based learning

Table 4.1:   Scaffolding Strategies for Teachers

Type	What the Teacher Does
Explanations	Explanations are explicit statements adjusted to fit the learners' emerging understandings about what is being learned; why and when it will be used (conditional or situational knowledge); and how it is used (procedural knowledge) (Duffy et al., 1986). In doing this, the language teacher would explain a grammar point clearly and offer rich examples to foster understanding.
Student participation	Learners are asked to join in the process that is occurring. As the teacher provides some background or foundational knowledge of the content, learners have opportunities to fill in the areas that they understand with their pre-existing knowledge. Students actively help to structure the lesson with their contributions. For example, as L2 learners listen to a lecture on science during a listening activity, the teacher can ask them to add information to the lecture and write about what they heard and what they know.
Verifications	Teachers check students' emerging understandings through oral or written production. For example, a teacher could ask students to put into their own words the concept just discussed. If it appears there is understanding, the teacher can move on. If not, the teacher can re-teach.
Modeling	Modeling is defined as a teaching behavior that shows how one should feel, think, or act within a given situation (Duffy, Sherman, & Roehler, 1977). In this case, if an L2 teacher wants students to role-play a conversation between a pharmacist and customer, the teacher should first role play the parts to model how it should or could look.
Think-aloud modeling	Learners are encouraged to think critically as they progress through a task and contribute their own thoughts to the process as it happens. This type of modeling focuses on making thinking visible. The L2 teacher could ask questions such as *Why do you think...? What do you think about...?* or *If you could imagine....*
Talk-alouds	Learners are shown how to act by the teacher, who talks about the task as it is completed. Students are invited to participate in the process and share with other students. This differs from think-alouds in that it is more about the action to be performed and how to do it rather than thinking about the concepts. Examples of questions might be: *How will you...? What will you do for...?* or *Can I do this by...?*
Performance modeling	Learners are shown how to complete the task with no think-alouds or talk-alouds but with active modeling. In this type of modeling, the teacher demonstrates reading and the enjoyment of the reading material. Some examples are when the teacher reads silently as the students read silently (USSR: Uninterrupted Sustained Silent Reading or DEAR: Drop Everything and Read).
Contributions	Students can contribute suggestions for reasoning through an issue or problem, as in offering recommendations on how to complete the task. Together, the teachers and students verbalize the process to its completion. For example, KWL graphic organizers (What do you **K**now? What do you **W**ant to know? What did you **L**earn?) are a way to draw on student knowledge and force students to think more about their prior knowledge and what they have learned throughout the lesson.

employs language-focused tasks as the primary framework for all aspects of language teaching and learning. Tasks, such as the Information Gap Task presented later in this chapter, are paramount. Grammar and all other aspects of language learning develop as a byproduct of engaging learners in highly interactive tasks.

Before exploring the characteristics and implementation of task-based learning, it is important to define *tasks*. Willis (1996) has defined a task as a goal-oriented activity with a clear purpose. With this definition in mind, Richards (2006) identified four key characteristics:

1. A task is something that learners accomplish using their existing language resources.

2. All tasks have targeted outcomes that are not simply linked to learning language. In other words, learners do something with the language they are learning, and language acquisition occurs as a result of completing the task.

3. Tasks need to be meaningful to the learners.

4. Tasks should be interactional in nature when they involve two or more learners. Communication strategies and interactional skills are as essential as language skills for successful task completion.

There are six types of tasks that can be successfully employed in task-based learning (Willis, 1996). They are: listing, sorting and ordering, comparing, problem solving, sharing personal experiences, and creative. These tasks are illustrated in Table 4.2. and focus on the teacher asking the students to think about various aspects of their hometowns.

Tasks can also be divided into pedagogical and real-world tasks (Richards, 2006). Pedagogical tasks involve the use of interactional and language-specific skills but have an outcome that is not similar to what learners will find in the real world. An example of a pedagogical task is shown in Exercise 4.1.

Table 4.2:   Examples of Task-Based Learning Tasks for Home Towns

Task	Example
Listing	Learners are asked to list 10 points of interest in their home towns.
Sorting and ordering	Learners list the most important points of interest for a group of tourists visiting their home towns.
Comparing	Learners compare their home towns with a town they have visited or lived in recently.
Problem solving	Learners identify a problem associated with their home towns and provide a solution to solve that problem.
Sharing personal experiences	Learners describe the happiest experience they had in their home towns.
Creative	Learners are required to prepare plans for the improvement of an area in their home towns (downtown, train station, airport, parks, etc.).

─────────────── **Exercise 4.1: Information Gap** ───────────────

Learners work in pairs. Each student is given a table with information missing. What is missing in one partner's table is filled in on the other partner's table and vice versa. Learners ask each other questions to discover what is missing in their tables to be able to fill in the gaps on the table. For example, students might ask, "Where is Mary from?" "What does Mary do on weekends?" or "What kind of movies does Mary like?" The primary purpose of this exercise is to practice listening and speaking with the goal of asking for information.

Learner A's Information

Name	From	Occupation	Weekends	Movies
1. Mary		scientist		thriller
2.		professor	hike	
3. Tom	Key West			action
4.	Tampa	truck driver	swim	
5. Janet	Jacksonville			

Learner B's Information

Name	From	Occupation	Weekends	Movies
1.	Orlando		watch TV	
2. Patrick	Miami			drama
3.		nurse	play football	
4. Sam				horror
5.		lawyer	read books	comedy

On the other hand, a real-word task is one that reflects the use of language and interactional skills in a situation that is plausible beyond the classroom. One example of this type of task could be a role-play in which learners, taking the part of college students, practice having a meeting with their academic advisor. If learners plan on enrolling in colleges in the United States, this task can be seen as a rehearsal for a real-world activity that they will have to perform in the future without any type of guidance from peers or language teachers.

A Framework for Task-Based Learning Implementation

How is task-based learning structured and implemented in the language classroom? In other words, are there specific steps language teachers need to follow for achieving successful task completion that will implicitly promote language acquisition? Willis (1996) has designed a sequence for task-based learning, which includes a pre-task phase and a task cycle, as well as a language focus component. Table 4.3 exemplifies these three components.

Based on one of the tasks illustrated in Table 4.2, Exercise 4.2 shows how the sequence proposed by Willis (1996) is applied in a language classroom where students are at the beginning level.

Table 4.3:   Task-Based Learning Sequence

Pre-Task Exercises	Task Cycle	Language Focus
Introduction to topic and task: Teacher explores the topic with the class, points out useful words and phrases, and helps learners understand task instructions. Learners are given time to prepare and may hear a recording related to the task.	**Task:** Learners perform the task in pairs or small groups. Teacher walks around the classroom and monitors, encouraging all attempts at communication, but does not correct. The emphasis is on spontaneous talk and confidence building within the privacy of the small group. **Planning:** Learners prepare a written or oral report for the whole class on how they did the task and what they decided or discovered. Because the report is public, learners will strive for accuracy. The teacher provides language advice and encourages peer editing and the use of dictionaries. **Report:** Some groups present their reports to the class while the rest of the class comments or adds extra points, or students can exchange written reports and compare results. The teacher comments on the content of the reports but does not provide overt public correction.	**Analysis:** Teacher sets language-focused tasks based on the texts learners read or transcripts of recordings they hear. Learners examine and then discuss specific language features. They can enter new words, phrases, and patterns in vocabulary notebooks or logs. **Practice:** Teacher conducts practice of new words, phrases, and patterns occurring in the data, either during or after the analysis.

─────── **Exercise 4.2: Celebrations/Festivals in Your Home Town** ───────

Task Type: Sharing personal experience
Task Example: Learners describe one festival or celebration that happens in their home town.

Pre-Task Exercises

The teacher asks students to think about their home towns.
The teacher talks about an event in his/her own home town. In addition, the teacher writes out his or her story, highlighting important vocabulary and language constructs.
The teacher introduces the task, which requires learners to describe a celebration in their home town.

Task Cycle

Students will work in pairs, and the outcome will be an oral presentation of their partner's description of the town celebration. Moreover, the teacher will provide students with a guiding worksheet that will assist students in organizing the information.

Guiding Worksheet **(Language Focus)**

1. Name of partner
2. Name of home town
3. Name of celebration
4. What do people do at the celebration?
5. When does the celebration take place?

Task-based learning and scaffolding are two exemplars of how sociocultural theory can be applied in the L2 classroom. The emphasis of scaffolding is on creating an atmosphere of classroom interactional support that is tailored to the level of the L2 learner, gradually decreasing that support as the L2 learner advances. Task-based learning also focuses on classroom interaction and support, with peer-based, organized tasks at the center of the language development process. Because sociocultural theory propounds that learning stems from using language in a supportive, interactional atmosphere, task-based learning and scaffolding are considered effective techniques in the L2 classroom.

This chapter looked at sociocultural theory and its influence on SLA. It discussed how sociocultural theory has particularly influenced two language classroom methodologies: scaffolding and task-based learning. To link theory with practice, the chapter illustrated several ways the two are utilized in the L2 classroom.

Summarizing Statements

1. Sociocultural theory, from the field of psychology, stresses the importance of socialization on cognitive development, which in turn has influenced learning in the L2 classroom.

2. Two learning theories grounded in the field of psychology have affected educational practices in the educational setting, particularly those based on Jean Piaget's research on individual development and Lev Vygotsky's research on social constructivism.

3. Vygotsky's Zone of Proximal Development is a powerful visualization of the difference between what an individual can do and what an individual can potentially accomplish with collaborative guidance, often used to guide L2 activities that focus on social collaboration.

4. Scaffolding is an important teaching technique commonly used in the language classroom whereby the teacher provides support to developing language learners.

5. Task-based instruction for L2 learners focuses on increasing language production and using social interaction as a basis for the acquisition of a second language.

REFLECTION AND APPLICATION

1. Do you agree or disagree with the application of Vygotsky's ZPD in the ESL or EFL classroom? Support your choice with specific reasons and examples.

2. Using the task-based learning framework developed by Willis (1996), create a language activity based on a problem-solving task.

3. Using the language activity you created in Question 2, what are some scaffolding techniques that would work well within that activity? Will the activity or scaffolding technique differ based on the context in which you are teaching, for example, EFL or ESL?

REFERENCES

Diaz-Rico, L.T., & Weed, K.Z. (2002). *The crosscultural, language, and academic development handbook: A complete K–12 reference guide* (2nd ed.). Boston: Allyn & Bacon.

Duffy, G., & Roehler, L. R. (1986). The subtleties of instructional mediation. *Educational Leadership, 43*(7), 23.

Duffy, G., Roehler, L., Meloth, M., Vavrus, L., Book, C., Putnam, J., & Wesselman, R. (1986). The relationship between explicit verbal explanation during reading skill instruction and student awareness and achievement: A study of reading teacher effects. *Reading Research Quarterly, 21*(3), 237–252.

Duffy, G., Sherman, G., & Roehler, L. (1977). *How to teach reading systematically.* New York: Harper & Row.

Piaget, J. (1953). *The origins of intelligence in children.* New York: Basic Books.

Richards, J. (2006). *Communicative language teaching today.* New York: Cambridge University Press.

Vygotsky, L.S. (1978). *Mind in society: The development of higher psychological processes.* Cambridge, MA: Harvard University Press.

Willis, J. (1996). *A framework for task-based learning.* London: Longman.

PART II

FROM NEEDS ANALYSIS TO GOAL SETTING, TO SYLLABUS DESIGN AND LESSON PLANNING

In order to take a comprehensive approach to curriculum development for the L2 classroom, a needs analyses and syllabi development must be part of the process. Chapter 5 defines a needs analysis, explains the importance of it in curriculum design, and shares various examples of needs analysis documents that L2 teachers can adapt to their L2 classroom for learners at different levels. In addition to discussing how to write goals and objectives for the L2 classroom, this chapter also addresses the process involved in evaluating an ESL/EFL textbook according to the standards set by ACTFL. Chapter 6 defines and gives examples of various approaches to L2 syllabus design, another important phase in the L2 curriculum development sequence. In addition, the chapter provides a template for lesson plan design and gives an example of a lesson plan based on that template.

Chapter 5
▲

Needs Analysis as a
Basis for Goal Setting

This chapter provides background on needs analyses and includes examples of documents that can be incorporated into the L2 classroom. According to West (1994), the term *needs analysis* was first seen in the literature around 1920, but it is in the 1970s that the needs analysis started to be implemented and researched within the context of the language classroom. Needs analysis for the second language classroom is a critical aspect of the language curriculum development process (Berwick, 1989; Seedhouse, 1995). To complement the needs analysis as an important part of goal setting in the ESL/EFL classroom, we also include a sample of a textbook adaption evaluation form in this chapter (see Figures 5.7 and 5.8).

Needs Analysis in the English Language Classroom

A **needs analysis**, or **needs assessment**, is a way to determine who your students are, where they are in their language development, what the content and goals of the course should be, how tasks should be accomplished, and what assessments are best for a particular class. "In the field of language curriculum design, needs analysis plays an important role, for needs analysis largely determines the goal and content of the course being designed" (Macalister, 2012, p. 120). This chapter will explore the various ways of conducting a student-based needs analysis, types of needs analyses, the important components of a needs assessment and how to conduct them in the L2 classroom, and example documents for varying levels of learners.

What Is a Needs Analysis?

Although there are many ways to collect information for a needs analysis (see Brindley, 1989; Macalister, 2012; Munby, 1978), a student-based needs analysis focuses on information that the

L2 teacher collects directly from L2 learners about their goals for the classroom. In Benesch's (1996) discussion of a needs analyses for the L2 classroom, she lists a number of ways to collect information that could be used as a part of any needs assessment, including student surveys, faculty input, assignment analysis, classroom observation, or a combination of all these factors. Lambert (2010) added the importance of using a needs analysis to understand the future language needs of the L2 learners (e.g., employment opportunities or educational advancement); the language being taught (in this case English); the experiences of the learners and teachers; and the type (i.e., EFL, ESL) of the program. The rationale for including a needs analysis in the language classroom according to Ann Johns is that "by identifying elements of students' target English situations and using them as the basis of . . . instruction, teachers will be able to provide students with the specific language they need to succeed in their future courses and careers" (as cited in Benesch, 1996, p. 723).

In this chapter we are going to focus on information that is gathered directly from the learner's perspective. We believe this focus is most important in the ESL/EFL classroom because it not only allows the learner to participate fully in the process of goal setting for the classroom but also puts the teacher in control of the process, data, and analysis. By taking a student-based approach to needs assessment using the various tools presented in this chapter, language teachers can effectively assess students' language, sociocultural, and personal needs in the classroom. This is a crucial step in creating the **scope and sequence** of a course. The scope and sequence of the course provides a brief outline of the language focus, the level of language complexity/fluency, and a recommended order for teaching the prescribed language concepts for a particular class. The needs analysis gives the teacher more refined information to determine the direction and depth of the content in the class within the scope and sequence. This can enhance L2 learner motivation, increase language proficiency, and satisfy the needs and priorities of the learner.

Let's start by looking at a student survey as a sample needs analysis document that could be used the first day of class based on Scenario 1 in Chapter 1. Remember Emily who has to develop an EFL curriculum in Turkey? Figure 5.1 is one example of a student-based needs analysis document that she could use in her job in Turkey for her writing classes. We will then discuss the student-based needs analysis process in more detail in the rest of the chapter.

Three Components of a Student-Based ESL/EFL Needs Analysis

Although the example given in Figure 5.1 focuses mostly on language and classroom goals, a needs analysis needs to account for more than just language goals. Personal and sociocultural goals should also be part of the process because they incorporate the fact that learners are functioning in a cultural environment. We recommend taking a more comprehensive approach to the needs analysis in the L2 classroom by including three components of an analysis: language needs, personal needs, and sociocultural needs.

Figure 5.1:   Intermediate EFL Writing Class: Needs Analysis Survey Sample

Dear Students, welcome to class! Please answer these questions to help me get to know you better and to understand your goals for this term. Please be honest and share as much detail as you wish. If anything is confusing, please ask me. **I will not share this information with anyone else, and it will help me to prepare this class.**

Part I: Personal Information

Name:	Where are you from in Turkey?	What languages do you speak other than English?	
Age:	How many years have you studied English?		Please circle one: Male or Female

How often do you use English outside of the classroom? Very often? Not often? Please explain your answer.

Part II: Language Learning

Please circle how comfortable you feel about each language skill.
1=very comfortable; 2=comfortable; 3=not comfortable
Then write one sentence why you chose this number.

Reading	1	2	3
Writing	1	2	3
Listening	1	2	3
Speaking	1	2	3

Part III: Classroom Learning

What writing activities do you enjoy in the English classroom? For example, do you enjoy pair work? Do you enjoy peer feedback in your writing? Do you like to give feedback to your peers? Please list the writing activities you enjoy most in the classroom.

Are there writing activities that you do not enjoy in the classroom? Please list any you do not enjoy and why they are not enjoyable for you.

What do you hope to learn in this class? I will list some of our goals in this Writing class. Please circle the ones you are most interested in, and write in any other goals you have for the class to the right.

Learn to choose a topic	**Learn to give feedback to peers**
Learn to brainstorm	**Learn to revise using feedback from peers**
Learn to outline	**Learn to proofread a final draft**
Learn to write the first draft	

Analyzing Language Needs

When addressing language goals in the needs analysis, the focus should be on determining where the students see themselves in terms of their language progress and where they hope to be at the end of the course. Because the goals will be different depending on the focus on the class— grammar, oral communication, writing skills, Business English, etc.—the language part of the needs analysis should be broad enough to address overall language goals yet contain specifics to address the pre-set curricular/program goals. When determining the language needs of L2 learners in any class, it is critical to allow students to share information about their past, present, and future use of language as well as their confidence in using the target language in various situations. If you look at Figure 5.1, the teacher asks students in Part II of the needs analysis survey to rate their language use at all skill levels and explain why they chose that rating.

Analyzing Personal Needs

Personal needs assessments allow students to share their individual journey in language learning, both inside and outside the classroom setting, and reflect on how they view their personal language journey. In the personal component of a needs assessment, students share how they interact in the language classroom—how they study, how they learn, and under what circumstances they thrive. This is not information that can be gleaned from grades, test scores, or even previous student work. It is only through a needs analysis targeting the personal needs of students that teachers can find out this valuable information, which will help them to set goals for the classroom. By recognizing that individual learning styles affect how ESL/EFL learners perform in the classroom, teachers can utilize the information from the personal needs assessment to optimize individual learning. If you look at Figure 5.1, you will see that in Part I the teacher asks students to share personal information related to using English outside the classroom and how they feel about their language journey.

Analyzing Sociocultural Needs

As discussed in Chapter 4, "sociocultural theory maintains that social interaction and cultural institutions, such as schools, classrooms, and so forth, have important roles to play in an individual's cognitive growth" (Donato & McCormick, 1994, p. 453). As a result, sociocultural factors are an important part of the needs analysis process. Looking at sociocultural factors in an L2 learner needs analysis will help determine the way that learners approach and feel about the L2 classroom structure and cultural environment. Language teachers can utilize this information to ensure that the classroom fosters language acquisition and takes into account students' cultural backgrounds and relationships. For example, if a student is not accustomed to working in pairs, particularly with students of the opposite gender, a needs analysis can make this information apparent. The teacher is then able to take concrete steps to quickly assist any student who is not comfortable in peer work. This part of the needs analysis addresses an identified sociocultural need on the part of the student and will ultimately result in more effective classroom activities where students are focused on acquiring language instead of making cultural adjustments. In Figure 5.1, you will see that the teacher asks students to share in Part III what they enjoy doing in the classroom and what they do not enjoy doing.

Types of Student-Centered Needs Analyses

There are many ways to conduct a student-based needs analysis in the L2 classroom. Here are some examples of the different types that can be utilized in the classroom based on using a student-centered approach. A student-centered approach focuses on the L2 learner and the learner's perception of his or her needs in the classroom and can include personal, sociocultural, and/or language needs depending on the L2 teacher's goals:

1. **Surveys/questionnaires** ask L2 learners to indicate their particular needs and interests and can be most effective in revealing much about the learner and his/her knowledge and experience. These are best used with learners who have the language capability to analyze and write about their own language needs. Figure 5.1 is an example of a survey instrument that can be administered in a written form.

2. **Open-ended interviews/informal observations on language performance** can be effective in understanding L2 learners' personal, sociocultural, and language needs. Interviews can be done on a one-to-one basis or in small groups and can provide valuable information about what learners know, what their interests are, and the ways they use or hope to use language. This is best used with learners who are focused on spoken language and in small classes where the language teacher has time to spend with individual students. Figure 5.1 is an example of a survey instrument that can also be administered as an open-ended interview.

3. **Learner-compiled inventories of language use** have a more open-ended purpose in that they aim to elicit the same information that most surveys/questionnaires offer except that L2 learners keep these lists of ways to use language and update them periodically throughout the course. This inventory works well with intermediate and advanced learners who use them to track their own language progress. This type of instrument focuses on language needs.

4. **Examining/reviewing reading materials** allows L2 learners to review and select what appeals to them. By choosing various types of reading materials (newspapers, magazines, books, other reading materials, etc.) and sharing them with learners, teachers can ask learners to rate which materials they would enjoy using in the classroom. This system works best for courses where the teacher has distinct control over classroom materials. Having students initially review potential reading material for the classroom helps the L2 teacher determine what subjects are of interest to the learners and what material will motivate them to read in English.

5. **Class discussions** are one way for L2 learners to express their preferences about the kind of language they want to learn and how it is relevant to their lives. Sample questions are "What do you want to learn in this class?" or "What do you need to learn for your career?" For classes where the learners are outspoken and confident in expressing their needs, this type of open discussion can foster class participation and individualistic expression.

6. **Personal/dialogue journals** encourage learners to engage in informal types of writing where they express their thoughts, opinions, insights, and beliefs about the English language classroom without fear of judgment or error correction. As a needs analysis approach, this works well throughout the class session, allowing the teacher to continually track and adjust course goals as students express their needs in a safe environment (see Auerbach, 1994 for more suggestions on what to include in a student-based needs analysis).

As you can see from these examples, a student-based needs analysis is a process that begins from the first day of class and can continue until the end of the term. The L2 teacher can use various methods to collect information for that needs analysis that can be utilized immediately in creating the goals and activities in the L2 classroom.

Steps in Conducting a Student-Centered Needs Analysis

The process involved in conducting a student-centered needs analysis are outlined in Table 5.1. The table displays the steps for the teacher to take and some sample questions that could be asked depending on the type of ESL/EFL program (see Chapter 1 for details about the various types of programs).

Combining Needs Assessment with Planned Course Content

One of the most important aspects of the needs analysis is reconciling the information from the needs analysis documents with the established curriculum. This steps leads to more comprehensive objectives for the course based on a combination of factors including content, curriculum, and learner needs, all of which can impact the success of the classroom (Grognet, 1997). It is therefore recommended that you plan your class in advance but leave some room on the syllabus/course plan so that you can fully integrate the results of the needs assessment as soon as possible after the start date.

The process of administering the needs assessment and compiling the results is easily integrated into the curriculum of the classroom. To see how this might be done, think again about Scenario 1 with Emily (from Chapter 1). She has completed the needs analysis survey from Figure 5.1 and now wants to incorporate that information into the Writing class curriculum. The class is using the *Great Writing 2: Great Paragraphs* textbook (Folse, Muchmore-Vokoun, & Vestri Solomon, 2010), but Emily wants to incorporate some of the needs analysis information

Table 5.1: Steps in Conducting a Needs Analysis

Steps	Example Questions/Activities		
	Language Needs	**Personal Needs**	**Sociocultural Needs**
In the **first few days** of the class, conduct a needs analysis. Some sample questions that you could ask are given and can be asked in written or oral from.	What experience do you have in learning English? What are your goals for this class?	What is a language skill you want to develop in this class? What activities do you enjoy in English class?	How do you feel about working in pairs in the English classroom? When do you use English outside the classroom? Do you need English for your job?
By the second week of class, utilize the needs analysis to prioritize objectives in the curriculum. Examples are given.	Students report a lack of oral communication experience.	Students report a desire to learn more about conversing with native speakers.	Students report concerns about whether group work is utilized in the classroom because they have never done this before.
By the second week of class, determine classroom activities, tasks, and assessments based on integrating the curricular goals and the needs analysis.	One previously set objective in the curriculum for the language class may be to improve oral language skills. Based on the needs analysis report, students indicate that they want more practice in conversational skills with native speakers. Therefore, include pair work with dialogues that contain certain informal, popular, or slang phrases, along with the dialogues already included in the textbook.		
Throughout the class, focus on instructional strategies that are learner centered, communicative, and include appropriate assessments.	In the needs analysis survey, students indicate they have concerns about group work because they have never done that before in class. Start by acknowledging these concerns openly and begin with guided pair work, which includes set dialogues, instructor modeling, and open discussion of effective pair work strategies. Include a student-centered evaluation of satisfaction with the pair work to track comfort levels and effectiveness.		
In the end, evaluate the effectiveness of the curriculum and needs analysis integration.	Include an oral interview with the final exam focused on language concerns indicated in the needs analysis at the beginning of the term.	Use midterm or end-of-term evaluation to determine if individual needs are being addressed. Use the information to adjust the curriculum if necessary.	Students fill out a midterm and final satisfaction survey asking about their comfort with pair and group work that was utilized in the classroom.
Use the needs analysis reconciliation to make adjustments in objectives and goals **for the rest of this class or in future classes.**	Use interview results to determine if enough class time is dedicated to oral communication.	Use evaluation pieces to determine if students are using the conversational language taught in the appropriate manner and setting.	Based on results, determine if more pair work guidance is needed, or if students reported comfort and satisfaction with group work in the classroom.

to enhance the class goals. The book recommends Seven Steps in the Writing Process, which Emily used in her student survey in Part III: Classroom Learning. She noticed that none of the students circled "Learn to give feedback to peers," which is one of the goals of the class based on the textbook. Emily decides that the teachers should give students some help in understanding why peer feedback is important, how it is accomplished, and how it can help their individual writing. In this way Emily is keeping the goals of the course yet using the needs analysis to enhance the learning in an area where students do not feel confident.

Student-Based Needs Analysis for ESL/EFL Students at Different Levels

It is important to note that any needs analysis should be adapted to each specific level, class, and curriculum. A needs analysis for an intermediate EFL class in Turkey will look different than one for an advanced IEP ESL class as you must adapt for language level, culture, learners, and curriculum. When choosing what needs analysis method to use for a particular class, it is essential to ensure that the material used in the analysis is applicable to the setting of the L2 classroom and comprehensible to the level of your students. For example, refer to the Figure 5.1 student survey. To ensure that is applicable in another setting, such as the beginner EFL class in Indonesia, how would you need to adjust it? You could include questions about Indonesian culture or ask specifically about course content from the textbook adapted for the classroom. Just as important is ensuring that the needs analysis is appropriate for the language level of the students and that they understand the documents. Figures 5.2, 5.3, and 5.4 and Table 5.2 describe what skills L2 learners in adult ESL classes generally demonstrate and give examples of student-based needs analysis documents for different levels of students.

Table 5.2 details some general language characteristics of each level of ESL/EFL learners and is followed by examples of needs analyses that may be appropriate for each level. These levels are based on the CASAS **Skill-Level Descriptors** for ESL (CASAS, 2012). The ESL Skill-Level Descriptors give broad generalizations about what adult ESL/EFL students should be capable of doing in English at that particular level. For a description of academic language skills by level of proficiency, TESOL professionals may consult the Common European Framework of Reference for Languages (CEFR) available at www.coe.int/t/dg4/linguistic/cadre1_en.asp for both children and adults, or WIDA's English Language Development Standards available at www.wida.us/standards/eld.aspx for K–12 L2 learners.

Examples of Student-Based Needs Analysis Documents

Beginning Students

For beginning students with limited language, a picture or simplified language needs analysis can be used. By pre-selecting the topics that are already determined to be part of the curriculum, you can then use the information from the needs analysis to focus in on the same topics to increase motivation on the part of the students. Figure 5.2 is an example of a needs analysis for beginning

Table 5.2:   ESL Level Descriptors

Learner Level	What a Learner Can Do at This Level	
	Listening/Speaking	Reading/Writing
Pre-beginning	Functions minimally, if at all, in English. Communicates only through gestures and a few isolated words.	May not be literate in any language.
Low-beginning	Functions in a very limited way in situations related to immediate needs; asks and responds to basic learned phrases spoken slowly and repeated often.	Recognizes and writes letters and numbers, and reads and understands common sight words. Can write own name and address.
High-beginning	Functions with some difficulty in situations related to immediate needs; may have some simple oral communication abilities using basic learned phrases and sentences.	Reads and writes letters and numbers and a limited number of basic sight words and simple phrases related to immediate needs. Can write basic personal information on simplified forms.
Low-intermediate to intermediate	Can satisfy basic survival needs and very routine social demands. Understands simple learned phrases easily and some new simple phrases containing familiar vocabulary if spoken slowly with frequent repetition.	Can read and interpret simple material on familiar topics. Able to read and interpret simple directions, schedules, signs, maps, and menus. Can fill out forms requiring basic personal information and can write short, simple sentences based on familiar situations.
Intermediate to high-intermediate	Can satisfy basic survival needs and limited social demands; can follow oral directions in familiar contexts. Has limited ability to understand on the phone. Understands learned phrases easily and new phrases containing familiar vocabulary.	Can read and interpret simplified and some authentic material on familiar subjects. Can write sentences related to basic needs and write papers based on instructions. Can fill out basic medical forms and job applications.
Advanced	Can satisfy most survival needs and social demands. Has some ability to understand and communicate on the phone on familiar topics. Can participate in conversations on a variety of topics but has limited use of idiomatic expressions.	Can read and interpret non-simplified materials on familiar topics. Can interpret charts, graphs, and some academic reading material. Can accomplish sustained writing on personal and academic topics.

Based on information in CASAS, 2012.

Figure 5.2: Example of a Needs Analysis Survey for Beginning Students

Why do you want to study English? Please put an X next to each one that is true.

Social

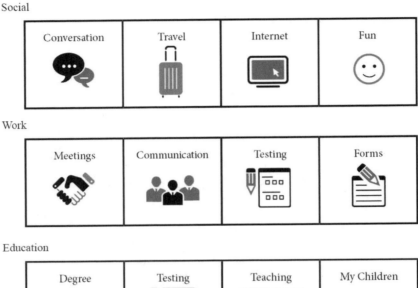

Work

Education

I am good at

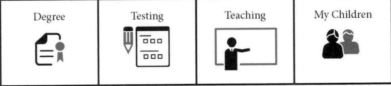

I need help with

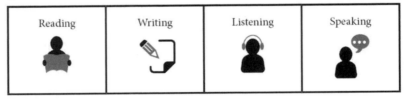

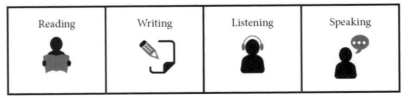

students that can be easily adapted for younger people or for some EFL contexts. Remember that when adapting a needs assessment for use in any classroom, you need to consider the local context when framing the assessment. For example, if you were teaching a test-prep class in Japan, you would include components of the test in your needs analysis to determine where your EFL learners feel they have strengths and weaknesses. If you are teaching children in an ESOL setting, the pictures in the needs analysis would include topics relevant to children such as playing games, going to the library, or eating in the cafeteria.

Low- to High-Intermediate Students

Because intermediate students can make more complex judgments about their language progress, a needs analysis survey instrument with a **Likert scale** can be a good option. A Likert scale is a psychometric scale most often used in surveys where respondents choose a set range of responses along a continuum. When using a class-specific questionnaire, Davies (2006) tells us that the "survey data contribute greatly to the aim of achieving more cohesive long-term course development. Over a period of time, data revealing learners' responses to a variety of tasks, content, materials, and so forth, will naturally reveal patterns of commonality between learners taking the same or similar courses, and contribute considerably to the goal of making the kinds of informed planning decisions needed to close any gaps that may exist between teacher and learner expectation of the course" (p. 4). By allowing students to focus on their perceived strengths and weaknesses, teachers can then individualize certain aspects of the curriculum or determine which topics to focus on first. The questions should be adapted according to the type of class being taught—for example, depending on if the class is an ESL or EFL class. Whereas an ESL needs analysis might include questions about using English in the community, an EFL needs analysis would include questions about seeking out opportunities to use English. Figure 5.3 is one example of a needs analysis survey with a Likert scale orientation for students at the intermediate level.

Advanced Students

Advanced students should have the language abilities to make known what their very specific language, personal, and sociological needs are. At this level, it is critical to determine the L2 learners' strengths, weaknesses, and needs to prevent language fossilization (language errors that continually persist) and to encourage them to make the transition from competent classroom skill to fluency and accuracy. Open-ended questions can provide complex language samples and be used to determine other needs at the same time. Figure 5.4 provides some examples of questions that might be included in a student-based needs analysis for advanced students.

The needs analysis, though, is just one step toward creating a curriculum that also includes the creation of the syllabus and the textbook analysis. Let's take a look at how to set goals according to the information gained from a needs analysis and then how to turn those goals into objectives for a lesson plan.

Figure 5.3: Sample Likert-Scale Needs Analysis (Intermediate)

Name:			Date:	
Class:				

Please put an X in the box with the answer that best describes you when using the English language. Please mark only one answer per statement.

Personal Goals	I'm excellent at this.	I feel comfortable with this.	I need to work at this.	I'm not interested in this.
Talking about myself, family, and friends				
Listening to English language TV, radio, or internet materials				
Meeting new people and having casual conversations				
Talking on the phone				
Finding, applying for, and interviewing for a job				
Completing my school work successfully				
Participating in groups in class				
Language Goals				
Correcting my language when I make mistakes				
Speaking in class when needed				
Speaking outside class when needed				
Listening and understanding in class when needed				
Listening and understanding outside class when needed				
Reading and understanding texts in class when needed				
Reading and understanding texts outside class when needed				
Writing in class when needed				
Writing outside class when needed				
Sociocultural Goals				
Shopping, eating out, or asking directions in the community				
Writing emails or letters for social reasons				
Going to the doctor or getting medical assistance				
Taking care of my apartment or car				
Feeling comfortable in social situations with speakers of other languages				

Figure 5.4:   Sample Student-Based Needs Analysis Questions (Advanced)

Personal and Sociocultural Needs
What experience do you have learning English?
In which situations do you use English?
With whom do you communicate in English?
Do you use English at work? If yes, give some examples. For example, do you write memos in English? Are meetings in English? Do you write emails in English?

Use this scale to answer these questions about your English. Write the number of your answer next to each item and then write 1–2 sentences explaining why you chose that number (1=somewhat comfortable; 2=comfortable; 3=very comfortable).How comfortable are you using English in these social or work situations?

Introducing and talking about yourself	Writing a work email or memo
Socializing with other language speakers	Speaking with colleagues
Making friends with other language speakers	Using the telephone for business

Language Needs

Use this scale to answer these questions about your English. Write the number of your answer next to each item and then write 1–2 sentences explaining why you chose that number (1=somewhat comfortable; 2=comfortable; 3=very comfortable). How comfortable are you using English in:

Reading?	Listening?
Writing?	Speaking?

What are your three main reasons for learning English?	1.
	2.
	3.

What do you find most difficult when learning English and why?
What experience do you have learning other languages?

Moving from Needs Analysis to Goal Setting

When setting goals for the language classroom, the teacher must keep in mind the age of the students, level of the students, setting of the school, overall goals of the language program, and goals for that particular class. Going back to Scenario 1 with Emily (see page 3), we see that she is teaching adults from beginning to advanced levels of English, and she is teaching EFL in Turkey. The school has decided to follow the model of an intensive program. For the purposes of needs analysis, Emily's focus is on her intermediate-level Writing class. After she administered her Likert scale needs analysis document to her class of 15 students on the first day of the class, the results that she compiled are displayed in Figure 5.5.

After Emily reviews the information, she wants to set the overall goals for the class based on the book she has been assigned in conjunction with the student-based needs as demonstrated by her needs analysis. Emily wants to focus on describing student behaviors associated with her class goals (Reed & Michaud, 2010). She wants to take a goal-based approach to her class to make clear to her students that their personal, language, and sociocultural needs for the course are incorporated into the overall class goals (Long, 2005).

Analyzing the Needs Analysis Results

Personal Goals

Under personal goals, it is clear that students want to work on a several issues. Students indicate that they want to improve their social skills, including interacting with people and interacting with social media. They are not interested in phone conversation skills, but they are definitely interested in job skills. A very positive note is how confident the students feel about their classroom skills.

Language Goals

As far as classroom skills, it is apparent that students feel confident about their speaking and listening skills, which differs significantly from their confidence of speaking outside the classroom. Since this is a writing class, Emily is particularly interested in the fact that they want to work on writing skills for both the classroom and outside of it. In conjunction with what students reported about job skills in Personal Goals, she definitely wants to focus on writing for academic, personal, and job-seeking purposes.

Sociocultural Goals

Emily sees that, in this category, students for the first time indicate some topics in which they are not interested. While students indicate that they are interested in writing for social purposes, they are not interested in some specific social situations, such as going to the doctor or renting an apartment. Emily chose these topics for the needs analysis because these topics were in some

Figure 5.5:   Results from a Sample Likert-Scale Needs Analysis

Name: N/A (compiled results from all 15 students)	Date: January 3		
Class: Intermediate Writing			

Please put an X in the box with the answer that best describes you when using the English language. Please mark only one answer per statement.

Personal Goals	I'm excellent at this.	I feel comfortable with this.	I need to work at this.	I'm not interested in this.
Talking about myself, family, and friends	1	3	11	
Listening to English language TV, radio, or internet materials	1	1	13	
Meeting new people and having casual conversations	1	4	10	
Talking on the phone	0	1	4	10
Finding, applying for, and interviewing for a job	1	3	11	
Completing my school work successfully	12	2	1	
Participating in groups in class	11	4		
Language Goals				
Correcting my language when I make mistakes	1	2	12	
Speaking in class when needed	11	3	1	
Speaking outside class when needed	2	4	9	
Listening and understanding in class when needed	10	4	1	
Listening and understanding outside class when needed	2	6	7	
Reading and understanding texts in class when needed	4	5	6	
Reading and understanding texts outside class when needed	1	1	13	
Writing in class when needed	2	3	10	
Writing outside class when needed	1	0	14	
Sociocultural Goals				
Shopping, eating out, or asking directions in the community	1	5	7	2
Writing emails or letters for social reasons	3	1	10	1
Going to the doctor or getting medical assistance			6	9
Taking care of my apartment or car			4	11
Feeling comfortable in social situations with speakers of other languages	1	2	12	

of the textbooks she was considering for her class (later on, this chapter provides information on how to choose a textbook for your language course). This information helps her to determine which of the topics in her chosen textbook she might want to decrease her focus on since her students feel these topics are not relevant to their lives. It does not mean that she need to drop these topics altogether, because it could be that the information becomes valuable at a later time. But, if Emily wants to motivate her students and show that their needs are being considered, she is going to choose those topics that students indicate are most important to them, and do it transparently. Now, Emily feels ready to write her course goals by putting together her needs analysis results with the school's set curriculum.

Setting Goals and Objectives in the L2 Classroom

Setting goals for the language classroom is a critical step in the overall curriculum development process. Goals set the general focus for the class and describe specifically what the students will learn during a certain period of time. The goals are also the foundation for the objectives for the class, which translate the student-focused goals into observable and measurable student behaviors (Reed & Michaud, 2010). The goals and objectives together specify the language forms to be taught (e.g., reading, writing, listening, or speaking), the tasks that will be accomplished (e.g., reading complex texts, writing paragraphs, listening to academic lectures, speaking in social situations), and the proficiency level necessary to complete those tasks (e.g., beginning level, intermediate level, or with 80 percent success rate).

Let's look at some sample goals as set by the *Great Paragraphs* book in the *Great Writing* series (Unit 1) to see how class goals might be set for a writing class. These goals are written keeping in mind the focus on the class (writing) and what the students will do to meet those goals.

Writing Unit	Goal
Unit 1	To learn the three main features of a paragraph
Unit 2	To learn how to brainstorm ideas for writing
Unit 3	To learn how to write a topic sentence

Goals in other types of classes could include:

Class	Goal
Reading	To read for the main topic of a paragraph To read for the details in a paragraph
Listening	To listen for certain sounds in the English language To learn how to identify the purpose of a spoken language segment
Speaking	To learn how to pronounce consonants in English correctly To learn about supragementals in English

Writing Objectives

Emily now wants to set her class objectives using needs analysis results in conjunction with the unit goals in her textbook (*Great Paragraphs*). The purpose is that her class flows smoothly with the book material and students are motivated by the goals indicated in the needs analysis. Objectives differ from goals in that they are operationalized to be measurable and observable (Reed & Michaud, 2010). Reed and Michaud recommend that objectives be written with the final outcome in mind and that the outcome be very specific. For example, instead of using subjective terms such as *know, understand,* and *learn,* student-focused goals should use concrete terms such as *state, respond,* or *write.*

Let's look at the objectives that Emily creates for her Writing class in Turkey using her textbook goals and student input.

Goal	Needs Analysis Input	Objectives
To learn the 3 main features of a paragraph	Personal Goals: Students are interested in job skills.	Given 4 different paragraphs (2 poorly written and 2 well written), students will successfully identify which paragraphs are effective. Students will write a paragraph with a topic sentence and 3 supporting details about their ideal job.
To learn how to brainstorm ideas for writing	Language Goals: Students are less confident about writing outside the classroom.	Given 5 job advertisements, students in groups will write 3 questions that they want to ask about the job. For homework, students will create a list of 10 ideas for writing a paragraph on this topic: What is the best job to have?
To learn how to write a topic sentence	Sociocultural Goals: Students are interested in writing for social purposes.	Given 4 different paragraphs that describe social media outlets (e.g., blogs, Facebook, Instagram, Twitter) and are missing topic sentences, students will write appropriate topic sentences for the paragraph. Students will write an effective topic sentence for a paragraph about their job skills.

Moving from Setting Goals and Objectives to Planning Lessons

Once the goals and objectives are created for the course, the teacher is ready to move to lesson planning. Reed and Michaud (2010) demonstrate the differences between lesson sequencing, which is simple plan based on time, and goal-driven lesson planning, which takes into account student goals and behaviors. Goal-driven lesson plans focus on a student-centered classroom where the needs analysis is utilized to motivate students in their classroom activities and where goals are adjusted as the teachers assesses student success (see Chapters 7–12 for more details on how to effectively assess students' performance in the classroom). Goal-driven lesson plans contain goals and objectives that are measurable and observable, making lesson planning, instruction, and assessment clear and focused, as shown in Table 5.3. (Chapter 6 will provide a more detailed template on lesson plan design.)

Let's look at an example of a goal-driven lesson plan. Note how the goals and objectives are clearly written and focus on student behavior. You will see embedded assessment and activities that motivate students and focus on their long-term needs and personal goals. You will learn more about syllabus and lesson planning formation in Chapter 6, but this is an example where you will see the focus on goal setting and objective writing. The basic components of an ESL/EFL lesson plan are listed in Figure 5.6, though, before you read about them in more detail in Chapter 6.

Table 5.3:   Lesson Sequences vs. Goal-Driven Lesson Plans

Lesson Sequences	Goal-Driven Lesson Plans
Focus on immediate student wants/interests	Focus on longer-term student needs
Include assessment only as an afterthought, at best	Contain built-in assessment
Include varied activities for high level of student interest	Include activities to advance students toward goals
Approach each lesson as an individual event	Approach lessons cumulatively
Remind teachers what to do in the classroom and when	Remind teachers when and why to do things
Draw on declarative knowledge	Draw on procedural knowledge
Use teachers' administrative functions	Use teachers' executive functions
Consider moment-to-moment tactics	Consider overall strategies

From *Goal-Driven Lesson Planning for Teaching English to Speakers of Other Languages* by M. Reed & C. Michaud, p. 51. Copyright © 2010, University of Michigan Press.

Figure 5.6:   The Lesson Plan

Setting: Here is where you will provide the basics of your class including age, level, number of students, genders represented, cultures, and language background if known.

Pre-Lesson Inventory: The inventory encourages you to track what your language learners have recently worked on and how this lesson fits into the overall goals and objectives of the previous lessons. This helps you to track what students have done and still need to do to meet language goals.

Goals: Set the general purpose of your lesson.

Objectives: Set your objectives for the lesson (they can be listed under Activities as each activity might address a specific objective).

Warm-Up/Review: During the warm-up, you can motivate students with a preview of the lesson in a fun way, such as showing them pictures, playing a game with a ball, or asking questions. This is also the time to review the previous day's lesson to determine if students have acquired the necessary language to move forward or if you need to re-teach any materials.

Presentation and Practice/Activities: Each activity should be set with clear and organized procedures and any language that is needed to complete the lesson.

Closure/Cool Down: At the end of each class, you should prepare a cool-down time where you can review the day's lesson and check for understanding.

Homework: Giving homework encourages students to use the language they have learned that day outside of the classroom and extends their learning.

Adapting a Textbook for Your Classroom and Students

The needs analysis revealed where your students are in terms of level, and now you have ideas about how to meet those needs through goal-driven lesson planning. However, you still have to make that work within your course objectives and textbook. It's important for students to see a connection between what they read and study and what they do in class. In some teaching positions, L2 teachers are assigned a textbook to use in their classrooms, while, in other cases, teachers are allowed to choose their own textbook, sometimes from a guide list. In any case, it is important for L2 teachers to analyze their textbooks to determine if they are appropriate for that particular class.

Textbook Evaluation Using the ACTFL Standards

The American Council on the Teaching of Foreign Languages (ACTFL, 2006) developed standards to create consistency in language content, delivery, and instruction around the world. The Standards are guidelines to review every aspect of delivery of L2 instruction. One such element to be considered is textbook selection. Based on the ACTFL Standards, textbook evaluation includes the 5 Cs (communication, culture, connections, comparisons, and communities), as well as the seven curricular elements of:

1. language systems
2. communication strategies
3. cultural knowledge
4. learning strategies
5. content from other subject areas
6. critical-thinking skills
7. technology

A number of ESL textbook evaluation checklists that L2 teachers may find useful are available (see Miekley, 2005; Skierso, 1991; Williams, 1993). One sample of a comprehensive textbook evaluation instrument that uses the ACTFL Standards' organizing principles and elements as the points of comparison among different textbooks is presented in Figures 5.7 and 5.8.

This chapter showed how curriculum development in the L2 classroom should involve careful assessment of learner needs. The needs analysis should evaluate language needs but also any psychological, social, and cultural factors that could influence the language classroom and the learning process. It is also very important to consider the language proficiency level of L2 students when choosing or creating a needs analysis instrument.

Figure 5.7:   Evaluating Textbooks According to the Five Cs

Communication

Questions	If Yes, exemplify:	No
1. Are L2 learners introduced to vocabulary and grammatical structures? 2. Is there a balance among listening, speaking, reading, and writing? 3. Do activities provide opportunities for individual, paired, or group learning? 4. Is the context for activities set age appropriate? 5. Are vocabulary and grammar points reviewed and practiced multiple times throughout the book?	1. 2. 3. 4. 5.	1. 2. 3. 4. 5.

Cultures

Questions	If Yes, exemplify:	No
1. Are there authentic, up-to-date visual images of the target culture? 2. Is the cultural information age-appropriate? 3. Does the teaching of the target culture incorporate the L2 learners exploring their own culture?	1. 2. 3.	1. 2. 3.

Connections

Questions	If Yes, exemplify:	No
1. Are there themes that encourage cross-disciplinary projects?	1.	1.

Comparisons

Questions	If Yes, exemplify:	No
1. Are L2 learners asked to look at their own native language and compare it to English? 2. Are L2 learners asked to compare their own culture and make comparisons with the target culture?	1. 2.	1. 2.

Communities

Questions	If Yes, exemplify:	No
1. Are L2 learners provided with role models or individuals who use English in their lives for personal interest and enjoyment? 2. Are L2 leaners given examples of ways they can use English beyond the L2 classroom?	1. 2.	1. 2.

Source: ACTFL (2006).

Figure 5.8:   Evaluating Textbooks According to the Seven Curricular Components

Language Systems

Questions	If Yes, exemplify:	No
1. Is the vocabulary appropriate for the language level in focus? 2. Is grammar presented clearly and in a way that is easy to understand? 3. Is there sufficient oral and written practice that promotes meaningful use of English?	1. 2. 3.	1. 2. 3.

Communication Strategies

Questions	If Yes, exemplify:	No
1. Are listening, speaking, reading, writing, and cultural strategies (such as paraphrasing, making and verifying hypotheses, making inferences, and predicting) presented and practiced?	1.	1.

Cultural Knowledge

Questions	If Yes, exemplify:	No
1. Is the cultural content accurate, current, and age-level appropriate?	1.	1.

Learning Strategies

Questions	If Yes, exemplify:	No
1. Does the text provide L2 learners with strategies to help them be successful listeners, speakers, readers, and writers of the language? 2. Does the text have a large number of pair and group activities? Are these activities meaningful?	1. 2.	1. 2.

Content from Other Subject Areas

Questions	If Yes, exemplify:	No
1. Are there activities/projects in every chapter/unit that connect language learning with other disciplines (science, history, geography, etc.)?	1.	1.

Critical-Thinking Skills

Questions	If Yes, exemplify:	No
1. Are students asked to do more than to memorize and recall? 2. Are the students asked to analyze, synthesize, and evaluate?	1. 2.	1.

Technology

Questions	If Yes, exemplify	No
1. Does the text have included technology (video, CD-ROM, website) that provides meaningful and interactive practice?	1.	1.

Source: ACTFL (2006).

Summarizing Statements

1. A needs analysis conducted at the beginning of any course is a critical step in determining the focus of the curriculum for that particular class.

2. Sociocultural, personal, and integrated language goals are also important components of the needs analysis process.

3. There are various methods for conducting a student-centered needs analyses, each one with unique properties and best used in different L2 classroom situations.

4. Before beginning the needs analysis, it is essential to ensure that the language is leveled for the students and appropriate for the language, cultural, psychological, and social factors that pertain to that particular L2 classroom.

5. It is important to use the needs analysis results to create goals, objectives, and goal-driven lesson plans for the L2 classroom.

6. When reviewing possible textbooks for the classroom, one approach inspired by ACTFL focuses on principles of the 5 Cs (communication, culture, connections, comparisons, and communities), as well as the seven curricular components (language systems, communication strategies, cultural knowledge, learning strategies, content from other subject areas, critical-thinking skills, and technology). The goal is for students to acquire functional language for academic achievement and for real-life communication as a result of the teacher having collected rich data through needs analysis and careful selection of a textbook appropriate for those needs.

REFLECTION AND APPLICATION

1. Think about a course you are teaching now or a course you would like to teach in the future. On your own, or in a group, list the age, level, and title of the ESL/EFL class. Brainstorm 10–15 questions you would like to include in a student-based needs analysis for that course. Discuss/write how this information will help you to determine the needs and curriculum for the class.

2. Table 5.2 details what language skills a student might be expected to have at various levels of ESL. In pairs or groups, create a fourth column that focuses on academic language skills using CEFR and WIDA resources listed in the chapter, and then list some class activities or assignments that would be appropriate for each level. Be prepared to explain the activities and how they are appropriate according to the table.

3. Use an ESL/EFL textbook you have or one shared by the instructor, and complete the textbook evaluation form in Figures 5.7 and 5.8. Were you able to answer most of the questions on the chart? Will the textbook work for a course you are teaching now or want to teach in the future? Discuss with the class, and share any experiences selecting materials for a course.

REFERENCES

ACTFL. (2006). *National standards in foreign language education project: Standards for foreign language learning in the 21st century.* Lawrence, KS: Allen Press. Retrieved from http://www.actfl.org/sites/default/files/pdfs/public/StandardsforFLLexecsumm_rev.pdf

Auerbach, E.R. (1994). *Making meaning, making change: Participatory curriculum development for adult ESL literacy.* Washington, DC, and McHenry, IL: Center for Applied Linguistics and Delta Systems.

Benesch, S. (1996). Needs analysis and curriculum development in EAP: An example of a critical approach. *TESOL Quarterly, 30*(4), 723–738.

Berwick, R. (1989). Needs assessment in language programming: from theory to practice. In R. K. Johnson (Ed.), *The second language curriculum* (pp. 48–62). Cambridge, U.K.: Cambridge University Press.

Brindley, G. (1989). The role of needs analysis in adult ESL programme design. In R. K. Johnson (Ed.), *The second language curriculum* (pp. 63–78). Cambridge, U.K.: Cambridge University Press.

CASAS. (2012). *CASAS skill level descriptors.* Retrieved from https://www.casas.org/product-overviews/curriculum-management-instruction/casas-scale-skill-levels-and-descriptors

Davies, A. (2006). What do learners really want from their EFL course? *ELT Journal, 60*(1), 3–12.

Donato, R., & McCormick, D. (1994). A sociocultural perspective on language learning strategies: The role of mediation. *The Modern Language Journal, 78*(4), 453–464.

Folse, K., Muchmore-Vokoun, A., & Vestri Solomon, E. (2010). *Great writing 2: Great paragraphs.* Boston: Heinle Cengage Learning.

Grognet, A. G. (1997). *Integrating employment skills in adult ESL instruction.* Retrieved from http://www.cal.org/caela/esl_resources/digests/eskilsqa.html

Lambert, C. (2010). A task-based needs analysis: Putting principles into practice. *Language Teaching Research, 14*(1), 99–112.

Long, M. H. (2005). Methodological issues in learner needs analysis. In M. Long (Ed.), *Second language needs analysis* (pp. 19–76). Cambridge, U.K. Cambridge University Press.

Macalister, J. (2012). Narrative frames and needs analysis. *System, 40*(1), 120–128.

Miekley, J. (2005). ESL textbook evaluation textbook. *The Reading Matrix, 5*(2), 1–9.

Munby, J. (1978). Communicative syllabus design. Cambridge, U.K.: Cambridge University Press.

Reed, M., & Michaud, C. (2010). *Goal-driven lesson planning for teaching English to speakers of other languages.* Ann Arbor: University of Michigan Press.

Seedhouse, P. (1995). Needs analysis and the general English classroom. *ELT Journal, 49*(1), 59–65.

Skierso, A. (1991). Textbook selection and evaluation. In M. Celce-Murcia (Ed.), *Teaching English as a second or foreign language* (pp. 432–453). Boston: Heinle & Heinle.

West, R. (1994). Needs analysis in language teaching. *Language Teaching, 27*, 1–19.

Williams, D. (1993). Developing criteria for textbook evaluation. *ELT Journal, 37*(3), 251–255.

Chapter 6

▲

Designing Goal-Based Syllabi and Lesson Plans

This chapter defines what a syllabus is in the larger context of a language curriculum and exemplifies syllabus components common to L2 syllabi, regardless of the teaching approaches. Several types of syllabi are discussed in the context of the language acquisition theories presented in Chapters 2 through 4. Grammar-based and communicative syllabi are addressed, as are eclectic syllabi and lesson plans.

Language Syllabi: Organizational Components

After deciding on the goals and objectives for a language course, the next step is to design a syllabus that will reflect those goals and objectives. A **syllabus** is a document that describes the order, content, and progression of what will be studied in the course based on the overall curriculum. The syllabus is a roadmap for the teacher and students that shows what will be accomplished over a period of a course. It is important to distinguish between syllabus design and curriculum design. When language instructors and administrators create a **language curriculum**, they must address all instructional and assessment activities for the program across many courses and language proficiency levels. Designing a syllabus requires a focus on a particular subject within the program. In other words, a syllabus for an advanced ESL Writing class in an Intensive English Program (IEP) will concentrate on the knowledge required for academic English writing, assuming that the goal of the students enrolled in that class is to pursue an academic degree at a U.S. college or university. That course syllabus is one part of the curriculum for that institution, which includes the goals, learning objectives, syllabi, materials, and assessment procedures for all classes taught in that IEP. Other courses at that proficiency level are considered, as are the courses that would precede or follow the advanced ESL Writing course.

Table 6.1: Common Components of a Syllabus

Component	Description
Basic course information	Course name/number, instructor name, meeting time and place, contact information, office hours
Goals/rationale	Type of knowledge and skills that will be emphasized, as well as an explanation regarding how and why the course is organized in a particular sequence
Learning objectives	What knowledge learners will gain from the course, sometimes phrased as *Students will be able to*
Student responsibilities	Policies on lateness, missed work, extra credit, exams, class requirements, participation, due dates, etc.
Materials and assignments	Required textbooks and readings and lists of assignments and their due dates (and possibly including length/content requirements, such as for a research paper)
Grading method	Statement of assessment procedures
Course content	Schedule/calendar, meeting dates and holidays, school policies, assignments, online components, as well as major topics

Syllabi for language classes tend to have the same components, as shown in Table 6.1.

Types of Language Syllabi

Seven types of syllabi tend to be employed in most L2 classrooms: structural, situational, topical, functional, notional, skills, and task-based (Brown, 1995; Dincay, 2011). Part I of this book identified three main directions in language acquisition theories and how they are reflected in L2 teaching methodology. Based on our analysis, there are three pedagogical orientations that are linked to the three major language acquisition theories previously analyzed in Part I of this book. The first one, associated with behaviorism, is grammar-based; the second one, linked to input theories, is communicative with an emphasis on the product of communication; and the third one, more connected with sociocultural theory, is also communicative but emphasizes the process of communication. Keep those major methodologies in mind throughout the discussion of language syllabi because some teaching circumstances require a combination of more than one approach to syllabus design (a fourth pedagogical approach); in other situations instructors are able to select their own course materials and are not required to teach using a pre-selected textbook. Table 6.2 lists examples of syllabi associated with the four orientations.

Table 6.2: Four Categories of Syllabi

Orientation	Example of Syllabus Used with Each Orientation
Grammar	Structural
Communicative product	Situational-topical Notional-functional Skills-based
Communicative process	Task-based
Eclectic	Layered Text-based

Grammar-Based Syllabi

Structural

Grammar is the organizing principle in a **structural syllabus.** The content for the syllabus is selected based on either the level of grammar complexity or frequency of grammatical forms. When L2 teachers decide to employ an approach that moves from easy to more difficult forms, they organize their content in the following manner: L2 learners are first exposed to simple structures, such as the simple present tense (*I read, you read, she/he/it reads*, etc.) before covering more complex ones, such as the present perfect progressive (*I have been reading, you have been reading*, etc.).

In addition to linguistic structures, the content of the structural syllabus may include the lexicon, or the vocabulary list, that is to be taught during the language class. Moreover, each element of the content to be covered in a structural syllabus is introduced in a linear manner, meaning that one grammar item is presented at a time and mastery of that item is required before moving on to the next. Figure 6.1 is an authentic structural syllabus for adult ESL learners in an IEP. Note how the syllabus components illustrated in Table 6.1 have been adapted to fit the needs of a course where there may or may not be a formal grading system in place.

Communicative Product–Oriented Syllabi

Situational-Topical

Unlike a structural syllabus, where grammar is at the core of language teaching, a **situational-topical syllabus** is based on the communication situations that L2 learners need to operate in and the topics they need to discuss. Some examples of communicative situations are being at the airport, at a hotel, in a restaurant, at school, etc. Determining which communicative situations to

Figure 6.1:   Structural Syllabus Sample

Intensive English Studies Program

Instructor: Florin Mihai

Contact Information: Email: FlorinMihai@iesp.edu

Office Hours: M–T 9–12

ESL Grammar 4 Syllabus for Spring 2016

Text: *Grammar Dimensions: Form, Meaning, and Use Book 4*
By Jan Frodesen and Janet Eyring

Course Description: The focus of this course is to present grammar as a supporting skill for reading, writing, listening, and speaking. There will be a strong emphasis on editing skills, paraphrasing, and summarizing. In addition, the class will provide extensive and varied language practice and will seek to balance form-focused language activities with opportunities for meaningful communication.

Student Responsibilities: Participate while in class and please, **be on time!** If you think you did not understand something, please ask for clarification or for more information to help you understand better. Please don't forget to be respectful and to show respect to the other students in your class.

Instructor Responsibilities: I will come to class prepared to teach the material and ready to address your questions or concerns. I will treat you respectfully, and I will be available to provide you with extra assistance out of class.

Class Calendar/Grammar Structures to Be Covered:
Week 1 Verbs: Chapter 1 Verb Tenses in Written and Spoken Communication, Chapter 2 Verbs, Chapter 3 Subject-Verb Agreement, Chapter 4 Passive Verbs

Week 2 Relative Clauses: Chapter 7 Relative Clauses Modifying Subjects, Chapter 8 Relative Clauses Modifying Objects, Chapter 9 Nonrestrictive Relative Clauses

Week 3 Organizing Text: Chapter 5 Article Usage, Chapter 6 Reference Words and Phrases, Chapter 14 Discourse Organizers

Week 4 Conditionals and Adverb Clauses: Chapter 15 Conditionals, Chapter 16 Reducing Adverb Clauses

Week 5 Gerunds and Infinitives: Chapter 18 Gerunds and Infinitives, Chapter 19 Perfective Infinitives

Week 6 Focusing and Emphasizing Structures: Chapter 23 Emphatic Structures, Chapter 24 Fronting Structures for Emphasis and Focus, Chapter 25 Focusing and Emphasizing Structures

Week 7 Review

cover in a course is based on the likelihood of whether or not the L2 learners will find themselves in those situations, which is typically indicated through the setting (e.g., adult education vs. academic setting) and the needs analysis (Bourke, 2006).

When sequencing situations, L2 teachers should consider a mixture of chronology and possibility of the situation happening (Brown, 1995). For example, suppose that you are teaching in an EFL environment and you want to make sure that your L2 learners are able to function in an English-speaking environment when traveling. Your syllabus would therefore include travel situations (e.g., being at the airport or train station, riding a bus or subway, taking a taxi) and social/interactive situations, such as visiting a museum, going to a party, or eating in a restaurant. To address these travel and social situations, an instructor might sequence the lessons on a situational-topical syllabus this way: (1) lesson focused on being at the airport, (2) lesson on taking a bus or subway or taxi, (3) lesson on checking into a hotel, (4) lesson on eating out in a restaurant, (5) lesson on going to a museum, and (6) lesson on attending a party.

In terms of the topic part of the situational-topic syllabus, the topics are selected based on the situations on the syllabus. For example, what kinds of things might someone need to be able to talk about at a party? Are there certain taboo subjects that need to be avoided? Or, if the communication situation relates to checking into a hotel, for example, the class would focus on the language needed to communicate in that situation: *I have a reservation. Can you help me with my luggage? Do you have free WiFi? What time is checkout?*

An example of a resource that demonstrates the attributes of a situational-topical syllabus is *Something to Talk About: A Reproducible Conversation Resource for Teachers and Tutors* by Kathleen Olson (2001). An excerpt from the table of contents shows the topic (Home) and the situations: describing your home in a lesson called "Home Is Where the Heart Is"; shopping for you and your family in a lesson called "Paper or Plastic?"; and choosing a home in a lesson called "Home Sweet Home." Figure 6.2 illustrates the content of one of these lessons.

Notional-Functional

Another way of organizing content in language courses is by using notions (concepts or ideas) and functions as key conceptual categories (Ahmed & Alamin, 2012; Wilkins, 1976). Examples of notions are general ideas such as time, distance, or duration or specific ideas such as pets or hobbies.

Functions, illustrated in Table 6.3, are communicative acts that employ language to achieve a purpose like making a request or asking for information (Finocchiaro & Brumfit, 1983). A **notional-functional syllabus,** then, puts communication first and does not consider grammar to be one of its organizing principles. It emphasizes communication by directing learners' attention to useful and socially appropriate expressions that they can use when communicating in a second language (Miranda García, Calle Martín, & Melendo, 2006).

When compiling a notional-functional syllabus, L2 instructors need to take into account the results of the needs analysis. The process of constantly accounting for what the students need in order to be successful is not unique to the notional-functional syllabus, but, in this case,

Figure 6.2:   Sample of a Situational-Topical Lesson

Home Sweet Home

Describe your childhood home.

Describe the house of your dreams.

- Where is it?
- What does it look like?
- What factors are most important in selecting your dream home?

The factors most important to Americans in selecting their
dream homes are

- size of house
- price
- appearance
- investment value
- size of yard
- proximity to work

Are the preceding factors for selecting a dream home the same as yours?

Is a garden important to you?

What interior features are most desirable to you?

Inside the home, storage space, a fireplace, an entertainment center, and a
pantry are considered most desirable by Americans.

Table 6.3:   The Five Types of Language Functions (Finocchiaro & Brumfit, 1983)

Type	Description	Example
Personal	Clarify or arrange one's ideas	Expressing love/joy/pleasure, fear/frustration
Interpersonal	Establish and maintain desirable social and working relationships	Extending and accepting invitations; refusing invitations politely or making alternative arrangements; making/breaking appointments for meetings; apologizing; excusing oneself and accepting excuses for not meeting commitments; indicating agreement or disagreement; interrupting another speaker politely
Directive	Attempt to influence the actions of others; accepting or refusing direction	Making suggestions in which the speaker is included; making requests; making suggestions; refusing to accept a suggestion or a request but offering an alternative; persuading someone to change his or her point of view; requesting and granting permission
Referential	Talk or report about things, actions, events, or people in the environment in the past or in the future; talk about language (metalinguistically)	Identifying items or people in the classroom, school, home, community; asking for a description of someone or something; defining something or a language item or asking for a definition; paraphrasing, summarizing, or translating (L1 to L2 or L2 to L1); explaining or asking for explanations of how something works; comparing or contrasting things
Imaginative	Include elements of creativity and artistic expression	Discussing a poem, story, piece of music, play, painting, film, or TV program

instructors should select the notions and functions that are the most relevant to their students. For example, for an ESL course for nurses who are learning English to work in an English-speaking environment, the syllabus might look like Figure 6.3.

Skills-Based

In a **skills-based** approach to syllabus design, L2 instructors organize their materials based on the academic and language skills that their L2 students need as identified through the needs analysis or the curriculum. For example, listening comprehension includes several skills—recognizing

Figure 6.3:   Example of Notional-Functional Syllabus, Nursing

---

Notions: Quantity and Duration

Functions:

► Talking about sickness: I feel pain in my___. I have a ___ache.

► Making a suggestion: Would you like to take one pill every 6 hours or one pill every 12 hours?

► Accepting or rejecting a suggestion: I think that's a great idea.

► Making a request: Could you give me something for my stomach ache?

► Agreeing to a request: Let's do that.

Figure 6.4:   Excerpt of Skills-Based Syllabus for Listening Class

---

Class Calendar

Week 1: Finding the right career

Day 1: Listening material: An excerpt from *The key to success? Grit* (TED Talks) by Angela Lee Duckworth

Listening skills included in this lesson: understanding cause and effect, sequencing events, identifying the main ideas, summarizing.

---

the topic, identifying the speaker, evaluating themes, finding the main idea, finding supporting details, making inferences, etc. (Brown, 2007). L2 instructors can select skills for the syllabus based on the needs analysis and then organize them based on chronology or frequency. An excerpt from a skills-based syllabus for a listening class is shown in Figure 6.4.

Communicative Process–Oriented Syllabi

The purpose of task-based learning is to use L2 learners' real-life needs and activities as learning experiences. The tasks involved in task-based learning bring real-world experiences into the classroom because language is not taught directly but supplied as needed for the completion of the task. Language learning happens mostly during the completion of tasks, which is why task-based syllabi are classified as process-oriented, as opposed to product-oriented. An example of a task would be determining the steps when applying for a program or job, which may entail obtaining the forms and information necessary to complete the process.

Just like the other types of syllabi previously discussed, **task-based syllabi** should be developed for each group of learners based on the results of a needs analysis. In addition, L2 instructors need to take into account the proficiency levels of their students when designing or selecting tasks.

Eclectic Syllabi

Layered

Many instructors and textbook authors combine two or more approaches in their syllabus when they organize content for their language classes, thereby creating an **eclectic syllabus.** An eclectic syllabus combines various approaches; a layered syllabus is one example. A layered syllabus has a primary syllabus and secondary or tertiary syllabi in layers operating under it, as shown in Figure 6.5.

The primary syllabus is the notional-functional syllabus, as represented by **actions in sequence** with the language functions of **describing actions** and **making predictions.** The structural part focuses on adverbs. Because of the importance of grammar instruction in many EFL settings for example, layered syllabi often include a communicative and structural outcome. The focus of the unit is how people spend their weekend. For **describing actions,** they can be required to listen to a conversation between two people who went to a barbeque and select the items they heard mentioned in the conversation. For **making predictions,** they can be asked to work in groups and predict what type of weekend activities might occur based on the weather forecast. For the structural focus, adverbs, they are asked to complete exercises like this:

Rewrite the sentences using a verb and an adverb.

He is a slow worker.   He works slowly.

1. He is a bad player.   _____ .

2. I am a terrible singer.   _____ .

3. She is a good dancer.   _____ .

Figure 6.5:   Example of a Layered Syllabus

Week 1
Unit: Actions in Sequence: Focus on Weekend Plans

Notional-Functional Aspects	Structural Aspects
Describe and discuss weekend activities Make predictions	Adverbs

Text-Based

Most of the approaches in syllabus design discussed so far assume the adoption and use of one textbook that will address the identified language and academic needs of L2 students, but text-based syllabi use a variety of texts and do not rely only on one textbook. Text-based syllabi are constructed around texts or samples of extended discourse, an approach often used when an overall context for language learning has been defined, such as in a specific workplace or a university. An example of a text-based syllabus for an advanced Reading class where the main textbook used is a novel is shown in Figure 6.6.

The first step in creating a text-based syllabus is to identify the texts for a specific context, which is followed by developing the units of instruction in relation to the texts. For example, suppose you are teaching a course preparing ESL learners to begin taking college or university courses. Following the needs assessment, the instructor would identify the texts to be used and then develop a sequence for them. Table 6.4 shows how an instructor would match texts to the syllabus.

As Krahnke (1987) has noted, no single type of syllabus is appropriate for all teaching settings because the needs and conditions of each setting are so distinctive that specific recommen-

---

Figure 6.6:   Example of Text-Based Syllabus, Reading Class

Navigating Stormy Weather: Advanced Reading

Goal: To get students to read for pleasure

Rationale for using an authentic text:
► learn how English speakers use English
► improve reading rate
► find examples of good writing in English
► learn new vocabulary
► learn about culture

Text: *Stormy Weather* by Carl Hiaasen

Objectives:
Students will be able to identify and follow the main plot line.
Students will be able to identify and follow all the characters presented in the book.

Activities:
Write the story (in groups).
Write about the characters (in groups).
Pick and describe their favorite character (individually).

Table 6.4:   Selecting Texts for Text-Based Syllabi

Units (Skills)	Possible Texts/Materials
Enrolling at university	Application forms
Discussing course selection	Advising: selecting courses from a university catalog
Attending lectures	Sample lectures and discussions (including transcripts)
Using the library	Library catalogues Online library support documentation
Reading reference books/academic content	Discipline-specific journal articles/books Dictionaries and encyclopedia
Writing essays/reports	Discipline-specific essays/reports Model essays/reports
Taking exams	Model exam papers
Participating in academic discussions/groups	Transcripts of discussions/groups

dations that will apply everywhere and to everyone are not possible. He also recommends that instructors:

> always chose the syllabus type that includes the broadest and most comprehensive representation of language functions and discourse types. In this way the syllabus designer ensures that two general goals of language instruction will be addressed. First, the bridge to communicative ability will be easier to cross because the problem of synthesis of knowledge and transfer of training is minimized. Secondly, the objectives the students are required to meet will not be so narrow as to handicap them when they are faced with actual occasions of language use. (p. 90)

Lesson Plan Template

Once instructors have identified their goals and objectives and finished putting together their syllabus, they need to think about designing daily instructional sequences, also called **lesson plans.** The structure of a lesson plan was introduced in Chapter 5 when it showed how the goals and objectives stemmed from the needs analysis. Lesson plans are developed by teachers to guide class instruction. A lesson plan template that includes all the necessary ingredients for a successful L2 class is shown in Figure 6.7 (pages 74–75).

Figure 6.8 (pages 76–80) is an example of a lesson plan based on this template.

Figure 6.7:   Lesson Plan Template

Setting: These factors, among others, will impact the content of your lesson plan. Keep in mind the students' age(s), proficiency level(s), cultural backgrounds, and needs; consider the class size, type of school, and overall goals of the program; factor in any constraints, such as a lack of adequate equipment, the potential for equipment to fail, and anything else you consider pertinent.

Pre-Lesson Inventory: This is an explanation of what was done in the previous classes, so that there is a clear/logical transition between what you did before and what you're doing next. Anticipate questions students might have about the material, and have extra examples prepared for explanations. Budget your time for each section of the lesson plan for good classroom management.

Goals: Set the general purpose of your lesson

Objectives: Set your objectives for the lesson. For example,
  Language objective: Students will practice the present progressive tense through readings, worksheets, and oral pair work.
  Theme objective: Students will role play going to the doctor with a fever and practice language appropriate for the situation.
  Skill objective: Students will watch a one-minute video of two friends talking, write the language that they hear, and practice with another student by using the informal language that they hear (e.g., *How ya doin'?*).

Warm-Up/Review: This is a short activity designed to prepare students for the lesson for the day. To tap into their background knowledge on the topic, ask students to look at pictures related to the topic, to skim a related reading passage, or to ask questions related to the topic to pique the students' interest in the subsequent activities.

Presentation and Practice/Activities: When presenting new content in the L2 classroom, be sure to
  ▸ Teach the language point clearly and thoroughly with the students' language abilities in mind.
  ▸ Include numerous and varied examples.
  ▸ Ask questions to check for understanding. Avoid broad questions such as "Does everyone understand?" Instead, ask specific questions to students about the new content.
  ▸ Allow time for students to ask questions and participate.
  ▸ Connect the material to the students in a personal way.

Figure 6.7: Lesson Plan Template (continued)

For practice, include a number of activities for students to practice the new language. Whenever possible, the activities should focus on all language skills (i.e., grammar, reading, writing, speaking, listening, or vocabulary) and should integrate skills when possible. For each activity, prepare in advance the purpose, procedures, and estimated time. Use these guidelines for the practice portion of the class:

- ► Practice activities should be varied and appropriate for the class.
- ► Use drilling and constant comprehension checks throughout the activities.
- ► Ensure that all students participate at some level and, whenever possible, that all language skills were used.
- ► Plan for students to work at increasingly higher levels of thinking.
- ► Allow students to use real language, not just academic-focused language.

Students should produce language related to the topic so that the effectiveness of the lesson can be evaluated. Production can include writings, oral production, worksheets, or pair/group work in an informal or formal manner. Focus on feedback and correctives in this area of the lesson:

- ► Ask students to complete an activity in which you can monitor their individual learning.
- ► Use correctives when needed and make sure they understand how, when, and why correctives are used.
- ► Use the extra examples that you have prepared if there are deficiencies in understanding.
- ► Be prepared to review the language taught or even re-teach using a different approach.

Closure/Cool Down: This is a short activity with the purpose of wrapping up the class. It should take only about 2 or 3 minutes. You can review the vocabulary, focus on the main aspects of a text (e.g., by asking questions about the article or asking students what they have learned during the class), or anything that brings a closure to the class. Be sure to use the same format as the other activities.

Homework: If appropriate, assign a piece of homework to give students further information/practice on the topics you covered in class. Be sure to give clear directions. You might want to include one more exercise here (e.g., "Find an article on the internet on the same topic and fill out the chart"). In this case, you would include this chart as a part of the lesson plan.

Figure 6.8:   The Lesson Plan: Telling a Story with Past Progressive

Setting:
   The class is a low-intermediate ESL class in an IEP. There are 16 students in the class from various parts of the world. Students range in age from 17–40, but most of the students are in their early 20s.

Pre-Lesson Inventory:
   This lesson comes at the end of a unit on the past tense. Students have spent three days learning regular past tense, irregular past tense, and past time clauses such as *I studied before I took the final exam* and *I was happy when I finished the exam*. Earlier in the week students:

   ▶   learned the way to spell past tense verb endings such as in the verb *study*.

   ▶   studied the past tense verb forms of common irregular verbs such as *see, hear, drink, eat, read, go, get, take, lose, have, sit, fall, make, do, begin, break, write, say*, and *buy*.

   ▶   practiced talking about past events by telling each other what they did on the weekend (e.g., *I did homework on Saturday. I played soccer on Sunday*).

   ▶   learned how to use past time clauses introduced by words such as *before, after, when*, and *as soon as* to order the sequence of events.

   ▶   practiced ordering the sequence of events by writing about the steps they took when preparing what they did to move to this country (e.g., *I bought a plane ticket before I went to the airport*).

Goals:

   ▶   To introduce the form and function of the past progressive tense using authentic language.

   ▶   To allow students to practice using the new language in an authentic context.

Warm-Up/Review: Hacky Past (group game)
<u>Goal</u>: To review, reinforce, and assess the past tense verb forms that the students learned earlier in the week and will need for today's lessons.
<u>Objective</u>: The students will stand up and say the correct verb form as prompted by the verb list.
<u>Procedures</u>:

   1.   Show a PowerPoint slide full of pictures that represent the irregular past tense words the students have learned this week (e.g., a man reading: *read*; a woman drinking water: *drink*; a green light: *go*; a child eating ice cream: *eat*; etc.).

   2.   Elicit the verbs from the students by asking "What did he/she do yesterday?" while pointing to each picture.

   3.   Ask students to stand in a circle.

   4.   Stand in the circle with the students and hold a hacky sack.

   5.   Say one of the verbs in the present tense (e.g., *go*).

   6.   Toss the hacky sack to a student and say the past tense (e.g., *went*), indicating that the student should say the past tense.

   7.   After the student says the past tense, tell the student to choose another present verb from the list of pictures.

   8.   When the student says the verb, ask the student to throw the ball to another student, who should now understand to say the past tense of the verb.

   9.   Continue the game **for 3–4 minutes** to let the students review the irregular past tense verbs and review their inhibitions.

Figure 6.8:   The Lesson Plan: Telling a Story with Past Progressive (continued)

Presentation and Practice/Activities:

Activity 1: Grammar Focus (spoken): Language Introduction: Past Progressive

Objectives:

- ▶ The students will see models of English sentences using the past progressive tense.
- ▶ The students will orally guess and say English sentences using the past progressive tense.
- ▶ The students will orally guess and use *while* and *when* appropriately.

Procedure:

1. Show a second PowerPoint slide with a picture of a man watching TV. The man's name, Mike, is typed underneath the picture. Elicit help from the students to build the scenario:

   Teacher: *What is this man's name?*

   Students: *Mike!*

   Teacher: *What did Mike do last night?*

   Students: *Watched TV.*

   Teacher: *What time did Mike watch TV?*

   Students: *He watched TV at 8 o'clock.*

   Teacher: *Did Mike (watch) TV for only 1 minute?*

   Students: *No.*

   Teacher: *How long did Mike watch TV?*

   Students: *1 hour. (Student answers may vary. Adjust your example based on their response.)*

2. Write *Mike watched TV: 8–9 PM* on the board.

3. Show a second PowerPoint slide that shows the same picture of Mike watching TV and a second picture of an older woman on the phone.

4. Continue the dialogue:

   Teacher: *(Point to the woman) Is this Mike's daughter?*

   Students: *No.*

   Teacher: *Who is she?*

   Students: *Mike's mother.*

   Teacher: *Ok, did Mike's mother send Mike an email?*

   Students: *No.*

   Teacher: *Did she go to Mike's house?*

   Students: *No.*

   Teacher: *What did she do?*

   Students: *She called Mike?*

   Teacher: *Very good. She called Mike at 8:15.*

Figure 6.8:   The Lesson Plan: Telling a Story with Past Progressive (continued)

5. Write *Mike's mother called: 8:15* on the board.

6. Continue the dialogue:

    Teacher: *Did Mike's mother call before he watched TV?*
    Students: *No.*
    Teacher: *Did Mike's mother call after Mike watched TV?*
    Students: *No.*
    Teacher: *Very good. Mike's mother called* **while** *Mike was watching TV.*

7. Repeat the sentence several times, and write it on the board.

8. Ask students to analyze the sentence. Ask them which activity was longer and which was shorter. Point out that we use **past be + verb + -*ing*** for the long action and **simple past** for the short action when two things happened at the same time.

9. Write this diagram on the board: *Short action (simple past)* <u>*while*</u> *long action (past progressive)*

10. Show three more sets of pictures to elicit this language:

    The boy fell <u>*while*</u> *he was riding his bike.*
    The neighbor came over <u>*while*</u> *the children were studying.*
    I left work <u>*while*</u> *it was raining.*

11. Reverse the sentences to teach *when*:

    Mike was watching TV <u>*when*</u> *his mother called.*

12. Again, ask students which activity is longer and which one is shorter. Emphasize that *while* comes before the long action, but if you change the order of the sentence *when* comes before the short action.

13. Write this diagram on the board: *Long action (past progressive)* <u>*when*</u> *short action (simple past)*

    The boy was riding his bike <u>*when*</u> *he fell.*
    The man was studying <u>*when*</u> *the woman came over.*
    It was raining <u>*when*</u> *I left work.*

Activity 2: Grammar Focus (written): Active Sentence Formation (class acting activity; individual writing activity)

<u>Objective</u>:
- ▶ Given a model demonstration, students will write appropriate sentences using the past progressive tense.

<u>Procedure</u>:
1. Ask for two volunteers.
2. Give one of the volunteers something to clean with, such as a feather duster or a bottle of Windex and instruct him or her to "clean" the room.

Figure 6.8:   The Lesson Plan: Telling a Story with Past Progressive (continued)

3. Give the other volunteer a camera, and ask him or her to wait for a minute and then take a picture of the student who is cleaning.

4. When they finish, ask the students to write a sentence about what happened. Sample sentences include:

    a. *Student A was cleaning when Student B took a picture.*

    b. *Student B took a picture while Student A was cleaning.*

5. Check their answers.

6. Repeat the activity with these scenarios:

    a. Volunteer A is listening to music on a pair of headphones. Volunteer B waits outside the room for a minute before entering the room. *Student A was listening to music when Student B entered the room.*

    b. Volunteer A is reading a book. Volunteer B pretends to call Volunteer A on the phone. *Student A was reading when Student B called him.*

    c. Volunteer A is talking. (He can just say *blah, blah, blah*). Volunteer B closes his eyes and starts to snore. *Student B fell asleep while Student A was talking.*

Activity 3: Speaking and Listening Focus: Information Gap (pair work)

Objectives:

▶   In pairs, students will form questions and answer questions using the past progressive tense.

▶   In pairs, students will convey information verbally according to their paper.

▶   In pairs, students will listen to gather information.

Procedure:

1. Return to the pictures introduced in Activity 2 to teach the question form. Ask students to repeat what you say and form their own questions as a group:

    What was Mike doing when his mother called?

    What was the boy doing when he fell?

    What did the neighbor do while the children were studying?

    What did you do while it was raining?

2. Put students into pairs.

3. Assign the students in each pair a role: Student A and Student B.

4. (Before class) cut each piece of paper into two pieces so you can give one side to Student A and the other side to Student B.

5. Tell Student A to ask questions to find out what the people were doing when each thing happened.

6. Tell Student B to choose the best answer, tell Student A what happened, and write the number of the question on his or her paper.

Figure 6.8:   The Lesson Plan: Telling a Story with Past Progressive (continued)

7. Be sure to walk around, help, and assess students as they complete the activity.

Student A	Student B
1. Karen _____ when her computer broke.	▸ clean the house ___
2. Bob and Eric_____ when Mark broke his leg.	▸ write a paper _____
3. Paul lost his wallet while he _____.	▸ study for a test ___
4. Melissa had an accident while she _____.	▸ play soccer _____
5. Lisa found her earring while she _____.	▸ shop _____
	▸ drive to work ____

8. Let the students compare their information gap cards to check answers.

9. Distribute the second set of cards so they can switch roles.

10. Repeat Steps 5–7.

Student A	Student B
▸ watch a horror movie ___	1. Frank _____ when he burned his finger.
▸ surf ___	2. Sarah _____ when she got scared.
▸ sleep ___	3. Chelsea _____ when she heard a noise.
▸ play a video game ___	4. Greg met Shakira while he_____.
▸ make dinner ___	5. Dave's mother came home while he _____.
▸ travel to New York ___	

Closure/Cool Down:

1. Ask students how they can use what they learned in class.

2. Review how to form past progressive:

   a. Do we use this when one thing happens before the other or when two things happen at the same time?

   b. Does the long action or the short action use **past *be* + verb + *–ing*?**

Homework: Write a paragraph about a time that you were frightened using simple past and past progressive and the words *when* and *while*.

Evaluating Lesson Plans

Once teachers have designed a lesson plan based on goals and objectives, they need to evaluate it to determine whether or not students will achieve those goals. First, lesson plans should include an explicit list of goals and objectives. These goals and objectives need to be student focused, measurable, and observable. One example of a focused, measurable, and observable objective is this one taken from the lesson plan on past progressive: "In pairs, students will form questions and answer questions using the past progressive tense." Teachers can make this objective even more focused by specifying the number of questions to be formed and answered by students. Second, the lesson sequence need to be ordered and specific, with activities that are achievable, student centered, and advance the stated goals and objectives. Third, activities should provide formal and informal assessment opportunities so that students can demonstrate their successful acquisition of the material presented in class.

To evaluate lesson plans, it is helpful for teachers to have a rubric that they could use when they examine their own lesson plans or are asked to evaluate other teachers' lesson plans. The rubric in Figure 6.9 (see page 82) is an example.

This chapter has looked at several types of syllabi and provided a more detailed presentation of lesson plans. The lesson plan example emphasized that lesson plans are based on goals and objectives that are a result of a solid needs analysis. Syllabi also include goals and objectives based on the same needs analysis findings. Because everything is connected, it is difficult to treat curriculum design activities separately from teaching activities or to sequence them in a linear way, curriculum design first and teaching second. When identifying goals and objectives, teachers should immediately think about what teaching approach they should use as well as how to design syllabi and testing materials. Teaching is part of curriculum, and it needs to be not only considered but also detailed in the course design process.

How can ESL or EFL teachers determine what type of syllabus they want to use? Moreover, what type of materials, such as textbooks or workbooks, should they select for their classrooms? At the lesson plan stage, what are they going to include as far as teaching activities and assessment? The answer to these questions is based on the goals and objectives identified during the needs analysis stage. For example, Scenario 3 describes Lindsey, who is a lead teacher for ESOL at her middle school (see page 4). Lindsey needs to create a new syllabus that should include new ESOL standards and choose the textbook and supplementary materials. The new standards are organized by language skill; for example, one standard for speaking states that students must demonstrate competence in speaking for effective communication in social and academic contexts. She also has to update every lesson plan to integrate the new ESOL standards.

The needs analysis that Lindsey has conducted, which took into account the required ESOL standards, indicates that a communicative teaching approach is the closest match to the identified goals and objectives, which incorporate the new ESOL standards. Keep in mind that syllabi are a result of decisions made about the teaching approach, which is connected back to language acquisition theories and based on course goals and objectives. Therefore, because of her

Figure 6.9:   Sample Rubric for Evaluating Lesson Plans

Goals and objectives	What will students know and be able to do after they complete the lesson? What are the goals and the objectives of the lesson? How are they linked to the needs identified in the needs analysis?
Resources	What materials will be used in learning and instruction?
Lesson introduction	How is the review of or connection to the previously taught material achieved?
Lesson sequence	Describe the instructional input, what you will do to check for understanding, and what students' guided practice will be?
Lesson closure	How is the review and clarification of major points of the lesson achieved?
Post-lesson practice	What is the homework or individual/group work after the lesson?
Learner assessment and evaluation	How will student understanding of the objectives be assessed? Will assessment be integrated throughout the lesson, or will it be at the end of the lesson? Will students have an opportunity to demonstrate their knowledge in a structured manner?
Other observations	

ESOL context, her identified goals and objectives for her ESOL classes, and her chosen teaching approach, Lindsey decides to design a communicative product–oriented syllabus. She has three options: situational-topical, notional-functional, and skills-based. Her ESOL context indicates to Lindsay that the skills-based syllabus is the closest to achieving the identified goals and objectives.

Next, to select her materials, Lindsey uses the ACTFL Standards' organizing principles and elements as the points of comparison among different textbooks. These principles are illustrated in Figures 5.7 and 5.8. At the lesson plan modification and design stage, Lindsay uses the evaluation rubric described in this chapter to identify any problem areas in the lesson plans currently in place. Then, using the lesson plan template presented in this chapter, she adapts or creates new lesson plans that not only include the new ESOL standards but also address the goals and objectives stemming from the needs analysis. The discussion of language plan evaluation emphasized the fact that the lesson sequence needs to be ordered and specific, with activities that are achievable, student centered, and based on the advancement of goals and objectives. Sometimes, materials that teachers use do not contain all the activities that address all the goals and objectives of the lesson. Therefore, many teachers will create their own activities. To help Lindsay create the best lesson plans with the best activities, the next section of our book includes very detailed teaching and assessment techniques for all language skills, strengthening the importance of teaching in the curriculum design process and the strong connection between those two.

Summarizing Statements

1. A syllabus describes the order and the selection and progression of what will be studied in a specific course and is a roadmap for both the teacher and the learner because it sets goals to be accomplished over a determined period of time.

2. Syllabi in L2 courses reflect the language teaching philosophies of the instructor.

3. There are four common types of L2 syllabi: grammar, communicative product, communicative process, and eclectic.

4. Some syllabi are eclectic and have multiple foci, combining two or more approaches in their design in their organization of content for their language classes.

5. Lesson plans should include an explicit list of goals and objectives, as well as a specific list of classroom activities that should be varied, student centered, and achievable.

1. Think of your current or future teaching situation. What elements from Table 6.1 have you used or would you use in your syllabus design? Explain your selection.

2. If you were to teach an Advanced ESL Writing course, what type of syllabus would you choose from the various types of syllabus design options presented in this chapter? Why? Will you choice be different if you were to teach an Intermediate EFL Reading course?

3. Design a speaking lesson plan for a class of L2 learners you are familiar with or would like to teach in the future using the lesson plan template presented in this chapter. Explain whether your lesson will integrate different language skills, and if so, how.

REFERENCES

Ahmed, S., & Alamin, A. (2012). The communicative approaches revisited and the relevance of teaching grammar. *English Language Teaching, 5*(1), 2–9.

Bourke, J. M. (2006). Designing a topic-based syllabus for young learners. *ELT Journal, 60*(3), 279–286.

Brown, H.D. (2007). *Teaching by principles: An interactive approach to language pedagogy* (3rd ed.). New York: Pearson.

Brown, J. D. (1995). *The elements of language curriculum: A systematic approach to program development.* Boston: Heinle & Heinle.

Dincay, T. (2011). Designing a learner-centered ESP course for adults and incorporating the learners' aims into a situational-based syllabus. *Ekev Academic Review, 15*(49), 235–247.

Finocchiaro, M., & Brumfit, C. (1983). *The functional-notional approach.* New York: Oxford University Press.

Krahnke, K. (1987). *Approaches to syllabus design for foreign language teaching.* Englewood, NJ: Prentice-Hall.

Olson, K. (2001). *Something to talk about: A reproducible conversation resource for teachers and tutors.* Ann Arbor: University of Michigan Press.

Miranda García, A., Calle Martín, J., & Melendo, A. (2006). Survival language learning syllabuses revisited: A customized functional-notional approach. *Porta Linguarum, 5,* 109–128.

Wilkins, D. A. (1976). *Notional syllabus.* London: Oxford University Press.

PART III

Instructional Activities and Assessment Techniques

This third part of the book details how specific language skills are taught based on the research and theory in language acquisition presented in the Part I of the book and the aspects of curriculum design discussed in Part II. The language skills included in this section are aural/oral (listening and speaking) and literacy based (reading and writing), with the addition of chapters on teaching grammar and culture. Each chapter defines the targeted language skill, discusses various approaches to teaching it, presents important information on assessment techniques, and shares model activities based on sound theory and pedagogy. All chapters in this section reflect the integrative approach used in this book. As a result, these chapters are about teaching language and go beyond simply using sound pedagogy. They follow a natural progression as reflected in our integrated approach, so they are directly based on and connected to language acquisition theories and curriculum design principles. This is the core of the direction taken in this book: We want to make sure that we do not leave the teaching aside and concentrate only on curriculum design. We also want to ensure that the teaching activities follow the curriculum design in a logical manner. To sum up, the direction taken here is language theory prompting language teaching and curriculum design simultaneously.

Chapter 7 ▲

Listening Activities and Assessment Techniques

This discussion of language skills begins with listening. The reason for this choice is to follow the acquisition order of language skills often seen in foreign and second language learning environments. A receptive skill, listening can be learned or acquired with or without formal instruction, as opposed to reading, which is a formally taught receptive skill. This choice of starting with listening is also connected to Krashen's SLA theory that emphasizes a necessary "silent period" where learners are not required to produce language. Instead, they need to be exposed to and comprehend spoken language.

As mentioned before, listening and reading are receptive skills, while speaking and writing are productive skills. As a result, there are similarities in the ways that listening and reading are taught and in the ways that speaking and writing are taught. The main function of listening courses is to help students understand spoken discourse. There are several characteristics of spoken discourse that language teachers need to consider when teaching listening. These characteristics of spoken language cast a light on why L2 listening can be very difficult for L2 learners. These characteristics are:

- ► length of phrases is fairly short
- ► formal discourse markers such as *while, whereas,* and *with regard to* are seldom present
- ► grammar and vocabulary are simplified
- ► there is a lot of repetition and redundancy
- ► body language and gestures are essential to convey meaning

In conversation, or even more so when listening to lectures, L2 listeners have very little control over the speed of what they are listening to. Because spoken discourse is often heard only once, they cannot go back and listen again. L2 listeners cannot pause a conversation to figure out the meaning of what they've just heard. Moreover, unlike the printed word, the same spoken word is produced in different ways depending on the speakers, who may have different dialects and accents.

Listening as a Skill

Before exploring listening activities, let's look at what the listening skill entails in general, as well as what Listening classes look like. Listening comes before speaking, as demonstrated in L1 and L2 acquisition settings that are not formal and classroom oriented. As a process, listening involves four steps:

1. L2 learners hear the message.
2. They attempt to understand the message.
3. Once the message is understood, L2 learners evaluate it.
4. Last, depending on the situation, they respond to it.

Listening is crucial for learning another language. Historically, there have been researchers who have emphasized the idea that listening is the way of learning another language (Krashen, 1981; Taylor, 1982; Terrell, 1982). According to them, listening gives the L2 learner information from which to build up the knowledge necessary for using the language. Only after the accumulation of sufficient knowledge can the learner begin to speak.

In the more recent L2 listening pedagogy, there is an emphasis on the integrated teaching of listening for communication and in conjunction with other L2 skills, such as speaking, grammar, reading, or vocabulary (Hinkel, 2006). One example of integrating listening with reading and writing is an activity where L2 learners need to fill out missing words in a provided text based on the teacher's dictation. This completion dictation activity starts with the teacher giving the learners several printed copies of the text they are going to hear. The first copy has a few words missing, the next copy has more words missing, and the third has even more words missing. The teacher distributes the first copy and reads the text while the learners listen and fill out the words missing on their first copy. Then the teacher collects the first copy and gives the learners a second copy that has more words missing than the first copy. The learners listen to the teacher reading the text again and fill out the missing words. The same process is repeated with the third copy. This activity integrates listening with reading and writing, an approach that is recommended by the current research on teaching L2 listening.

There are various descriptions of what leaners can do at different levels of proficiency levels when it comes to listening. ACTFL (2012) guidelines provide a very good set of descriptions or operations of all language skills at five major levels of proficiency: distinguished, superior, advanced, intermediate, and novice. Sometimes, it is not easy to define what a language skill entails. This useful set of descriptions does that. The operations associated with the listening skills, for example, may help curriculum designers in establishing goals and objectives for their Listening courses on the one hand and classroom teachers in their creation or adaptation of instructional activities on the other hand. To exemplify, here is the descriptor for the intermediate level of L2 listening (ACTFL, 2012):

> At the intermediate level, listeners can understand information conveyed in simple, sentence-length speech on familiar or everyday topics. They are generally able to comprehend one utterance at a time while engaged in face-to-face conversations or in routine listening tasks such as understanding highly contextualized messages, straightforward announcements, or simple instructions and directions. Listeners rely heavily on redundancy, restatement, paraphrasing, and contextual clues. Intermediate-level listeners understand speech that conveys basic information. This speech is simple, minimally connected, and contains high-frequency vocabulary. Intermediate-level listeners are most accurate in their comprehension when getting meaning from simple, straightforward speech. They are able to comprehend messages found in highly familiar everyday contexts. Intermediate listeners require a controlled listening environment where they hear what they may expect to hear. (p. 18)

What Happens in Listening Classes?

Now that you know what the listening skill entails, let's focus on what Listening classes are like and what listening students are expected to do in those classes. For example, in a Listening class for children, listening to stories is a typical activity. The L2 teacher chooses a story at the current proficiency level for the learners with only a few unknown words. At first, the teacher slowly reads the story to the learners, with most sentences read at least twice. The teacher is constantly checking for comprehension to see if the young L2 learners understand what they hear. When unknown words come up, the teacher writes them on the board and gives a quick explanation, using a translation (if the class is made of L2 learners with the same language background, also shared by the L2 teacher), a gesture, or a quick drawing or definition. If the same word appears in the story again, the teacher points to it on the board. At the end of the activity, the teacher asks comprehension questions to ensure that the story has been comprehended up to that point. In time, as learners become more familiar with the story, the teacher reads a little faster and reduces the repetitions and explanations.

In this Listening classroom for children, the material is at the right level for the learners so they are able to understand what they are listening to. In addition, because the material selected is age appropriate, the learners are interested in what they are listening to. There is a large quantity of language that learners are exposed to but learners are not required to produce a lot of language themselves. However, language production may occur as the teacher occasionally asks questions or gets the learners to anticipate what will happen, and as the learners ask the teacher to repeat, slow down, or explain. When unfamiliar words occur, learners understand them through context or teacher explanation, so they can follow the story without any breaks in comprehension.

Depending on proficiency and literacy levels, other Listening classrooms may be more integrative and require learners to actively use other language skills in addition to listening, as shown in the completion dictation activity. The ACTFL guidelines are very helpful in conceptualizing what an L2 listener is expected to do at different proficiency levels but do not provide pedagogical instructions to L2 listening teachers regarding what activities to use and what the level of integration with other language skills should be. One very helpful tool that could help L2 listening teachers with their teaching is a pedagogical framework that focuses on listener functions and listener response (Lund, 1990). Listener functions, listed in Table 7.1, are defined as the features of the message the listener tries to process.

Listener response is defined as what the listener does to demonstrate successful listening. Therefore, the listener's response has pedagogical importance for L2 classroom teachers because it helps them teach and evaluate listening comprehension of their L2 students. Table 7.2 illustrates the nine types of listener response.

Using Tables 7.1 and 7.2, L2 listening teachers can decide on the functions and responses they want to include in their lesson and can create a list of functions and responses for planning purposes. Using the listening to stories activity as an example, the list may look like this:

Function	Response
Main idea comprehension	Answering: respond to anticipatory questions about the story
Detail comprehension	Transferring: drawing a newly introduced story character based on a description provided at the beginning of a story chapter

Types of Listening Purposes

Listening activities are typically classified in three ways and are linked to **purpose:** (1) listening for main ideas, (2) listening for details, and (3) listening for and making inferences. Let's look at a dialogue teachers can use for a **main idea activity:**

Man:	Hello, Emily, how are you doing?
Woman:	I'm doing well, how are you?
Man:	Not bad. This week has been pretty hectic; I'm really looking forward to the weekend.
Woman:	Me too.
Man:	Susan and I are going to the movies this weekend. Do you want to come too?
Woman:	What are you going to see?
Man:	The new Tom Hanks movie.
Woman:	Tom Hanks? I love Tom Hanks.

Table 7.1:   Listener Functions

Listener Function	Example
Identification: focus on some aspect of the listening excerpt	Listing all the numbers in a listening passage about a trip schedule
Orientation: determine essential facts about the listening passage (the emotional tone, the situation, the general topic)	Listening to a radio recording and determining if the excerpt is a news program or a talk show
Main idea comprehension: define the main idea in a listening segment	Identifying the main idea in a lecture
Detail comprehension: identify specific information	Getting the departure times and gate numbers for several flights
Full comprehension: distinguish both the main idea(s) and specific details	Creating an outline of a lecture
Replication: reproduce the listening piece in its entirety	Responding to a dictation

Table 7.2:   Listener Responses

Listener Response	Example
Doing	Following directions (touch the board, go to the window, stand by the door)
Choosing	Putting pictures in order based on a story told by the teacher
Transferring	Drawing a picture based on a description narrated by the teacher
Answering	Responding to questions that are based on a listening passage (What time does the movie start?)
Condensing	Writing a summary of a movie review heard on the radio
Extending	Providing a solution in writing to a problem (an interview between a university student and a reporter where the student complains about a tuition raise)
Duplicating	Writing a phone message verbatim
Modeling	Creating a new ad based on an ad heard in class
Conversing	Responding to a comical ad presented in a focus-group format

In a main ideas teaching activity or assessment, teachers would ask L2 learners, "What is the main idea the man and the woman are talking about?" In order to respond, L2 learners need to understand the fact that the two speakers are talking about the possibility of going to the movies. The details of the conversation between the two are not important if the purpose of the activity is for students to get the main gist of the conversation to which they are listening. Clearly, longer and more complex dialogues or passages would increase the difficulty of the activity or assessment.

Next, let's look at a listening passage teachers could use for a **details activity.** This is from an anthropology lecture:

Professor: Perhaps the most distinctive human feature is the ability to speak . . . the ability to communicate ideas. Well, we, humans, are not alone in the use of symbolic communication. There are several studies that have shown that other animals . . . like apes and some species of birds . . . well, these animals make sounds and gestures that have comparable functions to human speech. However, these types of animal communication are not as complex as the one that we use on a daily basis. Ultimately, it is languages that allow people to preserve and transmit their culture . . . from generation to generation. Well . . . there is a branch of anthropology that studies human languages . . . and it is called linguistic anthropology. Linguistics anthropology may look at the way languages form sentences or conjugate verbs . . . in other words, it focuses on the description of language. Also, linguistic anthropology looks at the way languages develop and influence each other with the passage or time . . . or the history of language. Both directions of study give us valuable information not only about the ways in which people communicate, but also about the ways in which they understand the world around them as well.

In a details activity, teachers would ask questions such as "What do apes use for communication?" or "What is linguistic anthropology?" To answer these questions, L2 learners need to focus on the details presented by the professor in her lecture. The main idea of the lecture is not the purpose of the task, and in longer and complex passages, it would be easier to focus only on details.

Inference activities require L2 learners to listen for the message between the lines and focus on the inferred meaning of utterances. Let's listen to a conversation between a student and a librarian. They are discussing his late fees.

Student:	OK, so I cannot borrow any books from the library. I am pretty sure I paid the late fees for the book I borrowed last semester.
Librarian:	I'm really sorry…my computer says you didn't. You need to call financial services, or go there in person to straighten things out.
Student:	So, there is no way I could pay here. I really need this book…and I really don't have time to deal with financial services right now.

Librarian:	No, I'm afraid you have to go through them. I'm really sorry.
Student:	That's the last thing I needed. Well, it's not your fault; thanks for your help.
Librarian:	I'm really sorry. Look, I'll put a hold on your book so no one can check it out.
Student:	Thanks. Let me go ahead and call financial services.

If L2 learners were asked what the student's attitude toward the librarian is, they would not give a direct answer because this question is not covered in the dialogue. However, when listening to the context of conversation and concentrate on the tone and indirect language, L2 learners would realize that the student does not hold the woman responsible and he is not upset with her. Listening for inferred meaning is more difficult than the other two types of listening tasks because L2 learners tend to rely on semantic or dictionary meaning and are unfamiliar with inferences, which are heavily influenced by cultural norms. Ideally, L2 learners are more advanced before tackling complex inference activities. For beginning L2 learners, instructors should use simple inference activities and explain the intended meaning (the pragmatics) involved in conversations and monologues.

Bottom-Up and Top-Down Processing

For all three listening purposes, there are two types of processes involved in making sense of spoken discourse: bottom-up and top-down processing. Let's think of the following listening activity. The teacher says three or four words and the learner has to put those words in a sentence. It's an integrative listening-speaking activity where the student has to first decipher sounds, then put the sounds into words, and finally create a grammatically correct sentence using those words. For example, the teacher might say: *girl, reading, is, the*. Based on the language input provided by the teacher, the learner says: *The girl is reading*. This is an example of an activity that employs bottom-up processing. The **bottom-up processing** model assumes that listening follows a linear progression from sounds to words to sentences to discourse, as shown in Figure 7.1. In this view, meaning is derived at the end of the process, which uses the sounds of spoken discourse as building blocks for comprehension, and moves progressively from shorter to longer pieces of language.

To be able to process spoken discourse from the bottom up, L2 learners need a good knowledge of syntax and an extensive vocabulary. When designing bottom-up listening activities, the goal is for L2 learners to improve the retention of language they hear as they process it. In

Figure 7.1:   A Model of Bottom-Up Processing

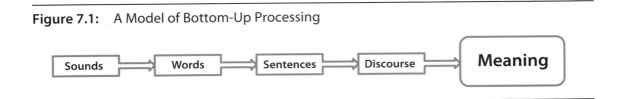

addition, they should expand their recognition of keywords, as well as key transitions in spoken discourse. To achieve the development of bottom-up listening skills, activities should require L2 learners to recognize time references (e.g., When did X happen?), identify referents of pronouns (e.g., in a dialogue, who does *he* refer to?), decide between positive and negative statements (e.g., Does the car belong to Jim?), or identify keywords in utterances (list all the nouns in a listening passage) (Richards, 2008). Let's look at an example of a listening activity in which L2 students are developing their ability to identify nouns in spoken discourse. From a listening purpose perspective, this activity can be labeled as listening for details, since students need to pay attention to discrete language points and not to the main idea of the passage. The passage is recorded or is spoken by the teacher.

Directions: Circle the words as you hear them in this listening passage.

Rome city Naples traffic gridlock Italy treasure destinations tourists

[Teacher plays recording or says:]

The third Italian city by size, Naples is a big city, with the world's worst traffic outside of Cairo. However, once tourists get past the initial gridlock, they'll find plenty of treasures, equaling and often surpassing many more popular destinations in Italy. It was founded between the 7th and 6th centuries BCE *by the Greeks and was named Neapolis, meaning "new city." The historic center of Naples has one of the biggest historical city centers in the world. There are over 400 historical churches, the highest number in the world for a single city.*

In contrast, **top-down processing** considers background knowledge and context to be crucial elements to understanding spoken discourse. For example, one effective activity that works with young learners is looking at pictures related to a fairy tale and talking about them before they listen to the story. This activity aids teachers in identifying whether the young learners are familiar with the vocabulary used in the story. This pre-listening activity where learners are looking at pictures and talking about them is a good way of introducing vocabulary that they may have forgotten or never known. It also helps them make predictions based on their previous experiences with the structure of a fairy tale. Here, L2 learners apply their previous knowledge (schema and scripts) to what they hear and match the meaning with language, as shown in Figure 7.2. Schema is defined as background knowledge or what we already know about a concept. A script is essentially a dynamic schema, a series of conventional actions that take place in a certain setting. There is a script for "Going to the dentist" and another script for "Ordering at a restaurant" (Piaget, 1928; Yule, 2014).

In top-down processing, prior experiences help learners construct the meaning carried by spoken discourse—meaning that facilitates their understanding of the language used to convey it. For example, let's suppose L2 learners listen to a conversation between a waiter and a customer. Based on their own experiences of having dinner at a restaurant that includes the actions

Figure 7.2:   A Model of Top-Down Processing

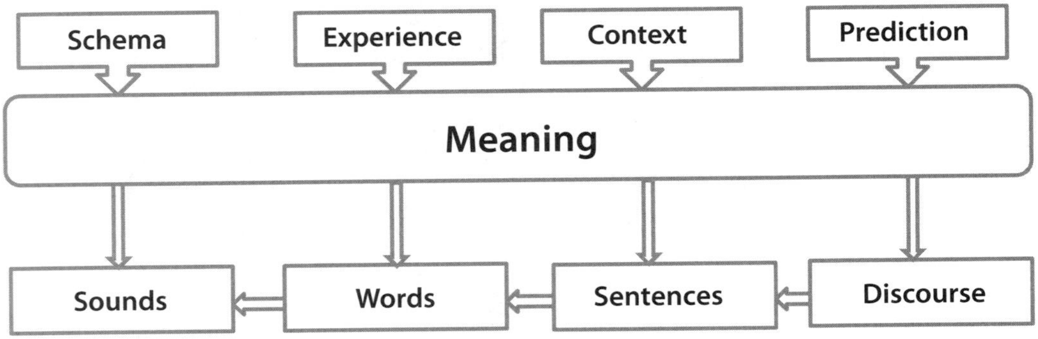

of booking a table, arriving at the agreed time, being greeted by a member of staff, and being shown to your table, learners may have the ability to anticipate the content of that conversation. When they hear the conversation, L2 learners confirm their expectations and fill in any details.

When designing top-down listening activities, the goal is to help L2 learners identify keywords that can help activate their prior knowledge of the situation or context. Another goal is to help them be able to infer important discourse elements (setting, cause/effect, role/goals of participants) that will facilitate their understanding of monologues, conversations, or lectures. To achieve these goals, there are several general types of activities that can be used in Listening classes. One activity asks L2 learners to generate a list of questions that they expect to hear about a given topic (differences between the United States and their home country) and then asks them to listen to a passage to see if those questions are answered. Another option is to ask L2 learners to create a list of things they already know about a topic and a list of things they would like to learn about it before they listen to a passage. An additional option is to give students a news headline and ask them to make predictions about the content; then L2 learners listen to the full news story and compare what they predicted with what actually happened.

Designing a Listening Activity

Previous chapters have explored how goals, based on needs analyses, are realized in language syllabi. The next step for language instructors is to create activities that reflect the language syllabus they have shaped. When designing listening activities for their classes, L2 instructors should ask three main questions:

1. How should the activities be structured?
2. What type of content should be included?
3. What should the students do in terms of language performance?

The Structure of Listening Activities

Listening activities have traditionally been organized as pre-listening, during-listening, and post-listening (Field, 2002). The pre-listening stage prepares students for the lesson through presentation of vocabulary and contextualization of content—in essence, they are preparing to do the listening activity by previewing vocabulary and the topic in general, including determining background knowledge. In the listening stage, L2 learners may complete **intensive listening** exercises where they listen for specific information in a relatively brief targeted segment of speech, or **extensive listening** exercises, where they listen to a longer and/or more complex passage for the overall message or to interpret the material. During the post-listening stage, L2 learners practice in more depth with the new vocabulary from the lesson and utilize any new language structures in unique ways. Post-listening is a review. Table 7.3 briefly summarizes these three stages and gives a sample exercise for each stage.

Pre-Listening Activities

Pre-listening activities are essential in helping L2 listeners find out what the purpose of the listening passage will be, as well as in providing them with the necessary background information. It is very important that learners activate their schema in order for them to predict the content of what they are about to hear. Accessing background knowledge is a top-down activity and L2 listening teachers should also include bottom-up activities, such as pre-teaching key vocabulary.

Pre-listening activities are typically short for two reasons. First, the more time needed for the pre-listening activities, the less time available for the actual listening task. Second, if too much vocabulary and too much context are introduced, the listening activity might be too easy. A common mistake is to provide too much support to L2 learners—for example, by attempting to define all the new words in the listening passage, which could make the activity less challenging. Generally speaking, five to ten minutes is an adequate amount of time for the pre-listening stage, although teachers should modify this as needed depending on the level of the students, the purpose of the task, and the difficulty level of the material. There are several activities that can be employed at this stage, as illustrated in the Table 7.4.

When designing listening activities, an important factor has to do with whether to give students the questions they'll need to answer before they listen to the passage or to wait until after students have listened. This is sometimes referred to as pre-setting the questions, which is one of the activities listed in Table 7.4. Field (2002) says that if questions are not given until after the passage has been heard, then L2 learners' listening will be unfocused because they won't know the level of detail required for their listening and they won't know what they are listening for in the context of the exercise. In Table 7.3, you can see that the questions were provided. In this case, the students knew what specific information in the phone call they needed to pay attention

Table 7.3:   The Three Stages of Listening Activities

Stage	Description	Sample Exercise for Low-Intermediate Adults: How to Make a Doctor's Appointment	
Pre-listening	Presentation/teaching of keywords. Discussion of the context associated with the spoken discourse learners are about to hear. Presentation of the comprehension questions.	Vocabulary *insurance* *ID number* *availability* *rash* *fever*	Context Discuss how, when, and why people need to make a doctor's appointment. Discuss personal experiences.
During-listening	Extensive listening activities Intensive listening activities Check responses to activities	Students listen to a sample phone call of a person making a doctor's appointment: *Receptionist*: Hello, this is Dr. Sloan's office. *Aziz*: Hi. I need to make an appointment. *Receptionist*: What's your name, please? *Aziz*: My name is Aziz Trusk. *Receptionist*: Mr. Trusk, how do you spell you last name? *Aziz*: T-R-U-S-K. *Receptionist*: What seems to be the problem, Mr. Trusk? *Aziz*: My foot's been bothering me for a couple of days now. *Receptionist*: Sorry to hear that. When would you like to see the doctor? *Aziz*: Will Wednesday afternoon work? *Receptionist*: Sorry, the doctor is fully booked that day. How about Thursday at 4:00? *Aziz*: Perfect. Let me give you my insurance information so you'll have the paperwork ready for me. I'm with Affordable Care, ID number 3346780. *Receptionist*: Thank you, Mr. Aziz. Then, students complete the intensive exercise by answering these questions: 1. What is the caller's name? 2. What insurance does the caller have? 3. What is the caller's insurance ID number? 4. What is wrong with the caller? 5. What is the date and time of the appointment? Students then share their answers with the class.	
Post-listening	Vocabulary practice Link functions with language	Students listen to the passage again, list any new vocabulary, infer the meaning of each new word, and create two original sentences using each of the vocabulary words. Students divide into groups of two and role play a caller making an appointment and the doctor's office personnel taking the phone call. They can volunteer to repeat this in front of the class.	

Table 7.4:   Pre-Listening Activities

Pre-Listening Activity	Description
Looking at pictures	The teacher finds a picture that is relevant to the listening passage to be heard and asks the students to predict what the passage will be about. The students can write their predictions in their notebooks and determine if they are right when they listen to the passage.
Reviewing and introducing vocabulary/grammar	The teacher asks the students to write down three words they associate with the topic and writes the words from all the students on the board. If a word is unknown, the student who came up with it provides a short definition, an antonym, or a synonym. If the keywords that are needed to understand the listening passage do not appear on the board, the teacher will pre-teach them. Also, the teacher will draw students' attention to essential grammar points, (e.g., past tenses in regular and irregular form) to make sure they understand the story happened in the past.
Pre-setting the questions	The teacher introduces the comprehension questions students will be asked to respond to in order to check listening comprehension at the while-listening stage.
Talking about the topic	The teacher introduces the topic of the listening passage and asks the students to talk about what they know in connection to the topic. While the students are discussing the topic, the teacher summarizes their answers on the board.
Miming the words	The teacher divides the class into two teams and asks one team to mime the words selected by the teacher from the listening passage.

to, which focused their listening. This also meant that they would have a better chance for success when completing the post-listening activities and wouldn't have to rely on their memories. Therefore, their listening will be done with a clear focus and they won't rely on their memory when answering the questions. Those who are opposed to pre-setting the questions say that, depending on the purpose of the activity, sometimes students ONLY listen for the material and do not therefore get an overall sense of what the listening passage is about. Some teachers allow students to listen to the passage the first time without any knowledge of comprehension questions or tasks—to let them get a feel for what the passage is about. Then, before they listen to it a second time, they give them the comprehension questions.

During-Listening Activities

At this stage, the students need to listen to the selected listening passage and process the information actively, as they will be required to perform tasks where their comprehension of the passage is measured. The purpose of during-listening activities is for students to understand the main idea of a text, as well as its important details. They do not need to understand every single word in the passage, but rather understand enough to collect the necessary information for the comprehension of the passage. During the during-listening stage, L2 learners respond to a listening text, either during or after they have listened to it. Their response can take the form of sequencing pictures in chronological order, filling in the blanks of incomplete text, determining if sentences based on the listening passage are true or false, comparing their predictions to the content of the listening passage, or writing short answers to questions. Several during-listening activities are presented in Table 7.5.

The during-listening activities can be categorized as extensive and intensive listening activities. As outlined in Table 7.3, in an intensive activity, students listen for specific information and details and focus on specific language forms in a short passage. In contrast, also stated in Table 7.3, in extensive listening exercises, learners listen to relatively long passages and are asked to identify the main idea of the passage or interpret the meaning of the passages. An example of an extensive listening exercise is where L2 learners listen to a lecture on a particular topic and must summarize and report the main ideas from that lecture material.

Table 7.5:   During-Listening Activities

During-Listening Activity	Description
Following instructions	The content of the listening passage provides students with instructions that students need to follow in order to show understanding (draw, write, check, underline, etc.).
Sequencing pictures	The teacher provides the students with several pictures that reflect the content of the listening passage. Students match pictures with the descriptions they hear in the listening passage (e.g., placing them in chronological order).
Comprehension questions	Students respond to a series of questions requiring them to identify the main idea and the important details in the passage (true/false multiple choice, matching, short answer questions).
Information transfer	Students fill out forms, grids, or maps based on the information presented in the listening passage.
Filling in the blanks	Students fill in the blanks of a transcript of the listening passage.

One question that L2 listening teachers may ask themselves is how many times they should play a listening passage. One possible answer is only one time since people don't have the luxury of rewinding conversations if some of their content has escaped them in real life. However, teachers must consider their students when they teach L2 listening (especially their anxiety level) and provide them with multiple opportunities to hear the language input. Some L2 listening teachers don't even require students to perform any kind of activity the first time they listen to a passage in order to reduce student anxiety. When deciding on the number of times to repeat a listening passage, consider its difficulty and length, as well as its pedagogical focus, which can be either listening for main ideas only, or listening for main ideas and details too. Perhaps playing the same passage more than three to four times is probably the maximum before students start to feel bored.

Post-Listening Activities

During the post-listening stage, teachers can ask L2 learners to try to use context to determine the meaning of new vocabulary from the passage as a way to practice and learn new words. For example, L2 learners may listen to a sentence and be asked to determine the meaning of specific words based on the context in which the words occurred. Additionally, at the post-listening stage, L2 teachers can direct the attention of L2 learners to the links between functions and language. For example, if requests for information were present in the listening passage, the teacher could ask students to practice using the words and phrases used for that language function.

Post-listening activities may also expand beyond the classroom. If students have listened to a lecture or audio/video recording (e.g., TV program or documentary) presenting a certain point of view regarding an issue such as global warming, teachers can ask them to do some research to identify opposing views and present their findings in class. Table 7.6 illustrates several post-listening activities.

Selecting Listening Content

Generally speaking, the best listening materials are authentic conversations or lectures. However, sometimes the proficiency level of the students requires teachers to adapt authentic materials to match the language levels and needs of the class. This does not mean that the material used is not authentic; it simply means that it's adapted since teachers are using it as the basis for their Listening class with some modifications.

Authentic material contains many of the characteristics that make spoken discourse unique, such as hesitations, false starts, and pauses. The closer the listening passages mirror real life, the sooner L2 learners can participate fully in real-world listening situations. Authentic materials can even be used with beginners under certain circumstances and always

Table 7.6:   Post-Listening Activities

Post-Listening Activity	Description
Summarizing	Students are given three short summaries and are asked to choose the best one that describes the listening passage. They can use the notes they have taken when they listened to the passage.
Integrating listening with speaking	Debates, role-plays, interviews are used as a follow-up activity based on during-listening activities.
Integrating listening with writing	Students are required to write a letter, email, or social media comment as a follow-up to during-listening activities.
Integrating listening with reading	Students are required to do internet research and come up with a list of three news stories related to the topic presented in the listening passage.
Creating and role-playing dialogues (multi-skill integration)	Based on the listening passage, students create and role play dialogues in class.

with the caveat that they should be told that they are not expected to understand everything. In these cases, teachers should try to simplify the listening task for beginners. For example, if the listening passage describes a Thanksgiving dinner in detail, the teacher would ask beginning L2 learners to only identify what food will be served, focusing on level-appropriate language.

In addition to selecting authentic materials, at the lesson planning stage L2 instructors may choose to concentrate on the micro-skills of listening when they select content for their listening activities. By doing this, teachers can identify the specific problem areas students need to work on and help students overcome their listening comprehension limitations in particular areas. The list of micro-listening skills illustrated in Table 7.7 is by no means exhaustive. For a more extended list, consult Richards (1983).

Table 7.7:   Listening Micro-Skills

Micro-Skill	Listening Activity
Discrimination of sounds that may change meaning	Directions: Put the pictures in order based on what you hear. First word: cheek Second word: chick
Identification of stressed and unstressed form of words	Directions: Listen to the word and place a check mark to the picture that is close in meaning to it. You hear: PREsent You see:  You hear: PreSENT You see: 
Recognition of reduced forms (*gonna* instead of *going to*) and word boundaries (where a word stops and another one begins)	Directions: Write what you hear and count the words. I'll getcha a sandwich. Whattyaya want? I gotcha that book you asked for. Djeetyet? Wanna come?

Table 7.7:   Listening Micro-Skills (continued)

Micro-Skill	Listening Activity
Detect keywords	Directions: Before you listen to the lecture, read and underline keywords in the questions that will test your listening comprehension; the keywords for understanding that sentence or question; and, when possible, the word(s) you are likely to hear when the speaker moves on to a new topic.

1. What is the main topic of the lecture?
   ► the discovery of a comet
   ► the structure of a comet
   ► the origin of a comet
   ► the evolution of a comet

2. What does the professor imply?
   ► He is going to talk more about the flood and ask for students' feedback.
   ► He is going to share pictures of a comet he saw long time ago.
   ► He is going to take a trip to Australia in the next semester.
   ► He is going to discuss the topic without showing the pictures.

3. According to the lecture, what is the composition of a nucleus?
   Choose two answers
   ☐ dust
   ☐ fluor
   ☐ ice
   ☐ mud
   ☐ fluor
   ☐ lead

4. Why do ions in a Type I tail reach speeds of hundreds of kilometers per hour?
   ► because of the solar wind
   ► because of Earth's magnetic field
   ► because of florescence
   ► because of sodium atoms

Table 7.7:   Listening Micro-Skills (continued)

Micro-Skill	Listening Activity
Identify main ideas or topics	Main Ideas Directions: Listen to the lecture and take notes. Then, in pairs, decide which one represents best the main purpose of the lecture: 1. to exemplify quantitative variables 2. to emphasize importance of statistics in economics 3. to identify differences between qualitative and quantitative variables 4. to define and discuss variables in statistics *Lecturer*: When we want to gather information for statistical purposes, we can do it in several ways. We can interview people, we can observe items, we can count objects, and so on. The characteristic we want to focus our attention on is called a variable. For example, grades on a test, heights of people, and weights of people . . . hair color . . . all these are examples of variables. In statistics, we can distinguish two types of variables. One type is represented by qualitative variables, whereas the second one is represented by quantitative variables. Let's start with the qualitative ones. A qualitative variable describes observations as belonging to one of a set of categories. For example, the color of an object is a qualitative variable. Or, when we toss a coin, the outcome can be either heads or tails . . . and it has no numerical value. Well, that's another example of a qualitative variable. Although a qualitative variable has no numerical value, we can assign numerical values to each category . . . for example heads can be 1 and tails can be 0. Now, let's look at the second category, the quantitative variables. A quantitative variable is defined as a value measured on numerical scale. Data collected for a quantitative variable is often referred to as metric data, another important statistical term to remember. For example, we can look at someone's height and we can say that the person is tall, medium, or short. See, these categories are all qualitative variables. However, when we express this height in meters or centimeters, or in feet and inches, the height of an individual becomes a quantitative variable. Other examples of qualitative variables are the price of a particular book in dollars, the annual revenue or profit of a company in dollars, or the waiting time in a restaurant in minutes or seconds, if you want to be very precise. Now, let's look at how we can further classify quantitative variables.

Students' Performance in Listening Classes

In addition to organization and content, L2 teachers need to plan what their students focus on in the listening activity. There are six different kinds of classroom listening performance activities, from simply repeating back what is heard to directly integrating listening with other skills (Brown, 2007). These activities are shown in Table 7.8.

Teaching Listening

In the Listening classroom, L2 learners at all levels need to develop the micro-skills of listening to enhance their overall listening skills. Teachers can foster language acquisition and skill in listening by organizing activities around targeted content and consistently using the stages of listening to set that content.

Table 7.8:   Types of Listening Performance

Type	Description
Reactive	Students repeat back what they hear.
Intensive	Students focus on components of discourse (sound, words, intonation, etc.) in relative short samples of spoken discourse. For example, students listen to a sentence or group of sentences and concentrate on a specified element such as intonation, stress, a contraction, a grammatical structure, etc.
Responsive	Students listen to teacher language that requires an immediate response. Examples of this type of teacher language are asking questions (*How are you feeling today? What did you do over the weekend?*) or giving commands (*Go to page 45 in your book*).
Selective	Students listen to longer stretches of discourse (monologues of a couple of minutes or longer) with the purpose of selecting specific information—for example, dates, events, location, situation, context, etc.
Extensive	Students listening to extended spoken discourse (lectures, conversations, etc.) with the purpose of developing a global understanding.
Interactive	Students participate in activities that integrate listening with other language skills, such as class discussions, debates, etc.

Listening Activities for the Classroom

The listening activities presented in the following section are designed for the L2 language teacher to use the pre-listening, listening, and post-listening stages to teach language and listening skills. These activities are based on the theoretical foundations presented in Chapters 2–4 (behaviorism, communicative approaches, and sociocultural foundations) and organized by syllabi presented in Chapter 6 stemming from that theoretical foundation (grammar, communicative product, communicative process, and eclectic approaches). Let's see some examples of activities that L2 teachers can use in their classroom.

─── Activity 7.1: A Pilot's Announcement ───

Grammar-Based Listening

Rationale: Because this is a grammar-based intensive listening exercise, the content is designed for a basic level of listening, with students listening for specific information in the text. It also includes the vocabulary that is to be taught during the language class.

Objectives: Students listen to a short announcement and fill in missing verb forms using their knowledge of *be* verb forms.

Pre-Planning

Pre-knowledge: Students should have been introduced to the *be* verb forms before this listening activity.
Materials needed: One copy of the text (flight captain's announcement) with the *be* verb forms in blanks
Language level: Low-intermediate
Recommended age group: Adults

Procedures

Pre-listening: The teacher introduces the topic (procedures before a flight) in order for the students to predict vocabulary and content. The teacher asks these questions:

1. Have you flown on an airplane before?
2. What do you remember happened before you took off?
3. Write three words you know about the topic.

In addition, the teacher writes on the board vocabulary items that will help with text comprehension so that students focus on *be* verb forms and numbers, and asks students if their words are the same as the words written on the board. Examples of vocabulary items to be discussed before listening are: *flight, captain, chance, temperature, crew, sit back*.

Listening: The teacher gives the students a handout of the announcement with the verbs missing and asks them to listen specifically for the *be* verb forms.

Content for Your Handout (Captain's Announcement)

Fill each blank with the correct missing verb form.

Captain: Good morning, passengers. This ___ your captain speaking. First, I'd like to welcome everyone to Safe Airlines Flight 50 going to Boston. Our flight time today ___ 3 hours and 15 minutes. The local time in Boston ___ 7:50 AM, and the current weather ___ cloudy with the temperature in the low 30s, Fahrenheit. There ___ a chance of snow later in the day. We'll arrive at Gate 19, and we will announce connecting flights on our approach to the Boston airport.

On behalf of Safe Airlines and the crew, I want to wish you an enjoyable stay in the Boston area or at your final destination. We ___ glad you chose Safe Airlines for your travel today. Sit back, relax, and enjoy the flight.

The teacher reads the passage without the blanks (that is, she adds in the correct *be* verb) at normal speed, and the students listen without taking any notes. The teacher reads it a second time, this time pausing after each *be* verb to allow students time to fill in the handout. When the teacher reads the text a third time, she pauses at the end of each sentence to give students an opportunity to double-check or correct their answers.

Evaluation

The teacher asks students to take turns reading the sentences with the correct verb form included. It is important to only correct the *be* verb forms as the focus of the lesson. It is an opportunity, though, to check overall pronunciation and note difficulties that could be addressed later. Instructors can also write the sentences on the board and ask students to fill in the blanks. Checking students' answers gives the teacher the opportunity not only to evaluate students' comprehension skills but also to diagnose problem areas in their comprehension—that is, were they able to distinguish the *be* verb forms and the accompanying information in the listening passage?

Post-listening: The instructor asks students to cover up or turn over their handout and then gives them a set of questions to focus their attention on the information after each *be* verb form.

1. Who is speaking?
   a. the captain
   b. the steward
   c. a passenger
2. How long is the flight?
   a. 3 hours, 50 minutes
   b. 3 hours, 15 minutes
   c. 2 hours, 5 minutes
3. What is the weather in Boston?
   a. windy
   b. rainy
   c. cloudy
4. What is the name of the airline?
   a. Boston Airlines
   b. Southern Airlines
   c. Safe Airlines

Homework: The instructor should find a website (such as www.soundsnap.com) that has an authentic clip from a pilot. Ask students go to that website and listen to the clip. Because it is authentic, low-intermediate students may not understand all the language, which is fine because students are getting exposure to real-world language. Students should be encouraged to listen to the clip as many times as necessary. They should write a short summary of the announcement that includes all the details and bring the information to the next class.

Activity 7.2: Applying for Financial Aid

Communicative Product Listening

Rationale: A communicative syllabus is based on situational-topical, notional-functional, or skills-based approach to student learning. This type of syllabus requires targeted, communicative language and vocabulary within specific topical situations, such as meeting people, or targeted notions-functions within the language, such as interpersonal functions (learning the pragmatics of accepting and refusing invitations). Students are expected to produce concrete, accurate language that is easily assessed during this extensive listening exercise. In this exercise, they answer questions based on an extended recording but must infer meaning and discern important information to answer those questions about the specific topic of financial aid for college.

Objectives: Students identify and infer details while listening to a conversation.

Pre-Planning

Pre-knowledge: Students need to have basic knowledge regarding the university advising and financial aid system in the United States.
Materials needed: A recording of a conversation between the student and the university advisor; one handout with the conversation script and one handout with listening comprehension questions
Language level: Advanced
Recommended age group: Young adults and adults

Procedures

Pre-listening: The instructor introduces the topic of the listening passage and asks these questions:

1. What do you know about the topic? Have you ever applied for financial support?
2. Write five words that you predict you'll hear in the conversation.

Next, the instructor writes the essential vocabulary (*financial aid, advisors, application, deadline,* etc.) on the board to prepare L2 learners for the activity.

Listening: To clarify the purpose, the instructor distributes the questions so students know what they will be listening for. The students should read quickly for the purpose of identifying and clarifying any additional unknown vocabulary that has not been discussed during the pre-listening stage.

Content for Your Handout

Questions

1. Why does the student want to talk with the advisor?

    a. to find out about financial aid

    b. to inquire about a graduate program

    c. to ask for an extension for a payment

    d. to discuss about the school's financial situation

Listen to part of the conversation for Question 2.

Advisor: Hmm. Let me check my schedule. Tuesday I have a workshop I need to attend. I'll be out of the office all day.

Student: How about next Thursday?

Advisor: Let me check. OK. Thursday looks good.

2. What is the advisor implying?

    a. The student can drop the application on Tuesday.

    b. The student can see the advisor on Tuesday.

    c. The student can submit the application on Thursday.

    d. The student cannot meet the advisor next week.

3. Why does the student want to quit his part-time job?

    a. because he wants to concentrate on schoolwork more

    b. because he thinks the job pays very little money

    c. because he hates the people he is working with

    d. because he found a job with more flexible hours

4. What determines who is eligible to get aid?

    a. school grades

    b. the income of grandparents

    c. financial need

    d. recommendation from professors

5. What are two mistakes people make when filing for financial aid?
   Choose two answers only.

    a. They don't send in a complete application.

    b. They don't file early enough.

    c. They don't submit the application in person.

    d. They don't edit their statement for grammatical errors.

    e. They don't capitalize their first and last name on the application.

    f. They don't attach their transcript.

After reviewing the questions, the instructor plays the recording. Students should listen to the conversation without taking notes.

Content for Your Handout

Student:	Good morning, Mr. Thomas.
Advisor: *(typing)*	Oh, hi, Jack, how are you? Give me a minute, please… I really need to finish this email.
Student:	Sure, no problem.
Advisor: *(finishing typing)*	Sorry about that, Jack. Now, you said you wanted to ask me a couple of questions?
Student:	Yes, I want to apply for financial aid next semester. I am working part-time and paying for school on my own, but I decided to quit my job next semester. I want to focus on school more.
Advisor:	That's a wise decision, Jack, you won't regret it. Your grades will definitely improve if you do that.
Student:	Yeah, but now I need to get some money so I can pay my tuition, my books—you know, all sort of things.
Advisor:	Sure, what do you want to know about financial aid?
Student:	First, do I need to file an application for it? How does it work?
Advisor:	Yes, you must apply each year. There is actually a deadline, but you're OK. You still have several weeks to finish up the application process. Here's the application; make sure you fill everything in.
Student:	Great, thanks. Now, if I apply, am I going to get it no matter what?
Advisor:	Well, not really. The primary factor in deciding who gets financial aid is financial need. Financial aid covers the gap between your own income, or whatever you get from your parents, and the tuition cost, room and board, books, and other school-related expenses.
Student:	OK, this makes sense. Are people turned down when they apply?
Advisor:	Well, if you want to get your application accepted, and let's say you do have strong support for financial need, then you need to make sure you don't make mistakes when you apply. You really need to read the directions very carefully. What else? Let me think. Oh, you must fully complete the application, and don't wait until the last minute. File as early as you can.
Student:	Got it. Now, if I get it, is it going to stay the same amount every year?

Advisor:	Well, not really. The amount changes as the tuition cost goes up. If it goes up, then, naturally, you'll receive more money. Also, if your family income changes, the amount of financial aid will change too. So, don't be surprised if you don't get the same amount next time around.
Student:	Thanks so much. You've answered all my questions.
Advisor:	You've got the application form, right? Don't forget to fill it out as soon as you can and you can drop it off here or, if you want, you can take it to the financial aid office. The deadline is a few weeks from now, but it doesn't hurt to do it before then. Don't wait until the last minute, you know, in case you need to make any corrections on your application.
Student:	I'll drop it off here next Tuesday if that's OK. Could you go over it with me then?
Advisor:	Hmm. Let me check my schedule. Tuesday I have a workshop I need to attend. I'll be out of the office all day.
Student:	How about next Thursday?
Advisor:	Let me check. OK. Thursday looks good.
Student:	See you then.

The instructor should play the conversation again so that students can take notes. Then, students should take a few minutes to answer the questions.

Evaluation

Post-listening: The instructor reviews the listening comprehension questions with the students and asks them to explain their answers. This allows the teacher the opportunity to evaluate students' listening comprehension skills and to identify problem areas in their comprehension (e.g., were they able to infer meaning?). To work on vocabulary development and listening strategies (inferring meaning from context), the instructor selects excerpts from the listening passage and asks students to provide synonyms or paraphrase selected words and phrases. For example, in this excerpt, the students are required to paraphrase the bolded phrasal verbs and replace the underlined words with phrasal verbs or other idiomatic expressions.

You've got the application form, right? Don't <u>forget</u> to **fill it out** *as soon as you can and you can* **drop it off** *here or, if you want, you can take it to the financial aid office. The deadline is a few weeks from now, but it doesn't hurt to do it before then. Don't <u>wait</u> until the last minute, you know, in case you need to make any corrections on your application.*

Homework: The teacher finds an example of a financial aid application form and asks students to fill it out for homework.

Activity 7.3: Seeking Advice

Communicative Process Listening

Rationale: In a communicative process–based syllabus, the organization of the curriculum is based on tasks. The task-based syllabi activities are focused on the language and language skill needed to complete a concrete task, such as applying for a program or job, or producing a class newsletter. This activity asks the L2 learner to listen to a personal problem that needs to be solved and to then give advice that helps solve the issue.

Objectives: Students offer advice about a problem, using listening, speaking, and writing skills.

Pre-Planning

Pre-knowledge: The students need to be familiar with advice columns, the U.S. holiday Halloween, and modal verbs.

Materials needed: Recording and handout of the listening passage

Language level: Intermediate

Recommended age group: Young adults and adults

Procedures

Pre-listening: The instructor discusses advice columns and introduces essential vocabulary from the passage, such as *Halloween* and *trick-or-treat*. The instructor asks students if they are familiar with Halloween and whether they have a similar holiday in their culture.

Listening: The instructor writes two questions on the board: *What is the question the man asks Abigail?* and *How would you answer his question?* Students should listen at least twice.

Content for Your Handout
Listen to the recording of a letter to an advice columnist.

Dear Abigail:
Since Halloween is nearly here, I have a question about trick-or-treating. Last year on Halloween, my wife and I decided to have dinner early so we wouldn't be disturbed by trick-or-treaters. While we were eating dinner around 4:30 PM, the doorbell rang. When I answered, four girls who live down the street asked me to give them the customary candy. I told them to come back later when I wasn't eating dinner. An hour later I received a call from the girls' mother scolding me for sending them away. I was just trying to get a bit of peace and quiet before the trick-or-treating started. Was I so wrong to ask them to come back later?
Signed,
Too Early for Trick-or-Treating

Evaluation

Post-listening: Give students time to write about how they would answer the question if they were Abigail.

Then put students into pairs and ask them to share their answers to the question. As the students are sharing, the instructor should move around the room and make sure they are on task. The instructor should also note any grammar or vocabulary problems students might have.

Then students should read their answers to the class, while their classmates take notes to compare their answers with their classmates' answers.

At the end of class, the instructor reads Abigail's response out loud twice and asks students to take notes. Then students will write a short compare-and-contrast paper using their answers and Abigail's response.

> Abigail's response: I think you should have answered the door with a welcoming smile. The girls' mother may not have wanted them out after dark, which is why she started them on trick-or-treating early. Part of Halloween is seeing the children's excitement and their costumes. On this day, it is a bit naive to expect peace and quiet in a neighborhood with kids. Think back when you went trick-or-treating and, when the doorbell rings, answer it and please don't make a fuss about it.

> If the teacher wishes, the students can turn in their written responses for a grade.

Homework: Students watch a TV program that focuses on finding solutions to people's problems (something like "Dr. Phil") and write proposed solutions to the problem.

— Activity 7.4: At the Public Library —

Eclectic Listening

Rationale: Many instructors prefer using various and mixed approaches in their design of the syllabus and curriculum. This activity takes an eclectic approach to listening because it focuses on grammar and communicative skills using a fill-in-the-blank dialogue. This activity is perfect before students are taken to the library for the first time or are being given a task that involves getting books or other materials from the library. This eclectic activity focuses on language used in a real-world setting and includes a strong grammatical focus.

Objectives: Identify main ideas and details in conversations; identify and use modal verbs in a real-world setting.

Pre-Planning

Pre-knowledge: The students should be familiar with the idea of finding books at the library. The students should understand modal verbs and other verb forms used in asking for permission and giving advice/direction (*can, should, would, ought to, have to, do*, etc.).
Materials needed: Audio player, dictation handout
Language level: Intermediate
Recommended age group: Young adults and adults

Procedures

Pre-listening: The teacher introduces the topic and asks students about their experiences finding books at the library. Depending on students' familiarity with vocabulary, the teacher might want to introduce vocabulary words that can potentially activate students' prior knowledge, such as a computer search.

Listening: The teacher should give students a handout to complete to familiarize themselves with the dialogue they are about to hear. In addition to the handout, the teacher writes these questions on the board and asks students to identify the main idea and a couple of important details:

> What is the conversation about?
>
> Why does the student need help?
>
> What books does the student like?

Students should listen the first time without taking notes. When they listen the second time, they should fill in the blanks.

Content for Your Handout

Listen to a conversation between a student and a librarian. Fill in the blanks with the correct modal verb.

Student:	Hello Ms. Mills. How _____ I find books I'd like to read?
Librarian:	Hi, Ahmad. First you _____ look for a book you like on the shelves.
Student:	How _____ I find books about lizards?
Librarian:	You _____ use the computer right here to do a computer search for books about lizards. It tells you where the book is on the shelf.
Student:	Wow that is cool! Thank you, I _____ start looking right now!
Librarian:	Have fun and let me know if I _____ help you.

After that, the teacher asks students to list the missing words and discuss their structure and usage. For each of the modal verbs in the passage, the students are asked to come up with an example of their own as shown here:

Content for Your Handout

For each modal verb, write an affirmative and negative sentence that is related to your own experience.

Example: I can play soccer. I cannot play the piano.

can

could

should

will

After the activity, the teacher directs students' attention to the three comprehension questions and replays the conversation. Working in pairs, students have five minutes to answer the questions and check their fill-in-the blank answers. The answers should be exact since they hear the words spoken.

Evaluation

Post-listening: The teacher checks the answers students provided for the modal verb activity as well as for the comprehension activity. Students can share other words that might work in the blanks as well. New words and phrases are written on the board, and students can then be asked to create new sentences in which these new words/phrases are used in various contexts. Students are asked to act out a dialogue between a student and a librarian, asking any questions about the library that they wish.

Homework: If possible, the teacher should arrange for a tour of the local library. When listening to the tour, students should take notes so they'll be able to answer the questions listed. If the librarian guide does not cover all the answers, students should ask for the missing information at the end of the tour.

How can I get a library card?

Are there any restrictions on a brand-new library card?

How often will my library card expire, and how do I renew it?

Is there a limit to the number of items I may check out at once?

Is there a limit to the number of holds I can place?

How long can I keep library materials?

How do I renew library materials?

Where can I return my materials?

What if I keep my library materials beyond the due date?

What if I lose or damage library materials?

Assessing Listening Comprehension

After looking at several L2 listening activities, what are some assessments L2 teachers could use to assess listening comprehension? When assessing listening comprehension in English, it is important to consider the three types of listening purposes:

1. listening for main ideas
2. listening for details
3. listening and making inferences

Classroom-based measurements and large-scale tests typically reflect these three purposes, regardless of proficiency level or teaching environment (ESL or EFL).

How to Assess Listening for Main Ideas

When designing assessments for this purpose, the goal is to measure whether or not L2 learners have the ability to identify the main topic, idea, or purpose of a passage—commonly, a conversation or lecture. Depending on the passage, the main point may be stated directly or it may be implied. If it is implied, learners need to put together all the information in the listening passage, consider all of the cues, and make an inference to determine what the main point is. This listening passage is an example of an implied main point:

> *Visual leaners tend to use graphs, charts, and pictures to learn new information. They can read body language well and are able to remember things that are written down. Auditory leaners retain new material through hearing and speaking. They often prefer to be told how to do things and then summarize the main points out loud to help with memorization. Kinesthetic learners like to use a hands-on approach to learn new content. They usually favor group work and prefer to demonstrate how to do something rather than explain it verbally.*

To check listening comprehension, the L2 listeners are presented with this question:

1. What is the main idea of the passage?
   a. Kinesthetic learners are more effective than visual learners.
   b. Auditory learners prefer group work.
   c. There are three learning styles.
   d. Teachers prefer to work with visual learners.

The answer is c, because the passage talks about three learning styles, and even though it does not have a topic sentence, the main idea is implied in the content of the listening excerpt. For conversations, typical questions on an assessment are:

What is the main purpose of the conversation?

What are the two people mainly talking about?

Why is the man/woman talking to the assistant/doctor/nurse/etc.?

For lectures, typical questions may be phrased as:

What is the main topic of the lecture/talk/class discussion?

What is the main purpose of the lecture/talk/class discussion?

What is the main subject of this lecture/talk/class discussion?

Here is an example of a main idea assessment in the context of a lecture:

Listen to the lecture.

Genetics plays an important part in the transmission of physical features from parents to children. From your parents, you inherit the color of your eyes and the thickness of your hair, but—and I know it sounds far-fetched—but you don't inherit the language they speak. Let me just say that you acquire, or we acquire, to make it a more general statement—we acquire the language we speak in a culture with other speakers, not from parental genes. For example, if a very young baby girl born in China is adopted by a French couple, who, naturally, speak French, then the child will speak French, the language of her adopted parents. She will not speak Chinese, the language of her biological parents. Of course, she will have the physical features of her Chinese parents, but her language will be French. We call this process where a language is passed from one generation to the next in a social context, um, we call this cultural transmission. So, language is culturally, not biologically, transmitted from one generation to the next. This process is essential for language acquisition. Human infants don't produce instinctive language if they are raised in isolation. No social and cultural contact means no language.

Question

1. What is the main topic of the talk?
   a. the process of language acquisition in infants
   b. the transmission of language through culture
   c. the shared physical features between parents and children
   d. the genetic differences between the French and the Chinese

---

How to Assess Listening for Details

The main goal here is to identify whether L2 learners understand the important details in a conversation or a lecture. Some examples of supporting detail questions are: What resulted from…? According to the speaker/the man/the woman/the doctor/etc., what is the main advantage of…? What are…? Which of the following is not true…?

Here is an example of two detail questions in the context of a lecture:

Listen to the lecture.

The Solar System consists of the Sun, and then we have nine planets, and a large number of smaller bodies, gases, and dust. Actually, sorry, I take that back. Now that Pluto is no longer considered a planet, we only have eight. Here's the order: the first one, which is the closest to the Sun, is Mercury. Then, we have Venus, Earth, Mars, Jupiter, Saturn, Uranus, and Neptune. Once again: Mercury, Venus, Earth—third rock from the Sun, right?—Mars, Jupiter, Saturn, Uranus, and Neptune. From Earth, five of them can be see without the help of telescopes, but Uranus and Neptune are too faint and we need the help of optical aids to observe them.

1. According to the lecture, how many planets are there in the Solar System?
   a. six planets
   b. seven planets
   c. eight planets
   d. nine planets
2. According to the professor, which two planets can be seen from Earth without the help of optical aids?
   a. Orion
   b. Mars
   c. Uranus
   d. Neptune
   e. Saturn
   f. Earth

How to Assess Listening and Making Inferences

This type of assessment requires L2 learners to listen between the lines and infer what the speaker's intended meaning is. Such listening comprehension questions focus on feelings, likes, dislikes, and whether the speaker is amused, bored, or anxious. This intended purpose is not always expressed clearly. For example, consider this example, adapted from Yule (2014):

Her: That's the doorbell.

Him: I'm in the bathroom.

Her: OK.

When taking into account only the literal meaning of the words in the dialogue, the exchange does not make any sense. There is meaning, but that meaning is inferred because it is stated indirectly. He expects her to answer the door because he is in the bathroom.

When designing an assessment for the purpose of making inferences, here are some examples of questions:

What can be inferred about the professor when he says X?

What does the man mean when he says X?

What is the student's attitude toward X?

Here is an assessment that measures making inferences. The context is a conversation:

Listen to a conversation between a student and an advisor. They are discussing the student's class schedule.

Student: OK. So, it's decided. I'll take 15 credit hours next semester.

Advisor: Sounds great. I'm glad you understood where I was coming from.

Student: You convinced me, but I still think I should've taken more hours. I really need to graduate as soon as possible.

Advisor: Well, you could if you didn't have to work so many hours in the lab. You know, if your course load is too heavy, your grades might suffer. That's why I think 15 is plenty for you.

Student: I guess you're right. But I would have liked at least two more credit hours. Maybe next semester.

Question

1. What is the student's attitude toward the schedule suggested by the advisor?

    a. He would have preferred to take more classes.

    b. He would have preferred to work fewer hours in the lab.

    c. He would have preferred an easier schedule.

    d. He would have preferred to work with a different advisor.

Here's another example.

Woman: Well, I mean, I know almost all parents with kids would love to go to Disney World in their summer vacation but I don't. True, it's the favorite vacation spot of a lot of Americans but it is not cheap—think of all park passes you'll need, and hotel costs, and food, and the gifts for the folks back home, and . . . . So there's no fun in going for me.

    1.   The woman thinks going to Disney World is:

        a.   gratifying

        b.   dangerous

        c.   fun

        d.   expensive

This chapter looked at the unique characteristics of listening and explored a few listening tasks and processes. It also introduced the structure, content, and student performance that L2 instructors should consider when designing listening tasks. Additionally, it provided examples of listening activities that were linked to the four orientations discussed in previous chapters: grammar-based, communicative product, communicative process, and eclectic. All listening activities should include assessment of listening comprehension skills. Listening offers ample opportunities for SLA, especially when instructors include post-listening activities in which language is practiced in meaningful contexts, as illustrated in the activities.

Summarizing Statements

1.   Listening comprehension is a receptive skill with the main function of processing spoken language.

2.   From the perspective of purpose, L2 listening is classified as (a) listening for main ideas, (b) listening for details, and (c) listening and making inferences.

3.   Typically, listening activities have followed a standard format (Field, 2002) with three main components: pre-listening, listening, and post-listening.

4.   The best materials to use when teaching L2 listening are authentic materials, either adapted or in their original form, because they accurately illustrate the characteristics of the spoken language.

5.   L2 instructors should take into account the sub-skills of listening as dictated by the listening situation (conversations or lectures) when they select content for and design their listening activities.

REFLECTION AND APPLICATION

1. The chapter discussed bottom-up and top-down processing. Do you think L2 learners employ them differently at different stages of their language proficiency? In other words, do lower-proficiency learners use more or less bottom-up strategies? Why? Why not?

2. In this chapter, we've learned that there are six types of listening that L2 learners complete in L2 classes. For each type, create a short listening exercise.

3. This chapter emphasized the importance of selecting, and in some cases, adapting authentic materials. Taking the activities provided in this chapter as an example, chose an authentic video clip from a popular sitcom and create a listening activity for a high-intermediate ESL Listening classroom. If your Listening class is focused on academic English, you can use a university lecture as content for your ESL Listening class.

REFERENCES

ACTFL. (2012). *ACTFL proficiency guidelines* [Electronic version]. Retrieved from http://www.actfl.org/sites/default/files/pdfs/ACTFLProficiencyGuidelines

Brown, H. D. (2007). *Teaching by principles: An interactive approach to language pedagogy* (3rd ed.). New York: Pearson.

Field, J. (2002). The changing face of listening. In J. C. Richards & W. A. Renandya (Eds.), *Methodology in language teaching: An anthology of current practice* (pp. 242–247). Cambridge, U.K.: Cambridge University Press.

Hinkel, E. (2006). Current perspectives on teaching the four skills. *TESOL Quarterly, 40*(1), 109–131.

Krashen, S.D. (1981). The "fundamental pedagogical principle" in second language teaching. *Studia Linguistica, 35*(1–2), 50–70.

Lund, R. J. (1990). A taxonomy for teaching second language listening. *Foreign Language Annals, 23*, 105–115.

Piaget, J. (1928). *The child's conception of the world*. London: Routledge and Kegan Paul.

Richards, J. C. (1983). Listening comprehension: Approach, design, procedure. *TESOL Quarterly, 17*, 219–239.

Richards, J.C. (2008). *Teaching listening and speaking: From theory to practice*. Cambridge, U.K.: Cambridge University Press.

Taylor, B.P. (1982). In search of real reality. *TESOL Quarterly, 16*(1), 28–42.

Terrell, T.D. (1982). The natural approach to language teaching: An update. *Modern Language Journal, 66*(2), 121–132.

Yule, G. (2014). *The study of language* (5th ed.). Cambridge, U.K.: Cambridge University Press.

Chapter 8

▲

Speaking Activities and Assessment Techniques

This chapter begins by describing the various forms of speaking, often called speech acts, starting with the simplest forms of sounds and broadening to a discussion about communicative competencies in the language classroom. The chapter includes speaking activities based on how natural speech acts occur. Assessment techniques are discussed in some detail, focusing on error correction, informal evaluation, and formal testing of oral speech acts.

Characteristics of Speech Acts

Speech acts occur whenever we utter language that performs some communicative function. It begins with **phonemes,** the smallest unit of sound produced using various organs of speech: the diaphragm, lungs, trachea, larynx, velum (soft palate), uvula, hard palate, alveolar ridge, tongue, teeth, lips, and nasal cavity all work to help humans produce sound. For example, [b] and [t] are two different phonemes of English beginning the words *butter* and *total,* respectively (see the Appendix for a detailed view of the phonemes in the English language). Phonemes do not necessarily carry meaning by themselves, but they do provide the building blocks for **morphemes,** which are the smallest units of language that carry information about meaning.

A morpheme can be a word by itself; for example, *cat* is a morpheme. It has a distinct meaning by itself, and morphemes that stand alone like this are called **free morphemes.** Another kind of morpheme that carries meaning but cannot stand by itself is the **bound morpheme.** The plural *–s* is a bound morpheme because it has meaning in that it tells us that something is plural. This is called a bound morpheme because it must be bound or attached to another morpheme. Another name for bound morpheme is **affix.** Bound morphemes/affixes can be **prefixes** (the bound morpheme attaches at the beginning of a word, such as *pre-* in the word *preview*), **infixes** (attach in the middle of a word), or **suffixes** (attach at the end of a word). An example of a suffix would be *–ed*, such as you would find in the word *worked*, which creates the meaning of past tense. English does not have infixes for bound morphemes, but other languages do, such as the language of Tagalog found in the Phillipines.

Bound morphemes often attach to root words, which in English commonly have Latin and Greek origins. For example, the Latin root of *act* has the meaning of "do," as we see in the English words *action* and *react*. *Action* also contains the bound suffix *–tion* (meaning "the action of") and *react* contains the prefix *re-* (meaning "again"). Another example from Greek would be the root *cosm*, meaning universe. You see this in English words like *microcosm* and *cosmonaut*. *Microcosm* also contains the prefix *micro-* (meaning "small") and *cosmonaut* contains the suffix *–naut* (meaning "sailor or voyager"). When L2 learners use these components (phonemes and morphemes) of language in consistent and meaningful ways, following the syntax (rules of grammar and structure) of English, they create English speech acts, like *Ah! I just saw a snake under the car.*

In analyzing speech acts, Austin (1962), proposed looking at them in three distinct ways. One aspect of the speech act is the **locutionary** aspect of the utterance. This is the physical action of voicing a meaningful set of words. Second, Austin analyzed the **illocutionary** aspect, or the **pragmatic** (social), meaning of the speech act. The meaning of the utterance for the speaker and the hearer is not only determined by the linguistic components but also the background, context, culture, or experience of the **interlocutors** (the persons participating in the speech event). Third, a speech act also has a **perlocutionary** aspect, which is the actual effect of the utterance on the hearer. For example, the speech act can convince the hearer of the speaker's argument or inspire the person to take a course of action. These three aspects of a speech act are illustrated in Figure 8.1.

Figure 8.1:   An Illustration of a Speech Act

"Wow, it's bright in here."
↓
(locutionary aspect)

Meanings

Locutionary	Illocutionary	Perlocutionary
Wow, it's bright in here.	*Speaker* says, "It's too bright in here for me." *Hearer* thinks, "She must not like the windows open."	The hearer closes the blinds on the windows.

Table 8.1:   Speech Act Intentions

Classification	Definition	Example	It Can Include
Assertives	Statements that can be judged true or false because their purpose is to describe an accepted truth.	*We are married.*	claims reports statements
Directives	Speech acts that direct the hearer to take action in some way.	*Marry me!*	commands suggestions advice requests
Expressive	An expressive act displays the speaker's emotions in some way.	*I'm so happy you are getting married!*	congratulations complaints thanks
Comissives	These speech acts commit the speaker to a future act.	*I will marry you.*	promises threats offers
Declaratives	Declaratives change the state of things through their vocalization.	*I now pronounce you man and wife.*	pronunciations decrees declarations

For L2 learners, understanding all aspects of a speech act is an important part of the process of developing speaking skills in the target language.

Speech acts can further be divided into different forms or intentions (Searle, 1975). Illocutionary speech acts can be divided into five classifications, each of which is defined in Table 8.1.

Oral Production in the Speaking Classroom

Brown and Abeywickrama (2010) further define oral production acts for the language classroom. For each type of production act, it is possible to create activities in the L2 classroom that specifically target, develop, and assess those speech acts. Table 8.2 lists five types of L2 learner speech acts, defines each one, and then briefly describes an L2 classroom activity or assessment targeting that oral production act.

Accuracy and Fluency

Regardless of the speech act being taught, the focus of oral communication in the language classroom is to develop both accuracy and fluency in speech. **Accuracy** in speech refers to the ability to produce correct language in the given context of the speech event. Throughout the process of learning a language, students' accuracy in speech will develop dependent upon their leaning of the vocabulary, structure, and grammar of English. **Fluency,** on the other hand, is concerned

Table 8.2:   Speech Act Types in the Classroom

Speech Act	Definition	Classroom Activity/Assessment
Imitative	To simply repeat what has been said	The teacher orally dictates words or phrases for low-beginner students to repeat; students develop listening and pronunciation skills.
Intensive	To produce short phrases or sentences, often targeted to specific language issues	For students to practice past tense verbs and markers, the teacher states a sentence in the present tense (*I eat oranges every day*) and asks the beginning student to say it back using the past tense (*I ate oranges yesterday*).
Responsive	To produce interactive speech, such as limited conversations or greetings	In a communicative activity, intermediate students work in pairs and role play a conversation. After preparing with sample vocabulary and dialogues, students break into pairs and role play ordering food in a restaurant with sample menus brought to class.
Interactive	To produce more complex interactive speech; it can include more participants and diverse topics that can be personal or informative	In a group setting, high-intermediate students play 20 Questions. Given particular categories from vocabulary being studied that week (occupations or academic programs), students must each choose a word within that category. Other group members take turns asking yes/no questions to guess the word. Students use diverse forms of questions and targeted academic vocabulary.
Extensive	To produce extensive oral presentations in formal settings or carry on prolonged conversations on various topics	In a formal setting, advanced students prepare a three-minute speech on a topic of their choice. After the speech, three students ask follow-up questions about the information in the speech that the student answers.

with the speed and smoothness of a person's speech. This skill is often dependent on the language ability and skill level of the speaker. During the process of developing language, accuracy and fluency will take on different levels of importance at different stages of learning and according to the language point/activity purpose being taught. Activities in the L2 classroom can be geared toward developing fluency; developing accuracy; or more often, a combination of the two. In combination with developing vocabulary and structure, language learners are moving toward their ultimate goal—communicating effectively in the target language.

Communicative Competence

While it is essential, of course, to learn the vocabulary and structure of language to produce the language, if no production actually takes place, language learners have not met the goal of communication. As Hunter (2012) has stated, the "perennial struggle for teachers is how to develop both accuracy and fluency in students' speaking since one often seems to come at the expense of the other" (p. 30). For example, this can be the case when looking at the differences between teaching an EFL classroom and an ESL classroom. In the EFL classroom based in another country, students may have many opportunities to speak in class—they converse with other EFL speakers, with their teacher, and they hear rich input from their EFL teacher. In other words, they often work on accuracy, following the material in the curriculum that portrays correct English. What they may lack, though, is the opportunity to use their speech outside the classroom, developing fluency in using the speech with English speakers in a spontaneous environment. ESL speakers, on the other hand, may have more opportunity to use their speech outside the classroom. As they go about their daily lives in an English-speaking country, they will use English in a spontaneous manner with native English speakers, developing their fluency in addition to the English input from the classroom setting. While these scenarios may not always be the case, English L2 teachers must always be aware when there is an imbalance between rich accurate input and opportunities for developing spontaneous and fluent speech.

Ultimately, the goal of the L2 classroom is for language students to demonstrate accuracy and fluency concurrently in their oral language production. When L2 learners demonstrate this oral confidence through the use of vocabulary, structure, accuracy, and fluency to use the language to convey ideas and respond to others appropriately, this is what Hymes (1966) defined as communicative competence.

Communicative competence is built through a variety of speaking activities that address both accuracy and fluency in oral language. While L2 learners might thrive in the safe classroom environment where they can rely on the textbook, the teacher, and other language learners to support and encourage their language use, this is only a small part of the equation. If the goal is for language learners to be able to communicate in real-world settings, then speaking activities must build accuracy and fluency equally. Let's start by looking at some common activities in a Speaking class that build accuracy and fluency, then address how to teach pronunciation in the ESL/EFL classroom, and finally discuss teaching overall communication skills in a Speaking class. The goal of all of these classroom activities is to develop L2 learners' communicative confidence, building from pronunciation to overall accuracy and fluency.

Speaking Classes

Speaking classes will vary depending on many factors, such as the age of the learner or whether the class is in an EFL or ESL setting, but one important component is that the class should revolve around student talk instead of teacher talk (Folse, 2006). Table 8.3 introduces some basic speaking activities in the L2 classroom that focus on fundamental speaking functions.

Table 8.3:   Speaking Functions and Activities

Speaking Function	Activity	Sample Activity Focus and Practice
Correct pronunciation and use of the sounds, tone, stress, and rhythm in English	Modeling and repetition activities	The teacher models correct pronunciation of various sounds or words in English and students repeat and practice what they hear, chorally and individually. Students develop listening and awareness of the differences between L1 and L2. Activities could include oral practice of words and sentences with certain target sounds, such as words beginning with the /f/ sound or words that have similar stress or tone (Grant, 2014). *Teacher:* Students, repeat after me—five. *Students:* Five. *Teacher:* Fairies. *Students:* Fairies. *Teacher:* Fight. *Students:* Fight. *Teacher:* Five fairies fight. *Students:* Five fairies fight. *Teacher:* Fabulous!
Sentence-level basic speaking including introductions, personal information, and simple conversations	Dialogue activities	The teacher provides models of simple dialogues between two people for students to imitate and practice. The models can be written and oral. *Teacher:* In pairs, you will practice this dialogue: *Student 1:* Hello, my name is Ines. *Student 2:* Hello, my name is Jorge. *Student 1:* It is nice to meet you. *Student 2:* It is nice to meet you too.
Vocabulary and negotiation of meaning	Information gap activities	Student pairs are provided with two different pictures or text that emphasize the vocabulary and grammar focus for that class. Students must ask each other questions to find out information their partner has. For example, the class is focused on going to the grocery store, so the teacher gives student pairs Picture A that contains all fruits and Picture B that contains all vegetables. Students must ask and answer each other to gather information about their pictures. Students should write what they hear and be prepared to report to the class. *Student A:* Do you have lettuce? *Student B:* Yes, I do. Do you have apples? *Student A:* Yes, I do. *Student A:* I don't know any more vegetables. What vegetables do you have? *Student B:* I have broccoli and carrots. What other fruit do you have? *Teacher:* Let's take turns sharing with the class the fruits and vegetables that are in our grocery store.

Table 8.3:   Speaking Functions and Activities (continued)

Speaking Function	Activity	Sample Activity Focus and Practice
Sustained communication and negotiation in specific situations, such as at the doctor's office or in a restaurant	Role-play activities	In role-play activities, students are given a particular role in a communicative situation and they must speak and listen in that role for a sustained period. It is important that the teacher prepare students for role-play, including introducing any critical vocabulary, modeling sentence structures for the activity, and giving students time to practice before completing the activity independently. *Teacher*: In pairs today, you are going to role-play that you are a patient in a doctor's office or that you are the nurse checking the patient in. We will go over some important vocabulary and structures to begin. Then, in pairs, you will practice so that you can role-play the dialogue for the class. Student 1 will be a patient coming in for an appointment due to a fever, cough, and chills. Student 2 will be a nurse who checks in patients and prepares them for the doctor.
Communicate opinions and information on a variety of topics, usually an integrated task that also includes prior listening	Oral presentation activities	Students create presentations based on information they have read, heard, researched, and prepared. Presentations can range from very basic informal tasks (e.g., Introduce yourself or What are your three favorite restaurants?) to complex research presentations (e.g., What are four different forms of world governments? and What are some similarities and differences between them?).

Communicative Competence and Teaching Pronunciation

Note: In this section, you may need to refer to the IPA chart in the Appendix for help when reading about sounds in English. Note that when using IPA, broadly transcribed phonemes are always in / / marks and narrow transcriptions are in [ ] brackets. English words and their sounds generally appear in italics or capital letters (especially to show stress).

The goals in teaching pronunciation in the ESL/EFL classroom have undergone changes over the years. The former objective of native-like proficiency in speaking has been superseded in many ways by the tempered goal of intelligibility and comprehensibility (Grant, 2014). **Intelligibility** refers to how well the speaker is understood by the listener, and **comprehensibility** is the level of effort the listener must make to understand the speaker's message.

Phonetics is the linguistics subfield that studies individual speech sounds (phonemes) and where (with which organs of phonation) and how (what types/manners of sounds) these phonemes are produced. For example, [b] and [t] are two different sounds/phonemes of English. The sound *sh* is a phoneme of English. It is articulated as one sound/phoneme; it is not the sound of [s] plus the separate sound of [h]. Voiceless *th*, as in *think*, is also a single sound/phoneme. There are approximately 44 phonemes in English.

Allophones are all the ways a particular phoneme is articulated. For example, the phoneme /p/ sounds different in the words *peach* (where [p] is strongly aspirated with an explosion of air from the lips when said at the start of word) and the word *type* (where [p] is non-aspirated; there is little/no explosion of air when [p] is at the end of word). We think of it as the sound of [p], but linguists recognize that the [p] sound has variations (allophones).

Speakers produce phonemes using various organs of speech: diaphragm and lungs, trachea, larynx/glottis/vocal folds, velum (soft palate), uvula, roof of mouth/hard palate, alveolar ridge, tongue, teeth, lips, and nasal cavity. There are several hundred different phonemes from the world's languages recognized by the International Phonetic Association (IPA) and transcribed into IPA. Of all the speech sounds that a human vocal tract can create, different languages vary considerably in the number of these sounds that they use. The total number of phonemes in languages varies from as few as 10 to as many as 141. These may range from familiar vowel and consonant sounds to sounds rarely heard by English speakers (such as clicks).

All speakers can also identify sounds that we have in English that other languages may not have, which can make them difficult for L2 learners to pronounce right away—for example, the two *th* sounds (voiceless as in *THanks* and voiced as in *THis*); the *sh* and *ch* phonemes that make *waSH* and *waTCH* two different words with different meanings because of the change in phoneme; or the American /r/ sound versus the alveolar or uvular /r/ sound of other languages. These all tend to be difficult English phonemes for many L2 learners to produce.

When teachers know the phonemes of English, how/where they are produced, and the English sounds that don't exist in other languages (or which commonly pose problems for L2 learners), they can start to predict and understand L2 learners' pronunciation/phonemic difficulties. This is a start in helping L2 learners to better hear, identify, and articulate the sounds of English.

Another issue to consider about phonetics when it comes to English is that, unlike Spanish, French, and many other languages, English has poor sound-symbol correspondence. This means that teachers cannot rely on a one-to-one sound-spelling correspondence. English has only five alphabet vowel letters *a-e-i-o-u* and 21 consonant letters, but it has more than 26 sounds. For example, the sound of [s] in a word is not always spelled with the alphabet symbol *s*. It could be spelled with a *c* as in *circus*. And in circus, the [k] sound/phoneme is not spelled with the alphabet symbol of *k*, but rather with *c*. The [f] sounds in *phone*, *cough*, and *fish* are all spelled differently (*ph-gh-f*). This is confusing for native English speakers and L2 learners alike. Thus, to be a good speller in English, one must learn not only phonics/sound-symbol relations but also memorize lots of spelling rules and irregularities. In many other languages, there is very good sound-symbol correspondence—words are spelled the way they sound, which makes spelling in those languages a piece of cake compared to English. Czech, for example, has exactly the same number of alphabetic symbols as it does sounds.

Phonology is closely associated with phonetics. Phonology describes the way the sounds are commonly combined in particular languages and how they are used to convey meaning. For instance, why might Japanese English learners tend to add vowel sounds to the ends of English words. The answer is because in Japanese phonology every word is composed of syllables made up of a consonant and a vowel, and words never end in a consonant sound except for words that end with an [n] sound. Likewise, why might Spanish speakers put a vowel sound in front of a consonant cluster in English? Unlike English, Spanish does not contain words that begin with s-consonant clusters such as *sp* or *st*; such consonant clusters are preceded by a vowel sound.

Most L2 learners, at least initially, transfer their L1 phonetic/phonological knowledge to the L2 and tend to say words in the L2 using the phonological pattern/system of their L1. Research shows that the one aspect of L2 learning where age alone seems to be a factor is in pronunciation. Younger does seem to be better when it comes to acquiring a native-like accent in an L2. Many older L2 learners will retain some L1 accent in speaking their L2, even when they are at advanced proficiency/fluency in the L2.

A final aspect of sound and meaning to be considered is how suprasegmentals can impact meaning. Suprasegmentals are those aspects of sound beyond the segmental (individual) phonemes. These are usually considered suprasegmental properties:

▶ stress

▶ intonation

▶ length

Stress

This refers to the part of a word that is given the most energy. Some languages have predictable stress patterns. For example, Czech stresses the first syllable of most words and Welsh stresses the next-to-last syllable. English word stress is often unpredictable and must be memorized for each word. Stress also adds meaning within sentences. Think of the differences in these three sentences depending on the stress placed on different words:

▶ HE didn't go to the store.

▶ He DIDN'T GO to the store.

▶ He didn't go to the STORE.

Stress plays a major role in distinguishing negative from affirmative sentences:

- ► I can SPEAK Swahili (the main verb is stressed in affirmative sentences)

versus

- ► I CAN'T speak Swahili (the negative auxiliary is stressed in negative sentences).

This is a very helpful hint for L2 learners who may think that native English speakers recognize negatives by hearing the *t* in *can'T*. Rather, native English speakers distinguish negative statements not by the *t* in *can'T* (which is often not articulated clearly) but rather by the stress pattern.

Intonation

In English, this usually refers to the rise and fall of stress and tone in sentences. For example, in English, statements and *wh-* questions have falling intonation at the end of the statement or question. Yes/no questions have rising intonation at the end. Choice questions have rising and then falling intonation. Surprise/disbelief is shown by a rise in the middle and again at the end. In other languages, however, tone patterns impact the meanings of words. Tonal languages include Mandarin and Thai. In these languages, the word *ma* has several different meanings, depending on the tone pattern used (flat, rising, falling, falling then rising, rising then falling). In contrast, in English, regardless of what tone you use when saying the word *Mom*, the word has the same meaning (though your feelings might be expressed by tone).

Length

In many languages, however, changing the length of a vowel or consonant sound changes the meaning of the word. For example, in Japanese, *biru* means "building" and *biiru* means "beer," and in Spanish *pero* means "but" and *perro* means "dog." In English, *live* and *leave* are good examples of how vowel length changes meaning.

Four Processes by Which We Produce Sound

The four main processes by which we produce sounds/phonemes are listed.

1. **Airstream**—movement of air through the vocal tract (via lungs, diaphragm, trachea). Most speech sounds use air; all English speech sounds do.

2. **Phonation**—the movement of the larynx/vocal folds to create voiced or voiceless sounds.

   - ► **Voiced** sounds—the vocal folds are together and rapidly vibrate open and closed (some English consonants and all vowels). To test whether a sound is voiced, put your fingers gently against your throat in the area of the Adam's apple; voiced sounds produce vibration. Another test is to plug your ears with your fingers and say the sound. If it is voiced, you will hear a loud buzzing in the head. You can help students correct voiced sounds by doing these tests.

▶ **Voiceless** sounds—the vocal folds are apart; no vibration. Sounds are produced with air and tongue/teeth/lips. A test for the correct articulation of voiceless sounds is to make sure there is no vibration of the vocal cords or that, when saying the sound with the fingers plugging the ears, there is no buzzing. Rather, the sound should produce a small puff or flow of air that will blow a piece of paper held in front of the mouth. This puff-of-air test will help L2 learners check if they are aspirating voiceless sounds correctly.

3. **Manner of Articulation**—different types of sounds that can be produced (how the sounds are made):

   ▶ **Nasal or oral sounds**—opening or closing of velum. For example, /m/ in English is a nasal sound.

   ▶ **Stops**—complete obstruction of air by lips, tongue, and velum. For example, /p/ in English is a stop.

   ▶ **Fricatives** (continuants)—partial obstruction of air, continuous hissing sound. For example, /s/ in English is a fricative.

   ▶ **Affricates**—quick explosions that begin as a stop but are released as a fricative. For example, /ʤ/ in English is an affricative, as in in the initial sound in *job*.

   ▶ **Liquids**—sounds such as /l/ and /r/ in English are both liquids.

   ▶ **Glides** (semi-vowels)—rapidly articulated vowel sound. For example, /y/ in English is a glide.

4. **Place of Articulation**—describes where sounds are articulated (where lips, teeth, and tongue are positioned)

   ▶ **Labial** (lips) sounds: bilabial (both lips)—/p /

   ▶ **Labio-dental:** lower lip and upper teeth—/f /

   ▶ **Dental or interdental** sounds: tongue between teeth—/ð/ as the initial sound in *the*

   ▶ **Alveolar** sounds: tongue touching alveolar ridge behind front upper teeth—/d/

   ▶ **Palatal/alveopalatal** sounds: tongue near roof of mouth—/ʃ/ as the initial sound in *she*

   ▶ **Velar** sounds: tongue touching near soft palate at rear roof of mouth—/ŋ/ as the final sound in *sing*

   ▶ **Glottal** sounds: whispery sounds; vocal folds as primary articulator—/h/

   ▶ **Uvular and pharyngeal** sounds—English doesn't have these sounds, but other languages do (e.g., the German [r] as in *rot*)

Pronunciation in the ESL/EFL Classroom

The last three processes described—phonation/voicing, manner of articulation, and place of articulation—are typically where the problems in English learners' pronunciation occur. Knowing how English sounds are produced can help teachers identify why mispronunciation is happening and help the L2 learner solve it.

▶ For example, often English L2 learners do not voice or incorrectly voice sounds (saying *bebsi* rather than *Pepsi*; *back* when they mean *bag*; or *crap* for *crab*). Teachers can help them practice the voiced /b/ versus voiceless /p/ by having them practice saying and hearing the sounds repetitively; learners can also use hands-on exercises (feeling for vibration, watching for puff of air on paper) for practicing correct voicing.

▶ Sometimes L2 learners make the wrong type of sound. They may say the affricate *ch* in *watch* for the fricative *sh* in *wash* or *choose* for *shoes*. Teachers can help them practice the longer fricative sound of [sh] versus the short explosive affricate sound of [ch] by demonstrating with their own mouths and tongue how to make the different sounds.

▶ Frequently the problem is just the wrong place of articulation. The L2 learner may not know where the sound should be made and may say *vater* for *water* (labiodental sound/lip and teeth /v/ vs. bilabial sound/both lips /w/); *sink* for *think* (alveolar /s/ vs. interdental /th/); or *light* for *right* (alveolar /l/ instead of alveopalatal /r/). In these cases, by demonstrating with their own mouths and using repetition of sound, teachers can show L2 learners where and how to make the sound.

Table 8.4 demonstrates how to take a systematic approach to teaching pronunciation presented and adapted from Linda Grant (2014).

Minimal Pairs as a Pronunciation Exercise

A very effective and useful type of pronunciation exercise in the L2 classroom is minimal pairs. **Minimal pairs** in the speaking classrooms are pairs of words that only vary in one sound. One example of a minimal pair is the pair of English words *it* and *eat*. These words only differ in the vowel sound, but the consonant sound is the same. Another example of a minimal pair is *hit* and *his*. These words only differ in the final consonant. Knowledge of minimal pairs will help you to put together exercises for L2 learners with pronunciation struggles. See Table 8.5 for some examples of minimal pairs.

Table 8.4:   Approaches to Teaching Pronunciation

Pronunciation Skill	Goal	Activity
Listening and awareness	To develop learners' awareness of the target pronunciation feature	Listen and Repeat: For beginning-level learners, ask them listen to a series of 3 words, only one of which contains the target sound. The learners must then circle the correct word with the sound. <u>Example</u>: Students, circle the words that contain the /sh/ sound: 1. sheet cheat cheap 2. push porch touch 3. show chow chomp
Control	To develop learners' control over the pronunciation of the target feature	Jazz Chants®: For all levels of students, Jazz Chants® are a great way to incorporate songs and sounds. Using chants, students repeat certain sound repetitively through song-like chants. Created by Carolyn Graham (1978), these chants use rhythm to promote good intonation, stress, and memory of new words and sounds. You can find these types of chants in many variations on the internet. Here is an example where students snap their fingers and add stress to each bolded word to practice stress: **I** *like* **cookies.** **I** *like* **tea.** **I** *like* **movies.** **English** *likes* **me!**
Practice	To develop learners' ability to produce the target feature in a range of different and increasingly difficult structured contexts	Targeting Problematic Sounds: At the intermediate level, ask students to practice a problematic sound in its various iterations. For example, because the sound /h/ is silent in some languages, this can be a problematic sound for students because it is sometimes pronounced in English and sometimes silent. First, ask students listen to as many words as possible with the /h/ sound at the beginning and middle of English words (*hat, hit, heat/behind, Ohio, ahead*). Ask them to identify the sounds on paper as you read the words out loud and then they read the words out loud. Then, you can go over certain words where the *h* is silent such as *ghost, honest, herb*, or *khaki*. Ask students to work in pairs to circle words with the letter *h* in them to determine if it is pronounced or silent.

Table 8.4:   Approaches to Teaching Pronunciation (continued)

Pronunciation Skill	Goal	Activity
Extension	To develop learners' ability to apply their new skills in a range of contexts	Because the past tense *–ed* suffix can be pronounced in three different ways, this can be difficult for L2 learners. Present the rules for pronunciation and then ask students to work with a partner to say them correctly. Rule 1: When the last sound in the present tense verb is voiceless, the *–ed* ending will sound like /t/. For example: *talked, baked,* or *laughed.* Rule 2: When the last sound in the present tense verb is a vowel or a voiced consonant, the *–ed* ending will sound like /d/. For example: *moved, turned,* or *opened.* Rule 3: When the last sound in the present tense verb is /t/ or /d/, the *–ed* ending will sound like /ɪd/). For example, *wanted, started,* or *counted.* After students understand these rules, put them in pairs and give them a paper with a series of present tense verbs to practice. For example: *cook* *play* *end* *stop* *start* *mail* *need* Students should first determine the correct pronunciation and work together to ensure they are saying it correctly. Then they should create sentences with each word and practice them together, working on accuracy and fluency.

Suggestions from *Pronunciation Myths: Applying Second Language Research to the Classroom Teaching* by L. Grant, "Myth 2: Pronunciation is not for beginning-level learners" (B. Zielinski & L. Yates) (pp. 56–79). Copyright © 2014, University of Michigan Press.

Table 8.5:   Minimal Pair Examples

/r/ – /l/	right – light	(different places of articulation)
/ɵ/ - /s/	think – sink	(different places of articulation)
/p/ – /b/	pat – bat	(same place of articulation, different voicing)
/s/ – /z/	sink – zinc	(same place of articulation, different voicing)
/k/ – /g/	back – bag	(same place of articulation, different voicing)
/t/ – /d/	bet – bed	(same place of articulation, different voicing)
/f/ – /v/	face – vase	(same place of articulation, different voicing)
/b/ – /v/	boat – vote	(different places of articulation, different manners of articulation)
/ ʃ / - /tʃ/	wash – watch	(different manners of articulation—fricative vs. affricate)
/ɪ/ – /i/	rich – reach	(the vowels have different mouth/lip shape and tongue location)
/æ/ – /ɔ/	map – mop	(the vowels have different mouth/lip shape and tongue location)
/ɔ/ – /ə/	dog – dug	(the vowels have different mouth/lip shape and tongue location)
/ɪ/ – /ɛ/	big – beg	(the vowels have different mouth/lip shape and tongue location)

Some rules for creating minimal pairs:

1. Only the target phoneme, the sound you want students to practice, can change; all other sounds are the same:

    ▶ *bit* [b ɪ t] and *bite* [b aɪ t] is a minimal pair; each has just three phonemes and the only difference is the vowel sound to be practiced — /ɪ/ and /aɪ/.

    ▶ These do not work:

       ▪ *bite* [b aɪ t] and *bright* [b r aɪ t]. There are three phonemes in the first word but four phonemes in the second word.

       ▪ *bat* and *car*; *cat* and *far*; *fat* and *bar*. None of these pairs work. Why? Because you're working on more than one sound change in each pair.

2. Keep it simple: *frightened/brightened* is a minimal pair, but it is not useful for pronunciation practice because it is long and has many sounds that L2 learners must have already mastered in order to work on: /f/ versus /b/, the *–en* sound, and then the past tense *–ed*. This is too difficult.

3. Don't choose confusing examples for pronunciation practice. For example: *bow (on a present)* [bo] and *bow (take a bow)* [baw]. They look alike but are pronounced differently and have different meanings. Don't confuse spelling issues with phonetic ones: *there, their,* and *they're* all sound alike but have different spellings and meanings. Again, this is a matter of memorization and practice, not pronunciation.

Remember, the goal of minimal pair exercises is to practice particular sounds. The focus should be on oral practice of target sounds, hopefully within a larger communicative competence framework. A great speaking and listening minimal pair activity is a Bingo game that uses the knowledge of minimal pairs to help L2 learners practice listening and speaking. Choosing four different minimal pairs (e.g., /r/ — /l/, /θ/ — /s/, /p/ — /b/, and /s/ — /z/), create Bingo cards like this sample with various minimal pairs. Learners must listen as you read aloud the words and cover the appropriate word with a game piece. Learners who have covered either a whole row, column, or diagonal will yell "Bingo!" The learners must then correctly pronounce the words that they have covered. A sample Bingo card is provided (Figure 8.2), and it can be scrambled to make other cards based on the words from these chosen sounds.

right/light	*though/sew*	*pea/be*
red/led	*thought/sought*	*sink/zinc*
reach/leech	*putt/but*	*sip/zip*
think/sink	*park/bark*	*sue/zoo*

Figure 8.2: Sample Minimal Pair Bingo Card

B	I	N	G	O
pea	think	sew	but	light
sip	led	thought	sought	sue
though	right	Free Space	be	zinc
putt	leech	bark	park	sink
bark	red	zoo	zip	reach

Designing a Pronunciation or Speaking Activity

Designing a speaking activity should always take into account the purpose and the goal of the activity. One way of looking at speaking tasks is to divide them into intensive and extensive tasks. One framework that applies to both types of tasks uses three important considerations that determine how you create those tasks (Folse, 2006):

1. one-way versus two-way tasks
2. planning time
3. open-ended versus restricted tasks

In one-way tasks, information flows in one direction, from one student to another. An example would be one learner introducing herself to another learner with the second learner acting as a passive listener. In two-way tasks, information flows back and forth between two students. For example, the learners in this scenario introduce themselves to each other, each one responsible for participating in the tasks. Two-ways tasks are considered more effective tasks for the speaking classroom, as they encourage negotiation and more communicative competence (Long, 1989, as found in Folse, 2006).

Planning time is also critical for L2 learners in the speaking classroom. If learners do not have the vocabulary or communicative competence to participate in a speaking task, then the effectiveness of the task to improve speaking skill is diminished. An example of a type of speaking task for which planning time is critical is a role-play, a speaking task where L2 learners take on different roles (such as waiter and customer) in a set scenario to practice dialogues. It is important to allow planning time for students to understand the vocabulary needed and hear models of the dialogues so they can participate fully in the task. When L2 learners must participate in such a task unprepared, the consequence is often classroom silence or dominance of the task by more proficient learners.

Open-ended tasks can also be more challenging and less effective than restricted tasks. Open-ended tasks can include broad discussions; for example, the L2 teacher asking the entire class, "What do you think is better, owning a dog or a cat?" This open-ended task has no specific solution and no right or wrong answer. Restricted tasks, on the other hand, require L2 learners to come to a final answer and provide a tangible result. An example of a restricted task would be learners being given a worksheet asking them to discuss the pros and cons of being a vegetarian. The learners would need to discuss the pros and cons in small groups and write at least three reasons in each category. In the end, they must decide whether they would become (or are) vegetarians and orally give a statement to class including two reasons for their answer from the list. In this case, they must come up with a finite and tangible solution using speaking and listening throughout the process.

The Structure of Speaking Activities

Before planning your speaking activity, you should consider the perceived needs of the L2 learners. When learners can relate to the topics being discussed or the language skills being practiced as relevant to their needs, then they become active participants in the lessons. Students may want to learn survival skills in English so that they can operate in the new environment or they may want to learn academic English so that they can enroll in a university/college abroad. If they are interested in academic English, then your lessons need to focus on skills such as taking part in discussions, asking for clarifying information from the instructor or peers, or taking notes from lectures.

There are a number of strategies that you can use in speaking classes to ensure that L2 learners are comfortable in speaking tasks. When engaging the students in communication activities, be sure to:

- ► use visuals to aid comprehension, such as pictures, videos, or realia
- ► speak at a normal pace or slower, not louder
- ► use sentence structure and vocabulary appropriate to the proficiency level of the students
- ► check for comprehension by asking students to rephrase, expand, or describe the content being addressed
- ► encourage participation of all students, not just the most confident

Techniques to Promote Practice

There are a number of techniques that are often used in the ESL/EFL classrooms to promote oral skills. Your lesson should be designed so that students will practice the language in the classroom in a non-threatening environment. Let go of the control by allowing students to interact with you and their peers. The biggest challenge for you as their teacher is getting them to practice the language. Always keep in mind that the language they are learning is not their native language that they hear and speak once they leave your classroom. You have to design your activities in such a way that the students are highly motivated to engage in the lessons. Here are some activities that are often used in language classrooms:

- ► **Discussions and dialogues.** Select a topic that is of interest to the students. It may be based on your lesson, a reading assignment, or a newsworthy event. Group the students so that they have an opportunity to actively participate in the discussion. Make your expectations clear so that the students know beforehand what their task is and how it will be evaluated.

▶ **Presentations.** Students are often required to present a report or speech in front of the class when they are in an academic setting. This activity can be very difficult for those who are at a beginning or high-beginning level of language learning. By giving students lots of opportunities to present to the class, they are getting valuable practice they can use later in other contexts.

▶ **Role-play.** The distinct advantage to this activity is that students interact with each other in a social/cultural context. Another advantage is that they have to be creative with the language. Students can act out solutions to problems presented to them or express their feelings about the topic.

▶ **Post-class assignments.** Encourage students to seek out English-speaking resources in their community. English films, television news shows, and the internet can expose them to other native speakers and serve as topics for discussion.

Students' Performance in Speaking Classes

In an oral communications skills class, students must be presented with different ways of practicing the language. The activities that you design for this class will provide students with the opportunity to interact with others in a meaningful way. Your lesson should introduce the features of the language that you want to students to acquire followed by a controlled practice so that students can familiarize themselves with the language being learned and, finally, provide an opportunity for them to express themselves in a meaningful way.

Some well-respected guidelines are:

▶ Model correct language appropriate to the students' level and needs.

▶ Check for comprehension.

▶ Allow students to practice the language in a non-threatening environment.

▶ Involve students in a highly motivating, creative activity.

▶ Encourage students' efforts.

▶ Provide context clues.

▶ Use non-verbal embellishment.

▶ Activate and expand students' prior knowledge.

Let's use these guiding principles to look at preparing successful tasks in the Speaking class. Table 8.6 looks at tasks for the classroom using pre-speaking, during-speaking, and post-speaking, just as teaching of language skills in the other chapters.

Table 8.6:   The Three Stages of Speaking Activities

Stage	Description of Task	Sample Exercise—Backpack
Pre-speaking	The teacher **motivates** students for the task. The teacher **introduce**s key vocabulary and language structures needed for the task. The teacher **sets** the context for the spoken discourse and the task guidelines.	In this activity, learners of any age get to share one item they choose from their purse, backpack, bag, or pocket and tell the class why they have that item. It can be simplified for beginners who can just say the name of the item or adapted for every level by allowing learners to share as much detail about the item as they want and are capable of doing. Teachers can **motivate** and **set the context** for students by first sharing an item that they have in their own bag, making it personal and interesting. Teachers can **introduce** potentially difficult vocabulary and structures needed during the introduction to the lesson by putting samples on the board and prompting learners with the *wh-* questions about the item—*what, when, where, why.* One model for the activity could be: *In my bag today I have a bracelet. I carry this bracelet every day because my grandmother gave it to me before she died. It is meaningful to me because she wore it almost every day of her life.*
During-speaking	The learners are **talking**, not the teacher. **All** learners **are engaged** in the task, not just a few. The learners are given a **timeframe** for the task, neither too short to complete the task nor too long so they become distracted or silent. The teacher is listening for both **accuracy** and **fluency** but is not correcting learners during the task. Learning is **extended** during the task to foster more language use.	After the teacher models the task, learners are asked to choose any item that they have with them. Explain that **all learners** will participate and should take time to find an item. Learners are asked to **talk** about the item in as much detail as they wish. Learners are given a **timeframe** of 30 seconds to 1 minute, depending on time. If learners do not know the word for the item, other learners should help first and then the teacher can offer assistance. The teacher should be listening, taking notes on **accuracy** and **fluency** during presentations, and prompting learners with questions. To **extend** the task, learners can ask questions of the presenter about the item, such as *Where did you buy it?*
Post-speaking	The learners have the opportunity to **assess** the task. The teacher provides **corrections** to accuracy and fluency. The teacher and learners **together** go over what was learned. Learning is **extended** after the task by making connections with the lesson or the real world.	After everyone has presented, the teacher **assesses** learning by asking the class to repeat some of the new vocabulary or information learned during the presentations. The teacher uses her or his notes to repeat and model any **corrections** to accuracy or fluency heard during the presentations. Words or phrases can be written on the board and modeled and repeated with the class **together.** Learning is extended by asking students to bring a small item that they keep at home (nothing valuable) or write a description of that item to the next class. Learners can then either describe the item for classmates to guess or share even more details orally with the class.

Speaking Activities for the Classroom

The speaking activities provided are based on various approaches to the language syllabus (grammar-based, communicative product, communicative process, and eclectic), integrate language skills, include assessment options, and emphasize real-world settings.

Activity 8.1: Oral Narratives

Grammar-Based Speaking

Rationale: Speaking activities that enhance grammar and vocabulary lessons are essential to enforcing the language and demonstrating the communicative potential of the language structures being learned. They also give the students exposure to a variety of language forms and give the teacher the opportunity to assess how accurately the language learners are using the grammatical structures and new vocabulary. Grammar-based speaking activities demonstrate to students the importance of grammar and vocabulary, not only in the academic setting but also in the communicative setting as well. This activity uses grammar as its main focus and allows the students to practice the various forms of grammatical structures in a creative way.

Objectives: Students follow visual/verbal cues to tell a story using past simple and past progressive tense.

Pre-Planning

Pre-knowledge: The students must already be familiar with both the uses and formation of the past simple and past progressive tenses, as these will be used while telling the story. Students must know both regular and irregular forms of the verbs.

Materials needed: One or two copies of a visual provided to encourage interest and language. The visual can be a photograph, picture, or even a webpage displaying a scene with lots of people or details. An example would be a picture of a park scene where people are engaging in various activities such as walking, riding bikes, playing Frisbee, and picnicking. You also need a whiteboard with markers and a ball of yarn that has knots tied into it at various lengths.

Language level: High-intermediate to advanced

Recommended age group: Pre-teens to adults

Procedures

Pre-speaking: Ask students to sit together in a circle, either on the floor or in chairs. Once everyone is situated, show them a printout(s) of the visual. The students can pass the visual around in order to see every detail. Give students time to view the visual and ask questions about anything they do not have the vocabulary to describe. You can add difficult vocabulary or wording to the whiteboard to assist students during the task.

As students are looking at the visual for the second round, ask them to describe the scene in more detail. Write the descriptive words they provide on the whiteboard so they have vocabulary to refer to as they tell the story. Encourage the students to create names and backstories for each character in order to make the story richer.

During-speaking: After the visual has been analyzed, tape it up where all can see it, and then tell the students that they are going to make up a story about what happened before, during, and after in the visual in past tense. Tell them to be creative and use their imaginations—the funnier, the better! Take the ball of yarn, and hand it to one of the students in the circle. Ask that person to begin the story while unravelling the ball of yarn. Once a student gets to a knot in the yarn, he or she must stop and hand the yarn to the person on the left, who then picks the story up where the other left off.

As the ball of yarn unravels and as each knot is revealed, the yarn should slowly travel around the circle, and a story based on the picture should take shape. The story will be successful if every student listens carefully and keeps the action going. When the yarn runs out, that student must finish the story (be sure that every student has had a chance to contribute).

Evaluation

Post-speaking: As the students are speaking, the instructor should be noting the errors in past simple or past progressive verbs. While student may make other errors, since the focus of this lesson is on a specific verb tenses, the other errors do not have to be recorded or noted. After the story, and after complimenting their work, the teacher can review the past tense verbs used. As a group, note any errors or pronunciation issues. This ensures that the students feel free to be creative during the storytelling, and yet there is feedback to ensure their language is accurate.

Homework: Ask students to write a true story from their past that they would like to share with someone in a typical conversation. This could be a funny story about their families, travels, or schools. Ask students to tell the story in the next class meeting, just as they would if they met someone at a party and they were getting to know each other with information and stories.

Activity 8.2: Getting to Know You

Communicative Product Speaking

Rationale: The syllabus has targeted, communicative language and vocabulary to use within specific topical situations, or targeted notions-functions within the language, such as interpersonal functions. Speaking activities within the communicative product syllabus are highly motivating to students since they are targeted and functional and the structures are predictable. In this activity, learners get to know their classmates, practice targeted language forms, and develop language confidence.

Objectives: Students use the present perfect tense to communicate with a fellow student and learn specific information about that student. They practice a dialogue specific to getting to know someone through his or her life experiences.

Pre-Planning

Pre-knowledge: The students must already be familiar with the present perfect tense and how to conjugate various verbs. Pass out the student sheet (Figure 8.3) with prescribed topics for the scenario

Materials needed: Student sheet and whiteboard/whiteboard markers. Some words are underlined to show students where the dialogue changes.

Language level: Intermediate

Recommended age group: Pre-teens to adults

Procedures

Pre-speaking: Write these dialogues on the board. With the help of a student, or using two student volunteers, model the two dialogues for the class. Students can practice with someone next to them until they feel more comfortable with the phrasing of the dialogues.

Model Dialogue in Affirmative

Student 1:   Hello, my name is <u>Kerry</u>. It is nice to meet you.

Student 2:   Hi, my name is <u>Florin</u>. Nice to meet you too.

Student 1:   <u>I am from Columbia</u>. Have you ever <u>been to Columbia</u>?

Student 2:   Yes, <u>I have been there</u>.

Student 1:   <u>Where did you go?</u>

Student 2:   <u>I visited Bogota.</u>

Model Dialogue in Negative

Student 1:   Hello, my name is <u>Kerry</u>. It is nice to meet you.

Student 2:   Hi, my name is <u>Florin</u>. Nice to meet you too.

Student 1:   <u>I am from Columbia</u>. Have you ever <u>been to Columbia</u>?

Student 2:   No, <u>I haven't been there</u>.

Student 1:   <u>Would you like to go?</u>

Student 2:   <u>I would like to visit Columbia</u>.

During-speaking: After some practice time, ask students to get into new pairs (not the same person as the earlier practice) and pass out Figure 8.3 to inspire new topics for the dialogues. Once the students have practiced one of the dialogues, they should write yes/no answers and the follow-up questions they used. They can switch partners after a certain amount of time or a certain number of questions.

Directions: Find out about the life experiences of your classmates. Ask a question using the present perfect and the experiences listed. When you find a student who answers yes, follow up with a simple past question, such as, "Have you ever ridden a horse?" If the answer is yes, the follow-up question could be, "Where did you ride it?" When you find a student who answers no, do the same. For example, if you ask, "Have you ever ridden a horse?" and the answer is no, the follow-up question could be, "Why not?" Fill in your follow-up question after the dialogue has taken place. Make notes so you can report to the class.

Evaluation

During- and post-speaking: As the students are speaking, the instructor should be moving around the room and noting the errors in dialogue or present perfect verb forms. While student may make other errors, since the focus of this lesson is on present perfect and the question-and-answer form, the other errors do not have to be recorded or noted. After practicing for some time, ask for volunteers to share their dialogues with the class. Students should hand in their student sheets for review.

Homework: Ask students to create dialogues using present perfect tense in different situations where they might be meeting people for the first time. This could be at work, at a party, or through a friend at school. They should prepare potential follow-up questions for yes and no answers and come prepared to practice the dialogues with another student.

Figure 8.3: During-Speaking Student Sheet

Life Experiences	If Yes, What Was the Follow-Up Question?	If No, What Was the Follow-Up Question?
Ride a horse?		
Sail in a boat?		
Drive a motorcycle?		
Play on a sports team?		
Act in a play?		
Eat spicy food?		
Go hunting or fishing?		
Paint a picture?		
Write a story or poem?		
Read a book in another language?		
Play in a band or music group?		
Traveled to another country?		
See snow?		
Go camping?		

Activity 8.3: Collaborative Process Interviewing

Communicative Process Speaking

Rationale: In the communicative process–based syllabus, the organization of the curriculum is based on tasks. The task based–syllabi activities are focused on the language and language skill needed to complete a concrete task. One way for students to develop their interpersonal and academic language skills is to ask them to interview members of the school staff, public, or other persons in the community. This provides a great opportunity for students to practice their oral, listening, and cross-cultural skills. It forces students to move outside of the classroom to demonstrate that they can use their language ability in an authentic setting. This activity uses integrated skill practice to complete a focused task.

Objectives: Students collaborate while orally interviewing a member of the community and gather information using pre-planned questions and procedures.

Pre-Planning

Pre-knowledge: None
Materials needed: A recording device if possible
Language level: High-intermediate and higher
Recommended age group: Pre-teens to adults

Procedures

Pre-speaking: First, ask students to brainstorm their own particular personal interests on various topics. Students can form pairs based on these shared interests. Help them to choose a topic (i.e., social networking, sports, arts, movies, books, engineering, business), and assist them in looking for local organizations that have a focus on that topic. For example, contact a student's group on campus, a community organization such as the Department of Veterans Affairs, a senior citizen center, or a women's business group prior to the assignment to line up potential participants.

Then students should work together to form questions for a 5–10-minute interview. Students should have the chance to edit their work so their questions are appropriate and grammatically correct. You can easily have them focus on any particular question type you are currently studying (*wh*-questions, such as *Why did you decide to become a business owner?*; *to be* questions, such as *Are you happy with your choice of career?*; or those focusing on the subjunctive case, such as *If you were young again, would you pick the same career?*). They should then practice interviewing their classmates in preparation for the real event, getting feedback and refining their technique.

Set the criteria so that students are evaluated during each step, with rewards for refining and editing their own work. Help them to set up the interview but, when possible, students should take the lead in the project. Students should be required to contact the person and set up the interview themselves once some candidates have been selected. While students may be rejected, this is good practice for students to refine their persuasive skills or learn how to accept rejection politely. If students are having trouble finding an acceptable candidate, step in with some back-up candidates that you have available.

Ideally, students should tape their interview with their interviewee so they can create actual transcripts of the session. The school will hopefully have equipment that students can share or they can use the recording device on their phones. The recordings can be used and transcribed to evaluate the success of the project. *Note:* In this project, students will need assistance throughout the project with demonstrations of appropriate techniques and skills for the students being critical. For example, students may have no idea how to request an interview, how to negotiate when they do not understand, what questions are appropriate in the culture in which they are residing, or how to report on what they have learned. Lots of classroom role-play will be critical to the success of the project. The skills they learn will be invaluable for their future academic or job careers, especially in working with instructors, professors, and professionals in various areas.

Some sample questions that students can use when developing their own questions are listed; these will, of course, need to be made more specific to the context and person being questioned.

Sample Questions

Background

> What can you tell me about yourself?
>
> What made you choose this career?
>
> What best prepared you for this career?

Education

> What is your educational background?
>
> What kind of education do you recommend for this career?
>
> What educational opportunities are available in this field?

Career

> What kind of skills do you need to do this job?
>
> What is your day like?
>
> What kinds of opportunities are in this field?

Personal Views

> Do you enjoy your job?
>
> What is the best part of your job?
>
> Are there things you would like to change about your career?

Openers

> Thank you for agreeing to this interview.
>
> I appreciate your time.
>
> May I tape this interview for my own personal use?

Closers

> Thank you for being interviewed.
>
> Thank you for your time.
>
> Thank you for helping me with my class project.

Evaluation

Students should complete these six tasks and report on their work and progress as they complete each part.

Pre- and During-Speaking:

1. **Topic development:** Choose at least three topics of interest and explain how an interview with someone in those fields will help you understand the topics better.

2. **Community research and contact:** Using the internet, class resources, group discussion, and community engagement (talking with those in the school or community who could help you develop contacts), research groups and individuals whom you might contact to conduct an interview. Create a list of emails, phone numbers, and addresses for each group or individual.

3. **Question creation:** Develop a series of questions based on your curriculum background knowledge that you would like to ask your interviewee. Your questions should be clear, organized, in perfect English, and follow a pattern. You have been given examples of question types in class to help guide and inspire you. Keep in mind your interview should only be approximately 5–10 minutes long.

4. **Collaboration:** With your partner, share your contact list and your questions. Then, together, come up with a strategy for phoning or contacting the person you want to interview. Role play setting up and conducting the interview with a partner. You should practice your pronunciation, questioning technique, and negotiating skills.

5. **Interview:** If given permission, tape the interview so you can create a complete transcript of the interview. During the interview, be polite, ask your questions, and use your best interpersonal skills to gain the information you desire in a timely manner. Wrap up the interview politely.

Post-Speaking:

6. **Interview analysis and report:** After the interview, you should complete an analysis of what you accomplished, what happened, and what you learned. Prepare a transcript and evaluate what you learned both about the topic and about interviewing someone. What speaking skills did you learn that you can use in the future in your personal, academic, or professional career?

Homework: A final evaluation of the project should be turned in so students reflect on their learning.

Activity 8.4: Weekly Oral Evaluation

Eclectic Speaking

Rationale: Many instructors prefer using various and mixed approaches in their design of their syllabus and curriculum. In an eclectic approach to the language classroom, the syllabus may contain a diverse number of activities, such as giving directions based on a map, but may also include language-specific goals, such as the introducing the past tense within the same framework. Teachers like this eclectic approach because it allows them to meet various learner needs and adapt the curriculum to class-specific goals. This weekly evaluation form that students fill out is both a language assessment activity and a self-assessment report. It benefits the instructor and the L2 learners by encouraging monitoring of language progress over the term.

Objectives: In small groups, as a class, or individually with the teacher, students will express what they did that week, what they learned, and what they need to study further. Students express personal experiences orally using past tense verbs.

Pre-Planning

Pre-knowledge: None
Materials needed: Prepared questions
Language level: Must know and use the past tense
Recommended age group: Age 6+

Procedures/Evaluation

This activity has three options:

1. In one-on-one sessions with each student, particularly young students who cannot write, orally ask these questions and record their answers. Take time to evaluate each success with each student and discuss how that student wants to address each problem.

2. In small groups, students fill out the written evaluation form, discussing with classmates the weekly activities, and then turn in the form.

3. Individually, students can fill out the form and turn it in for evaluation.

The weekly evaluation form (see page 152) is a tool to continually document students' learning. Its purpose is to promote L2 learner self-reflection and to provide information about the curriculum. The learners appreciate the interest shown in their progress, and instructors gather information about students and their learning process. It can be adapted to be more manageable and more focused on the learning objectives for that week.

Sample Weekly Evaluation Form

Name:

Hrs in Class:

Week Ending:

1. In class or out:

I learned these new words:

I practiced this grammar:

My biggest problem was:

My biggest success was:

2. What/where/when/how often:

I read:

I spoke:

I wrote:

I listened:

3. Class activities this week:

The most fun:

The most boring:

The most helpful:

The most confusing:

4. I need help with:

Feedback and Error Correction in the Speaking Classroom

In addition to creating speaking activities, L2 instructors need to determine the most effective treatment of oral errors in the Speaking classroom, such as during class activities or discussions. This is not only important for the Speaking classroom but also important for any L2 classroom. There are many ways to correct speaking errors, and it is never appropriate or possible to correct every one made in the language classroom. This is de-motivating and can inhibit fluency. At the same time, errors can fossilize (become permanent) when students consistently make errors in oral production and do not receive correction. L2 teachers can use a number of direct and indirect techniques to address oral errors in the L2 classroom. Let's look at some examples of error correction for different levels, ages, and contexts of L2 learners.

Indirect Correction

▶ **Pinpointing**, coined by Cathcart and Olsen (1976), involves the teacher, when hearing an error in the student's speech, immediately repeating the phrase exactly as the learner stated it, pausing right before the error to give the student the chance to self-correct. Using higher tone or exaggeration before the error can also direct the student to the issue with the language.

Student: I goes to the store every day.

Teacher: I ……….goes to the store every day.

▶ **Rephrasing**, suggested by Holley and King (1971), also allows the student to self-correct. The teacher hears an error and the rephrases it back to the student, either correcting the error or asking the student, *Did you mean . . .?* It is critical that the teacher give the student the opportunity to correct the speech with encouragement.

Student: I goes to the store every day.

Teacher: Did you mean *I go* to the store every day?

▶ **Cueing** (Holley & King, 1971) is more teacher directed in that the instructor makes it clear there was an error in speech, offers cues as to the potential corrections, and then allows the student to repeat the phrase correctly.

Student: I goes to the store every day.

Teacher: Would you say *goes* with *I*? Would you like to try again?

▶ **Questioning** (Burt & Kiparsky, 1972) occurs when the teacher repeats exactly what the student said, including the error, but in a question form that makes it clear there was an error that needs to be corrected. The teacher can emphasize the error with tone or inflection.

Student: I goes to the store every day.

Teacher: *I goes* to the store every day?

- ▶ **Repetition** occurs when the teacher repeats exactly what the student said, including the error, but not in the form of a question. While the teacher may give a clue to what the error is, it is more purposely ambiguous to encourage L2 learner self-correction (Walz, 1982).

  Student: I goes to the story every day.

  Teacher: I goes to the store every day. (Pause)

Direct Correction

Teachers can also choose to directly correct students with the word *no* after an error or by telling the student specifically what he or she should have said. This is an unambiguous way of providing oral feedback that is prompt and direct, but this may or may not be a comfortable way for learners to be corrected in the classroom, as there is a risk to inhibiting participation in class. Each L2 teacher must carefully evaluate whether the particular class of students is used to, or open to, direct correction; must discuss it with the class in advance; and must then be judicious in choosing which errors to correct.

Other Correction Forms

- ▶ **Self-correction:** L2 learners can be given the opportunity and training to listen to themselves carefully, pause, take time to reflect on the accuracy of their speech, and learn to correct their own errors before anyone else has to do so. With practice, learners can develop skill in self-correction.

- ▶ **Peer correction:** Fellow students may be able to assist in correcting some mistakes made by their peers. Students could be asked to listen for errors and correct them respectfully and judiciously. It is critical, though, to make sure that peer correction is a positive and profitable experience for all involved.

When making a decision about which error correction method to use in the classroom, it is essential that the L2 instructor be fair, open, and consistent. Teachers must take into account culture, level, curriculum, EFL/ESL setting, and psychological/social dynamics in every class. What works for one class may neither be appropriate nor effective in a different setting, which is why the instructor should use careful judgment in each class and pay attention to body language and other clues that can demonstrate whether certain techniques are working. Many teachers use different techniques depending on the characteristics of that particular class, but there is no reason not to discuss error correction with students who are capable of understanding and negotiate with them on how they would like to be corrected.

Assessing Oral Communication

In order to target all areas of oral communication, assessment of speaking activities and speaking skills must not only focus on knowledge, structure, skill, and accuracy but also on overall communicative competence. A fundamental question to ask when creating evaluation procedures for the classrooms is what is the construct of the assessment? In other words, what is being assessed and does the assessment actually target that particular skill? Speaking activities that focus solely on developing specific skills in the limited classroom setting must be supplemented with the goal of encouraging and evaluating L2 learner communicative performance, as real-world communication acts integrate more than one language skills in addition to other cognitive abilities (Frost, Elder, & Wigglesworth, 2012).

Assessment of Pronunciation

Pronunciation is often a matter of developing good listening skills that translate into good speaking skills. Good pronunciation also involves the training of the vocal apparatus to create sounds that may be different from those of childhood. While it may not be possible to strive for perfect, native-like pronunciation in one classroom setting, it is possible to help students develop their ear for English sounds and develop their vocal apparatus for creating those sounds. In order to assess pronunciation, it is important for the teacher to create opportunities for students to listen and speak using targeted phonemes so that the teacher can give feedback. This feedback can consist of the teacher providing repetitive pronunciation of English sounds (rich input) and then listening to the student output to determine if the student is comprehensible or needs to work on that particular sound.

Informal Assessment

Teachers use **informal assessment** in teaching speaking when they want to track and note speech development in students without having formal consequences such as grades. Known as **running records** in the elementary classrooms, a great way to informally assess L2 learners' speaking abilities is to create a journal or record of their participation level and errors in the classroom. This requires L2 instructors to create situations where they can take notes on when, how, how often, and how accurate learners' speech acts are. For example, during small group or peer-to-peer discussions, teachers should be walking around and not just listening to students, but actually recording their speech acts. They can then use this information in one-on-one sessions with students or keep records of consistent errors that were heard, so the entire class can correct them at the end of the class period. Either way of correction is non-threatening and yet works with students to correct errors. Running records also tracks L2 learner progress and improvement by providing information on learners who are very quiet in class, something that can make it difficult to judge informal communicative competence.

L2 learners can keep **speech records** of their own so that they quantify and qualify how often they are speaking English inside and outside of the classroom. When these records are reviewed, the teacher and learner may both be shocked at how little time the learner spends speaking in English except when required in the classroom. Finding ways to pair students with native speakers or requiring them to complete formal activities with native speakers (e.g., interviewing a native speaker from school, calling for information, interacting with someone at a cultural event, or seeking out a conversation at the library to get help to accomplish a task) are great ways to foster communicative competence and to ensure students use their emerging speaking skills in real-world situations.

Formal Assessment

Formal assessments involve formal feedback to L2 learners, such as assigning a score or grade to the learner's classwork, homework, quiz, or test. There are many formal standardized tests that now include a speaking or oral communication component when assessing overall language skill. With advances in technology, it is now possible to capture samples of L2 learners' oral production and evaluate the proficiency level of those samples even on large-scale standardized tests.

At the local classroom level, the formal assessment of pronunciation and speaking skills still poses challenges for teachers with limited one-on-one time for evaluating individual proficiency. Further, the subjective nature of communicative competence skills, such as fluency, make it difficult to assess formally. Brown and Abeywickrama (2010) delineated categories of oral tasks and the purpose of each type of tasks within speaking assessment. Table 8.7 demonstrates these categories and gives specific examples of the tasks for the Speaking classroom.

This chapter defined what oral skill development means in the language classroom, including defining what speech is, how speech occurs, and how it is assessed. The chapter also refined the variety of speech acts, including types, intentions, and forms and demonstrated how the acts can be practiced in the classroom. Additionally, teaching pronunciation was discussed in detail. Communicative competence was presented in terms of how language activities can help develop L2 learner competence. Four oral skill development activities that are focused on different domains of oral speech were shared. A critical component in the L2 Speaking classroom, assessment of oral speech, was covered in terms of error correction techniques, informal assessment, and formal evaluation.

Table 8.7:   Oral Task Assessment

Oral Task	Student Production	Focus	Example
Directed response tasks	Student responds to a simple request to transform a sentence or give information.	pronunciation grammar mechanics	*Teacher:* Students, make this statement into a question: "I like rain." *Students:* Do you like rain?
Read-aloud tasks	Student reads aloud a piece of text, from sentences up to multiple paragraphs.	reading structure pronunciation fluency, tone, intonation	Learners take turns reading aloud the poem "Thinking" by Walter Wintle, while the other learners highlight on their paper copy every time they hear a contraction.
Completion tasks	Given an incomplete text, learners fill in the appropriate information and then produce the material orally.	reading structure pronunciation fluency, tone, intonation accuracy	In pairs, learners are given these dialogues with words missing. The learners must first fill in the missing words and then practice the dialogue together. *Student 1:* What _____ you do tomorrow? *Student 2:* I will _____ to the store for some milk. *Student 1:* Oh, well, how about the next day, what _____ you doing then? *Student 2:* I'm _____ to the movies with a friend. Why? *Student 1:* Do you _____ to go to the movies with me instead?

Oral questionnaires	In an interview-style situation, learners respond to questions or commentary.	structure
		pronunciation
		fluency, tone,
		   intonation
		accuracy
		overall language
		   competency
			Using the structure from Brown & Abeywickrama (2010) for the oral interview (warm-up, level check, probe, and wind-down), work one on one with each learner in the classroom to determine their speaking progress in the language. Some sample questions from each type are:
			Warm-up (to prepare students for speaking and make them comfortable)
			How are you today?
			How was your morning?
			Level check (to focus on particular content that learners are currently studying in the classroom).
			Here you are checking on the present perfect:
			How has your family been?
			How has school been lately?
			Probe (where you want to stretch your learner and see what she/he is capable of)
			Have you seen any good movies lately?
			What was it about?
			What did you think?
			Would you recommend it to a friend
			Wind-down (wrap up what you have accomplished)
			How do you feel our interview went?
			Do you feel you have done well in class so far?

Table 8.7:   Oral Task Assessment (continued)

Oral Task	Student Production	Focus	Example

Picture-cued tasks	Given a graph, map, picture, or cartoon, the student must respond to questions about the material.	structure
		pronunciation
		fluency, tone,
		   intonation
		accuracy
		overall language
		   competency
		inference skill
			Give learners a map of a town center. Put them in pairs, and ask them to give each other directions to various places on the map:
			How do I get to the library?
			How do I go from the theater to the store? Where is a good restaurant?

Extended speaking	Using open-ended questions, a dialogue, or a role-play situation, the student must respond with extensive and appropriate language.	structure
		pronunciation
		fluency, tone,
		   intonation
		accuracy
		overall language
		   competency
		inference skill
		cultural
		   competency
			Tell learners they are going to role play buying a car. Model some dialogues and show them some information at first so that they understand the vocabulary and context. Then, in pairs, students will create dialogues for buying a car that they can then demonstrate in front of the class.

Integrative tasks	Using an audio/video prompt or a piece of text, the student must first use listening or reading skills and then respond orally with extensive and appropriate language.	structure
		pronunciation
		fluency, tone,
		   intonation
		accuracy
		overall language
		   competency
		inference skill
		cultural
		   competency
		integrated
		   language skills
			Give learners the lyrics to a song with about 20–30% of the words missing (most song lyrics are available for free online). Ask them listen to the song a couple of times to fill in the missing words and then discuss it as a group. Ask the group to sing the song with the music and discuss some of the meanings in the lyrics.

Translations	Given a word, phrase, or sentence in the native language or in English, the student translates the material accurately into English or their native language.	structure
		pronunciation
		fluency, tone,
		   intonation
		accuracy
		overall language
		   competency
		inference skill
		cultural
		   competency
		integrated
		   language skills
		language
		   translation
		   skills
			Learners can choose a fable or poem that is written in their first language. At home, they translate the text into English as best as they can, and then bring in both texts to the classroom. In small groups, learners can share the original and then the English version, discussing any difficult parts to translate to understand the nuances of the language.

Summarizing Statements

1. Speech can be defined and discussed in many different ways, including types of speech acts and intentions of the interlocutors.

2. Pronunciation is a specific skill that depends on the knowledge and use of the phonemes in a language.

3. L2 instructors can identify which speech act types to focus on in the classroom and target instruction to foster communicative competence development.

4. Assessment of communicative competence can be accomplished through informal evaluation, formal testing, and error correction infused throughout the L2 curriculum.

5. Regardless of how oral error correction is integrated into the language classroom, it is important that the teacher take into account psychological, social, and cultural factors in determining which indirect, direct, or eclectic techniques to consider.

REFLECTION AND APPLICATION

1. Reflect on each of these different teaching situations in L2 teaching:

   a. teaching EFL to adults in Indonesia

   b. teaching ESOL to third-grade Spanish speakers in a public school

   c. teaching speaking in an Intensive English Program (IEP)

   d. teaching speech to young adults in an English for Academic Purposes (EAP) program

   e. teaching ESOL to young adults wanting to get their high school diploma

   Now, review Table 8.2, which lists five typical speech act exercises in the ESL/EFL classroom. Individually or in a group, create two speech act activities from the table for each scenario.

2. This chapter discussed the difference between accuracy and fluency in speech. Consider beginning ESL/EFL students. Do you think it is more important to focus on developing their accuracy in oral communication skills or their fluency? Or do you feel both accuracy and fluency should be developed at the same time? Does the level of the student make a difference in whether you focus on accuracy, fluency, or both in developing speaking skill?

3. What is the difference between informal and formal assessment of oral communication skills? Table 8.7 lists a number of oral tasks. Use the information in this table and create your own task ideas for each category. Share your ideas with the class and see how many different speaking tasks you can create.

REFERENCES

Austin, J. L. (1962). *How to do things with words*. Oxford, U.K.: Oxford University Press.

Brown, H. D., & Abeywickrama, P. (2010). *Language assessment: Principles and classroom practices*. White Plains, NY: Pearson Longman.

Burt, M. K., & Kiparsky, C. (1974). Global and local mistakes. In J. H. Schumann & N. Stenson (Eds.), *New frontiers in second language learning* (pp. 71–80). Rowley, MA: Newbury House.

Cathcart, R. L., & Olsen, J. (1976). *Teachers' and students' preferences for correction of classroom conversation error in TESOL*. Retrieved from ERIC database. ERIC document 138089.

Folse, K. (2006). *The art of teaching speaking: Research and pedagogy for the ESL/EFL classroom*. Ann Arbor: University of Michigan Press.

Frost, K., Elder, C., & Wigglesworth, G. (2012). Investigating the validity of an integrated listening-speaking task: A discourse-based analysis of test takers' oral performances. *Language Testing, 29*(3), 345–369.

Graham, C. (1978). *Jazz chants*. Oxford, U.K.: Oxford University Press.

Grant, L. (Ed.) (2014). *Pronunciation myths: Applying second language research to classroom teaching*. Ann Arbor: University of Michigan Press.

Holley, F. M., & King, J. K. (1971). Imitation and correction in foreign language learning. *Modern Language Journal, 55*(8), 494.

Hunter, J. (2012). 'Small talk': Developing fluency, accuracy, and complexity in speaking. *ELT Journal, 66*(1), 30–41.

Hymes, D. H. (1966). Two types of linguistic relativity. In W. Bright (Ed.), *Sociolinguistics* (pp. 114–158). The Hague: Mouton.

Long, M. (1989). Task, group, and task-group interactions. Paper presented at RELC Seminar, Singapore.

Searle, J. R. (1975). A taxonomy of illocutionary acts. In K. Günderson (Ed.), *Language, mind, and knowledge* (pp. 344–369). St. Paul: University of Minnesota Press.

Walz, J. (1982). *Error correction techniques for the foreign language classroom*. Retrieved from ERIC database. ERIC document 217706.

Chapter 9
▲

Reading Activities and Assessment Techniques

This chapter defines reading comprehension in a second language and describes different types of reading purposes and the processes involved in reading comprehension. It also presents the components of reading activities and various ways that reading comprehension is assessed.

The Reading Skill

Like listening in a second language, reading in a second language is a receptive skill (speaking and writing are productive skills). Reading is a cognitive process that involves understanding written texts. During this process, the reader receives and interprets language that is encoded in print. As a result, reading comprehension takes place when the L2 reader successfully decodes and interprets the information contained in the text. Obviously, when a student is decoding in a new language, it is much more difficult to interpret the information.

When discussing the processes that define reading, Grabe (2009) found that fluent reading is rapid and efficient. Reading is essentially a comprehending process, where readers work with text to understand the writer's intentions. This last aspect makes reading an interactive process between the writer and the reader. The writer conveys information that the reader is expected to understand, while the reader brings a lot of background knowledge to reading that is very useful in determining what the author's intended meaning is. Efficient readers are equipped with strategies that help them anticipate, organize, and summarize information, which make the reading process strategic in nature. Moreover, we read to learn new information and rely on written text, adding two more processes that define reading: a learning process and a linguistic process as well.

What are the characteristics of written discourse, the backbone of the reading skill? These characteristics are:

► continuous flow of discourse

► use of formal connecting markers

► standard and consistent form

► complex vocabulary and morphological structures

► lack of paralinguistic information (body language, intonation), repetition, and redundancy

► uniformity in register usage

Chapter 7 looked at the ACTFL (2012) Standards and described a set of descriptors of what leaners can do at different proficiency levels when it comes to listening. To recap, the ACTFL Standards provide descriptions of all language skills at five major levels of proficiency: Distinguished, Superior, Advanced, Intermediate, and Novice. We recommend that teachers consult this resource because of the potential difficulty of defining what a language skill entails, especially for novice L2 teachers who want to create new instructional activities or adapt existing ones. To exemplify, here is the descriptor for Distinguished level of L2 Reading (ACTFL, 2012):

At the Distinguished level, readers can understand a wide variety of texts from many genres including professional, technical, academic, and literary. These texts are characterized by one or more of the following: a high level of abstraction, precision or uniqueness of vocabulary; density of information; cultural reference; or complexity of structure. Readers are able to comprehend implicit and inferred information, tone, and point of view and can follow highly persuasive arguments. They are able to understand unpredictable turns of thought related to sophisticated topics.

Readers at the Distinguished level are able to understand writing tailored to specific audiences as well as a number of historical, regional, and colloquial variations of the language. These readers are able to appreciate the richness of written language. Distinguished-level readers understand and appreciate texts that use highly precise, low-frequency vocabulary as well as complex rhetorical structures to convey subtle or highly specialized information. Such texts are typically essay length but may be excerpts from more lengthy texts.

Distinguished-level readers comprehend language from within the cultural framework and are able to understand a writer's use of nuance and subtlety. However, they may still have difficulty fully understanding certain nonstandard varieties of the written language. (p. 21)

Reading in L1 and L2: Similarities and Differences

Do L2 learners go through the same processes when they read as the reading processes of native speakers of English? Reading researchers have supported a Reading Universal Hypothesis, which states that reading processes in L2 are very similar to reading processes in L1. There are, indeed universals of reading abilities, as identified by Grabe (2009).

The first universal is linked to the cognitive nature of reading. All readers in all languages use pattern-recognition skills, working memory, and long-term memory. Therefore, reading in L1, as well as reading in L2, is a cognitive process. Second, all writing systems are based on spoken language, and phonological decoding is an essential element of reading in all languages, including those that do not use alphabetic script. For example, one aspect of phonological awareness, syllable awareness, seems to be very strongly related to the ability to read Chinese characters (Chow, McBride-Chang, & Burgess, 2005). The third universal of reading abilities is the extent to which transfer in L2 reading is facilitated by the similarities between L1 and L2.

When L1 and L2 share similar linguistic properties, then L2 reading comprehension will be greatly improved. In a research study conducted by Muljani, Koda, and Moates (1998), Indonesian students speaking Indonesian Bahasa were faster than Chinese students in English word recognition because of their previous alphabetic experiences, especially when the English words conformed to the syllable structures of their L1. Finally, reading processes in all languages rely on background knowledge and culture in order to make sense of print and incorporate the new information into existing knowledge and linguistic systems.

There is strong evidence of similarities between reading in L1 and reading in L2, but that does not mean that there is an absolute similarity between the two. The fundamental difference between the two processes is revealed in the nature of L2 reading. Reading in L2 involves two languages. They continuously interact and make reading in L2 more complex than reading in L1 (Koda, 2007). In most cases, L2 learners bring to the L2 reading process their L1 language background. However, L2 reading is not just a transfer of L2 learners' first language abilities. It is true that L1 has a very important part to play in L2 reading proficiency. However, most issues of L2 reading development can be associated with L2 language proficiency, L2 language and print exposure, and L2 processing skills development. In fact, these issues are the important differences between reading in L1 and reading in L2.

August and Shanahan (2006) synthesized nearly 300 studies into a number of important findings on L2 reading. Their review of studies showed that first and second language speakers learning to read can develop word-level literacy—that is, decoding and spelling, at equal levels. A disparity exists, however, in text-level skills. For example, L2 readers do not attain reading comprehension at the same level as native speakers. They also found that L2 oral proficiency is essential for L2 reading comprehension. This includes vocabulary knowledge, listening comprehension, syntactic skills, and metalinguistic knowledge.

The panel determined that L2 readers have additional factors involved in reading comprehension in the L2, including first language literacy and L2 oral proficiency. Oral English proficiency is necessary for reading in English, and any literacy instruction should also encompass developing listening and speaking skills. Research has demonstrated this because L2 learners with strong L1 reading skills do not read at the same levels in English as their native-speaking peers. Certain errors occur because of differences between L1 and L2, but on the positive side, literacy skills in L1 facilitate L2 literacy development. Some language transfer issues are more likely to affect L2 literacy development than others and at certain stages of literacy development.

Contrasting the Spanish sound system with the English sound system illustrates how the native language can transfer to the L2, resulting in errors in reading and spelling (Bear, Invernizzi, Templeton, & Johnston, 2004). English vowel sounds that do not exist in Spanish include the vowels /æ/ as in the word *man* or /ɛ/ as in *pen*. Additionally, English letters that represent different sounds in Spanish are another area of contrast. For example, the letter *a* as in *cake* is represented by the sound /e/ in Spanish. Similarly, the letter *e* as in *bean* is the sound /i/ in Spanish.

L2 Reading Classes

After examining the reading skill, as well as some important similarities and differences between reading in L1 and reading in L2, let's look at what L2 reading classes are like and what L2 reading students are expected to do in those classes. Traditionally, an L2 reading class requires students to work with a piece of text in class under the guidance of their L2 reading teacher. The class is typically divided into pre-, during-, and post-reading activities that are centered upon a piece of text that should not present major comprehension challenges to learners. The first part of the class is assigned to pre-reading activities where the teacher's purpose is to introduce the topic of the reading material in order to make connections between the text to be read and the students' background knowledge. Essential vocabulary is introduced at this stage to facilitate text comprehension. One example of an activity that is appropriate at this stage is Creating Sentences. The teacher selects eight to ten words directly from the text that are to be read, mixing words the students know with some that they do not. The teacher asks the students to create sentences that might be found in the upcoming reading using the selected words. After reading, the teacher asks students to compare the sentences they have created with the ones in the text and explain the differences and similarities.

After pre-reading activities, students read the text and complete during-reading activities, the purpose of which is to clarify content and vocabulary of the text on the one hand and to focus on purpose and structure of the text on the other hand. For example, an activity like Most Important helps students identify the most important facts in the text. As they read, they underline the sentences they think are important to each paragraphs in the text. After reading, they choose the one sentence they believe is most important for the whole text and write it on a piece of paper, along with their explanation to why they think it is important. Students then discuss their sentences in small groups, explaining their reasoning, listening to others' explanations, and determining the most important sentence in the text.

After the text is read and discussed in class, students are typically assessed their comprehension of the text ideas and vocabulary (multiple choice answers, true/false, fill in the blanks), which can be part of either during- or post-reading activities. An example of homework and a post-reading activity is the creation of a graphic organizer that synthesizes the main ideas and important details in the text.

Reading teachers may want to flip their classroom and use a format that is different from the traditional sequence just exemplified. In a flipped classroom, reading is done at home and tasks that are usually assigned as homework are done in class. An example that uses a flipped model for Annotating as You Read, which is a during-reading strategy (Lockwood, 2014; Lockwood & Sippell, 2012), is shown in Figure 9.1.

Similar to all pedagogical orientations, flipped reading classes have benefits and drawbacks. In terms of benefits, students are able to process reading materials at their own speed. Reading at home allows students to process information at their own pace without worrying that they read too slowly. The flipped classroom also allows teachers to have more control of their class time and create activities where students go beyond the surface understanding of ideas or vocabulary. In addition, flipped classrooms promote collaboration among students by encouraging them to teach and learn concepts from each other with the guidance of their teachers.

Perhaps the biggest disadvantage is that flipped reading classrooms are dependent on whether students come prepared to class and read the materials at home. That is not the case with more traditional reading classrooms where reading is done in class and not at home. Additionally, a flipped classroom could add an extra workload on teachers. In a flipped classroom, new activities need to be developed as there is not as much reliance on reading texts being the primary source of class activities. Despite these drawbacks, the flipped classroom can still be a very effective way of improving student achievement and involving them in their own learning.

Types of Reading Purposes

In both traditional and flipped L2 reading classrooms, there are several identifiable reading purposes for all readers: Readers read for enjoyment, to learn new information, or to locate specific information. When readers read novels, newspaper articles, or blogs, they read for enjoyment or pleasure. In these cases, readers read for general comprehension or to get the gist of the text and are not preoccupied with remembering all the important details. To be proficient in this type of reading takes time, but ultimately, fluent readers read for general comprehension almost effortlessly. However, when it comes to L2 readers, it does not mean that this type of reading is easy. Rather, fluent readers have achieved reading fluency as a result of considerable (in both time and quantity) extended reading. Grabe and Stoller (2011) describe extended reading as way to teach L2 reading in which L2 learners read large quantities of texts (books, articles, magazines) that are within their linguistic competence. Because the texts are not linguistically challenging (too much above the level of proficiency of the L2 readers), the level of frustration due to difficult vocabulary/syntax issues is kept low and the incentive to finish the text is high.

In academic contexts in particular, L2 students read to search for specific information. They scan through texts to find out a specific date a historical event occurred, the name of the person

Figure 9.1: Example of Annotating

During Reading Strategy: Annotating as You Read

Annotating is basically summarizing the most important information in each paragraph as you read by making notes. You cannot summarize without understanding what you've read, so it is a useful way to check comprehension. In addition, you are creating a useful study guide that you can use to participate during class discussions and to study for tests. You can write your notes in the margin or on sticky notes. You can also circle, highlight, or underline main ideas and definitions.

You might want to note the purpose of some paragraphs; for example, you could mark a story used to explain a point as "example" or "ex." An example of how Paragraph 1 of Reading 2 could be annotated is shown.

The fundamental distinguishing characteristic of the most enduring and successful corporations is that they preserve a cherished (valued) core ideology while simultaneously stimulating progress and change in everything that is not part of their core ideology.	fund char.—keep core ideology, start progress
Put another way, they distinguish their timeless core values and enduring core purpose (which should never change) from their	value & purpose—never change
operating practices and business strategies (which should be changing constantly in response to a changing world).	strategies—always changing
In truly great companies, change *is* a constant, but not the *only* constant. They understand the difference between what should never change and what should be open for change, between what is truly	great companies know the diff.
sacred and what is not. And by being clear about what should never change, they are better able to stimulate change and progress in everything else.	sacred = something held dear, same as cherished

From *4 Point Reading and Writing: Intro to English for Academic Purposes* by R. Lockwood and K. Sippell, p. 22. Copyright © 2012, University of Michigan Press.

who wrote a famous novel, or the researchers who created a life-saving medicine. Most of the time students read to locate specific new information with the purpose of using it in an academic task that is scheduled immediately after the reading or in the future.

Another purpose of reading is to learn new information, another generally academic task that involves not only the comprehension of the main points but also the recall of the crucial supporting details. For all readers, the rate when doing a "reading to learn" task is usually slower than when doing a "general comprehension" task. When students read to learn, they use supporting information; create outlines that organize information by cause/effect, compare/contrast, or other criteria; and consciously use their background knowledge.

Chapter 7 identified three main goals of listening: for main ideas, for important details, and for making inferences. Similar goals can be applied to reading activities, as illustrated in Table 9.1.

Bottom-Up and Top-Down Processing

Like listening, reading can be done bottom up and top down. The **bottom-up** reading **model** assumes that readers follow a linear development, from part to whole. L2 readers identify letters, combine letters to recognize words, link words together to understand sentences, and move from sentences to larger blocks of written text, as shown in Figure 9.2.

To develop students' decoding skills, L2 instructors need to assign activities that develop bottom-up strategies (Abbott, 2006). Bottom-up strategies can be used with L2 learners who have problems with basic reading in English to give them a chance to work on basic coding

Table 9.1: Reading Activities in L2 Classrooms

Activity	Description	Goals
Skimming*	L2 readers sample parts of a text to achieve a general understanding of its meaning.	Reading for main ideas
Scanning*	L2 readers locate particular pieces of information without necessarily understanding the rest of a text or passage.	Reading for details
Intensive reading	L2 readers read shorter texts (articles, book chapters, etc.) for getting the gist of the text and specific details or information.	Reading for main ideas Reading for details Reading for making inferences Reading to learn
Extensive reading	L2 readers process large quantities of texts and read widely to gain a general understanding of what is read.	Reading for main ideas Reading for making inferences Reading to learn

*Activities typically included in intensive or extensive reading activities.

Figure 9.2:   A Bottom-Up Reading Processing Model

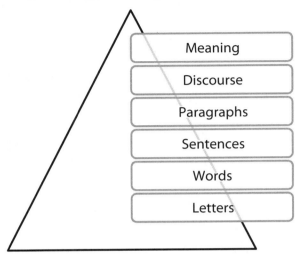

using the English alphabet. The goal is to allow automaticity and reading fluency to develop. For example, in this bottom-up activity, words are presented in groups that share similar sound/spelling patterns.

The teacher writes these words on the board in two columns. Then, the teacher says a word and asks the students to tell her if it is in Column 1 or Column 2.

1	2
hat	hut
mad	mud
dabble	double
sadden	sudden

This offers students systematic knowledge about the English language. Note that reading in these types of activities is often related to pronunciation and spelling.

Table 9.2:   An Inventory of Bottom-Up Reading Strategies

Strategy	Suggested Activity
Break lexical items into parts	Break words into smaller units to promote comprehension. For example, identify all the parts in the word *underdevelopment.*
Scan for explicit information	Scan the text for specific details or explicitly stated information requested in reading comprehension questions.
Identify a synonym or a paraphrase of the literal meaning of a word, phrase, or sentence	Identify or formulate a synonym or a paraphrase of the literal meaning of a word, phrase, or sentence in the text to help answer reading comprehension questions.
Relate verbal information to accompanying visuals	Match verbal information in the text to visual information in reading comprehension questions.
Match key vocabulary in the reading comprehension question to key vocabulary in the text	Highlight key vocabulary or phrases in the reading comprehension questions.
Use local context cues to interpret a word or phrase	Use the words in a sentence that precede or follow a specific word or phrase to understand a particular word or phrase.

Table 9.2 contains other examples of bottom-up strategies and suggested activities to teach these strategies to L2 students.

Figure 9.3:   Vocabulary Ladder Puzzle

Before class, the instructor selects five words that all have the same number of letters. Each selected word differs from the word immediately above or immediately below by only one letter. The five words will be the vocabulary ladder. Here is an example of a vocabulary ladder:

| big |
| bag |
| bat |
| mat |
| man |

These five words are the answers to the word ladder puzzle created by the instructor. If L2 learners do not know one word, they skip that clue and go to the words above and below the unknown word. Once they have the answers above and below the word, they can rearrange the letters to discover the missing word.

Directions: The five missing words in the vocabulary ladder all have three letters. Each word differs from the word immediately above or immediately below by only one letter. Use this information and the clues to solve the puzzle.

_ _ _   The United States is a ___ country.

_ _ _   I put my clothes in a ___.

_ _ _   You need a ___ to play baseball.

_ _ _   I bought a ___ for my yoga class.

_ _ _   My grandfather is an old ___.

Vocabulary is essential for L2 learners to move from words to larger blocks of written discourse. Vocabulary size can be increased through vocabulary development and word recognition exercises, on the one hand, and teaching various cohesive devices (*first/at first, last/at last, finally/ultimately*), on the other hand. The exercise in Figure 9.3 aims to develop vocabulary for beginning L2 students.

The **top-down model** views reading from a different perspective, with the emphasis on what readers bring to the text. The progression of the reading process is from whole to parts, as shown in Figure 9.4. L2 readers apply their previous knowledge to what they read. Moreover, they identify letters and words only to confirm their assumptions about the meaning of the text (Dechant, 1991).

Because background knowledge or schema is crucial to interpreting meaning from texts, L2 instructors need to focus on developing the skill of using previous knowledge in comprehending and interpreting written texts (Abbott, 2006). In addition, other top-down specific strategies that L2 instructors may employ in developing top-down reading skills are shown in Table 9.3.

Figure 9.4:   Top-Down Reading Processing Model

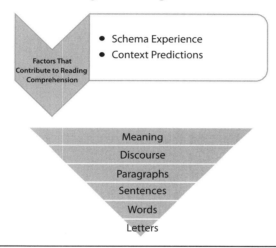

Table 9.3:   An Inventory of Top-Down Reading Strategies

Strategy	Suggested Activity
Skim for gist/identify the main idea, theme, or concept	Summarize the main concept in reading passages.
Connect or relate information presented in different sentences or parts of the text	Relate new information to previously stated information; synthesize dispersed information (for example, students are required to create paragraph outlines).
Draw an inference based on information presented in the text	Make an inference, draw a conclusion, or form a hypothesis based on information not explicitly stated in the text.
Speculate beyond the text	Employ background knowledge to speculate beyond the text (for example, students are asked to relate the text to a personal experience or an anecdote).
Recognize discourse format	Use discourse format or text organization to answer questions (for example, students discriminate between fact and opinion or cause and effect).

One type of exercise that can be used to help L2 learners employ background knowledge before reading is an anticipation guide exercise (Readence, Moore, & Rickelman, 2000; Vacca, Vacca, & Mraz, 2013), shown in Figure 9.5.

Figure 9.5:   Anticipation Guide

The primary goal of this activity is to raise readers' expectations about meaning prior to reading text. The process for instructors is:

1.   Before class, analyze the material to be read and determine major ideas, both implicit and explicit.

2.   On the computer, or on a piece of paper, write those ideas in short, clear declarative statements.

3.   Create an anticipation guide based on the identified statements to elicit anticipation and prediction making.

4.   Distribute the anticipation guide before reading, and ask learners to respond to the guide individually. Then, form groups and ask learners discuss their predictions and anticipations.

5.   Distribute the text and ask learners to evaluate the statements listed in the guide and take into account the author's intent and purpose. Finally, ask learners to compare their predictions with author's intended meaning.

ANTICIPATION GUIDE: *Before you read the excerpt, write a Yes or No next to each statement. After you read the excerpt, write Yes or No again and see if you have changed your mind.*

Statement	Before Reading	After Reading
People want to have perfect families.		
Family always looks out for one another.		
Only children have fears.		
Most people have perfect families.		
Friends accept you for who you are.		

Designing a Reading Activity

During the process of designing reading activities for their reading classes, L2 instructors are generally guided by three elements: structure of the activities, content in the readings, and students' language performance.

The Structure of Reading Activities

Typically, reading activities include both bottom-up and top-down techniques and follow a general format that includes pre-reading, during-reading, and post-reading, as described in Table 9.4.

Table 9.4:   The Structure of Reading Activities

Stage	Scope	Reading Activities
Pre-reading	Introduces the reading topic Provides learners with background knowledge necessary to comprehend the text Introduces essential language features (vocabulary, type of text) to activate background knowledge	Learners predict the content of the text from the title of the text. The teacher introduces essential keywords and the grammar in the text before students start reading. Learners skim to find the main idea or theme. The teacher pre-sets or introduces the comprehension questions to focus attention on finding relevant information while reading.
During-reading	Clarifies content and vocabulary of the text Focuses on purpose and structure of the text	With the teacher acting as a facilitator and a language resource, learners: ► guess word meanings by using context, cognates, or affixation (prefixes and suffixes). ► identify topic sentences containing the main ideas in paragraphs. ► recognize connectors.
Post-reading	Strengthens and reflects on the content read Relates the text to the students' own knowledge/interests/views Provides a starting point for practice of other language skills, such as speaking and writing	Under the teacher's guidance, learners: ► compare original predictions to what the text actually communicated. ► discuss the information learned from the text. ► create graphic organizers to synthesize the main ideas and important details in the text.

Pre-Reading Activities

Pre-reading activities are very important in preparing L2 learners for reading. These activities have the potential to build interest, confidence, and motivation for reading the text, and, from a language perspective, can facilitate reading comprehension. At this stage, schema plays a very important role. Instructors should acknowledge the different experiences and background knowledge that learners bring to a text. Knowing what learners already know, L2 teachers can help students make connections between their knowledge and the text information and address learners' gaps in their background knowledge. Keene and Zimmerman (1997) found that students comprehend better when they make three different types of connections: text-to-self, text-to-text, and text-to-world. Text-to-self connections are personal connections that readers make between a reading and their own experiences or life. Text-to-text connections occur when readers are reminded of other books or stories that they have read. Text-to-world connections are the larger connections that a reader brings to a reading situation. An example of a text-to-world connection would be when a reader says, "I listened to a program on the radio that talked about the topic of this reading." Table 9.5 shows examples of questions that can be used to facilitate L2 student connections.

One possible exercise that will help elicit L2 learners' prior knowledge before reading is called a **word splash** (Readance, Moore, & Rickelman, 2000). For this exercise, L2 instructors need to follow these steps:

1. Read the text you want to use for your reading activity.

2. Select keywords, phrases, and concepts in the text that will provide cues for your students or that may need clarification.

3. Create a one-page handout and distribute it to your students.

4. Allow students to read through and discuss with others the listed words and phrases. Allow them to make predictions about the text.

5. Ask them for their predictions.

Table 9.5:   Facilitating Text Connections

Text-to-Self	Text-to-Text	Text-to-World
What does this remind me of in my life?	What does this remind me of in another book I've read?	What does this remind me of in the real world?
What is this similar to in my life?	How is this text similar to other things I've read?	How is this text similar to things that happen in the real world?
How is this different from my life?	How is this different from other books I've read?	How is this different from things that happen in the real world?
Has something like this ever happened to me?	Have I read about something like this before?	How did that part relate to the world around me?
How does this relate to my life?		

Previewing is another pre-reading activity that helps students read and learn from texts. The teacher draws attention to these features of the text:

1. Title (used to activate prior knowledge and predict the content of the reading passage)

2. Information about the author and source of text (used to establish text-to-text connections)

3. Subtitles and subheadings (used to give students ideas about what information may be found under specific headings)

4. Graphic aids in the form of photographs, drawings, charts, graphs, tables (used as resources to summarize important information)

In another activity, Vocabulary Preview, unfamiliar keywords are taught to students before reading. In this activity, the teacher provides students with a list of all the words in the reading passage that may be important for students to understand. Then, the teacher arranges the words on the board to show their connections to the reading topic. In addition, the teacher adds words based on students' vocabulary knowledge of the reading topic to link what is known to what is unknown.

Pre-reading activities have a very important role in facilitating student comprehension as well as increasing their confidence. Similar to pre-listening activities, teacher may not want to spend weeks only on pre-reading activities, but they are absolutely necessary in order to ensure students' comprehension of the reading passage.

During-Reading Activities

As they read, L2 learners should be encouraged to verify their predictions, gather and organize information, and get a deeper understanding of the reading material. One during-reading activity is a Double-Entry Journal, similar to the Cornell method, which is a note-taking system created by Walter Pauk, a Professor of Education at Cornell University. The reading teacher creates a double-column note sheet, as shown in Figure 9.6. The left column is used for main ideas and key terms, while the right column is used for details and facts found in the reading. At first, to develop students' note-taking strategies, the teacher may fill out the left column (key terms/main ideas). Conversely, the teacher may give the students the details and ask them to develop the main ideas as they read. In time and with practice, L2 students will be able to identify both the main ideas and important details from the text. Teachers may also differentiate their reading instruction by giving lower-proficiency students more support/information in the journal.

It's important that students think critically while reading, determine important information in the text, and find evidence to support their thinking. An example of an activity that encourages this process is Key Sentences. This during-reading activity directs students' attention to identify the most important information in the text. As L2 students read, they mark sentences

Figure 9.6:   Reading Journal Format Example

Reading Title/Topic:	
Key terms/ Main ideas	Details/Facts

they think are important to the text. After reading, they choose the one sentence they believe is most important and write it down on a piece of paper. The teacher collects all the sentences/paper and writes them on the board. Then, the students explain why they think the sentence each of them selected is important. As a variation, the discussion can be done as a group activity, where students discuss their sentences with other students. Another variation of this activity would be to allow students to write the most important sentence on one piece of paper and their favorite sentence on a different piece of paper.

A during-reading activity that allows L2 readers to go through a textbook or a longer article with subheadings in a structured manner is SQ3R. It is named for its five steps: survey, question, read, recite, and review. Because it encourages students to develop questions prior to reading a text, SQ3R could also be used at the pre-reading stage. When completing this activity, students are finding answers to their own questions, rather than ones the teacher or textbook created. Its steps are outlined here:

1. **Surveying:** Before reading, students survey the text, looking at pictures, headings, graphs, and other key text features.
2. **Questioning:** Based on headings and subheadings, students formulate questions that could be answered in the text.
3. **Reading:** The students read the text in order to find the answers to their questions.
4. **Reciting:** The students answer their questions in their own words either orally or in writing without looking back at the text for support.
5. **Reviewing:** The students review the text and the information they wrote to make sure they did not miss any key facts.

Sometimes, during-reading activities tend to be overlooked by teachers and material developers on spite of the fact they are a *sine-qua-non* (meaning "without which not") condition for reading comprehension. If L2 learners do not accurately understand a text, post-reading activities relying on students' careful analysis of the text will be unsuccessful (Hedgcock & Ferris, 2009).

Post-Reading Activities

During post-reading, learners have the opportunity to integrate their comprehension of the text with their schema or background knowledge and analyze the quality of the information gained from the reading. L2 learners will benefit from their reading more if they are required to not only analyze the text critically but also use its content in language production activities that focus on speaking and writing.

Summarizing a text is a very good review and comprehension check tool. The Paired Review exercise provides students with practice in summarizing what has been read and learned. During this activity, students work with a partner, taking turns being the "talker" and the "listener," and review a text that they have read. The procedure for instructors is:

▶ Pair students as Student A and Student B.

▶ Student A begins by describing something interesting from the text and talks for 60 seconds, while Student B listens.

▶ After 60 seconds, tell students to change roles. Student B becomes the speaker and cannot repeat anything said by Student A.

▶ After Student B has spoken for 60 seconds, partners switch again. Student A now has 40 seconds to continue the review. Nothing stated already can be repeated. After 40 seconds, switch roles where Student B gets 40 seconds.

▶ To recap, follow the same procedure allowing each student 20 seconds.

To develop critical-thinking skills as well as to connect reading to speaking and listening, L2 reading teachers could use the Think-Pair-Share activity. First, after the during-reading activities are completed, the teacher poses a question or a problem that is based on a text-to-world connection to students. Individually, the students think about their responses and write them on a piece of paper. Then, the teacher asks students to pair up with a partner to discuss their answers. At the end of discussion, they generate a summary of their answers to the question/problem posed by the teacher. Last, the teacher asks students to share their summaries with the entire class. The main points of each summary are written on the board by the teacher.

Incorporating writing activities at the post-reading stage is one effective way of making connections among language skills, developing critical-thinking skills, and fostering language development. For example, individually or in pairs, L2 learners can write an imaginary conversation between two characters in a story they've read. If they've read a non-fiction text, they may be asked to complete an activity such as A Day in the Life, where they are asked to write a "day in the life" account of an animal or an atom, for example. Writing letters can also be used in a variety of ways in the L2 reading classroom. For example, students can be asked to write correspondence that might have occurred between characters from different stories. L2 reading teachers can also ask students to write letters to local businesses, local or national politicians, famous athletes, or the author of the reading passage.

Post-reading activities can and should be creative and stimulating for students. They should go beyond the traditional question-and-answer comprehension questions. While comprehension questions have a place in teaching and assessment, they should be supplemented with post-reading practice that moves beyond the text and the reading skill. By doing so, teachers are ensuring that the new language and content knowledge from the reading passages are integrated in the students' L2 and schema.

The Content of Reading Activities

When selecting the content for reading activities, L2 reading instructors need to keep in mind the type of reading their students will have to do. If they select content for intensive reading activities (see Table 9.1 for a definition of intensive reading), instructors should focus on items that occur in a large range of reading materials. In other words, they should focus on items (grammar, vocabulary, type of text, etc.) that are high frequency in the language as a whole. Low-frequency vocabulary items such as *isotope, mitosis,* or *lithosphere* should be either ignored or briefly explained since they have very little impact or reading comprehension due to their infrequent usage. L2 teachers should teach these words as the need arises for comprehension in specific content areas.

Focusing on the sub-skills of reading is another factor influencing content selection for intensive reading activities. Doing that will help L2 teachers diagnose the problem areas their students need to work on. In terms of essential sub-skills, L2 readers need to be able to identify the topic of the text, as well as its purpose, type, and organization. Moreover, they need to identify and understand the main idea or the gist of the text, as well to distinguish key information and details from less important information. They should also be able to understand the author's attitude, follow the development of an argument, and track the sequence of a narrative. Other reading sub-skills include understanding words and identifying their grammatical function, recognizing grammar features, and guessing the meaning of unknown words from context (Brown, 2007).

In addition to knowing the details of reading processes and skills, L2 reading teachers need to determine the vocabulary level of their L2 students. They could use the Vocabulary Levels Test, which will assess the current level of vocabulary knowledge of L2 readers. Using this information, L2 reading teachers can then select graded readers for their L2 reading classes, which have vocabulary development activities included in the pre-, during-, and post-reading stages. Graded readers are books that are simplified or "graded" in the sense that their syntax and vocabulary are based on the L2 learners' current level of proficiency to make the content accessible.

For all reading activities, it is absolutely essential not to introduce an abundance of new words that will make comprehension virtually impossible. The vocabulary knowledge that students possess will become evident in extensive reading activities. Extensive reading is defined as the reading of large quantities of text conducted during or outside the L2 reading classroom. During extensive reading, L2 learners are reading with their focus on the meaning of the text rather than on learning the language features of the text, as it is the case in intensive reading activities.

According to Hu and Nation (2000), L2 learners are able to comprehend text without additional help only if 95 to 98 percent of the words in a text are already familiar. When 90 or 95 percent of the words are known, only few learners are able to gain adequate comprehension. At the 80 percent level of unknown words, learners are not able to comprehend the reading material. As a result, L2 learners at the low stages of vocabulary proficiency can do extensive reading only when they read graded readers that have been specially designed for their level. Nation (2009) suggests several guidelines, outlined in Table 9.6, that L2 reading instructors should consider when developing and implementing extensive reading activities.

Table 9.6:   Guidelines for Developing and Implementing Extensive Reading Activities

Guideline	Description
Frequency	Regardless of their proficiency level, L2 readers should read at least one graded reader every week to allow unknown vocabulary to be repeated.
Minimum number per level	L2 readers should read at least five books at one level before moving to books at the next level to be exposed to all the vocabulary introduced at that level.
Quantitative progression	L2 readers should read more books at the later levels than the earlier as the vocabulary of the earlier levels occurs very frequently in the books at the later levels.
Total number per year	L2 readers should read at least 15–20 and preferably 30 readers in a year to allow repetition of the vocabulary and occurrence of most of the vocabulary several times.
Unknown vocabulary	L2 readers may need to study directly the new vocabulary at the lower levels or make use of a dictionary because of the higher number of unknown vocabulary at the lower levels.

Students' Performance in Reading Classes

In addition to organization and content, L2 teachers need to think about learners' reading performance. Brown (2007) has discussed two types of classroom reading performance: The first is represented by **oral reading,** which is when learners read aloud to check on L2 learners' pronunciation or to employ bottom-up reading processing skills; the second and most common type of reading performance is silent reading, as illustrated in Figure 9.7.

The reason for discussing student performance in L2 reading classes is make teachers aware of the different skill sets needed for both oral and silent reading. This awareness should be translated into a balanced approach to activity design so that both types of student performance are addressed.

Reading Activities for the Classroom

The reading activities presented in this section address all levels of readers and are structured following a pre-, during-, and post-reading design. These activities are based on the theoretical foundations presented in the first part of the book and organized by the syllabi presented in Chapter 6.

Figure 9.7:   Silent Reading Performance

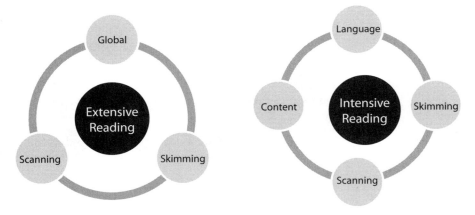

Activity 9.1: Which One Is Which?

Grammar-Based Reading

Rationale: A grammar-based approach is based on the level of grammar complexity or frequency of grammatical forms. Therefore, this activity focuses on applying the grammatical knowledge associated with parts of speech to a reading passage that has been selected based on the learners' vocabulary level.

Objectives: Learners identify various parts of speech in a reading passage using context.

Pre-Planning

Pre-knowledge: Learners should have been introduced to parts of speech before this reading activity.
Materials needed: One copy of the handout. Parts of speech labeled in bold letters by instructor.
Language level: Advanced
Recommended age group: Young adults and older

Procedures

Pre-reading: The teacher introduces the topic by asking the learners what they know about the link between the brain and reading. This is done to help learners predict vocabulary and content. In addition, the teacher introduces vocabulary items that help with text comprehension, such as *dominance, lateralize*, and *theory*.

During-reading: Students are given the handout with this content:

> The left and right brain dominance is an important issue in a developing theory of learning. As the child's brain matures, various functions become lateralized to the left or right hemisphere. The left hemisphere is commonly associated with language functions and logical thought, with mathematical and linear processing of information. The right hemisphere perceives and remembers visual, tactile, and auditory images. It is also more efficient in processing holistic, integrative, and emotional information.

As students read, they are asked to:

1. use a highlighter to show the main ideas.
2. circle key vocabulary words.
3. circle words they do not know.

Based on oral responses, the teacher gives feedback and writes the main ideas on the board, as well as the key vocabulary (Main Ideas and Key Vocabulary columns). Also, the teacher writes all the unknown words on the board. If the word is known by another student, that student explains the word to their classmates and the teacher places the word in the Unknown Words (Solved) column. If there are words that are unknown to all students in class, the teacher writes them on the board under the Unknown Words (Unsolved) column.

Main Ideas	Key Vocabulary	Unknown Words (Solved)	Unknown Words (Unsolved)

In pairs, students create a visual representation for each unknown word, using the model illustrated in Figure 9.8. The newly created visual representations are posted on the classroom walls.

Evaluation

Post-reading: Using the visual representations for each unknown word, the class discusses other possible parts of speech for the same words in a different context. Then the teacher pairs learners and asks them to find a meaning different from the meaning explored in the analyzed text and to create a sentence with the new meaning. The pair with the most meanings and sentences wins.

Homework: Learners are asked to write an imaginary dialogue between the left and the right hemisphere of the brain.

Figure 9.8:   Vocabulary Diagram

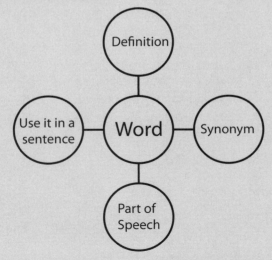

Activity 9.2 The Importance of Fairy Tales

Communicative Product Reading

Rationale: A communicative product syllabus is based on situational or notional-functional approaches to student learning. The syllabus has targeted, communicative language and vocabulary to use within specific topical situations, such as at a doctor's office, or targeted notions-functions within the language, such as interpersonal functions (learning the pragmatics of accepting and refusing invitations). This activity uses authentic text to help students identify the main ideas in the reading. There is no emphasis on grammar or teaching structural points. Rather, the emphasis is on communication and collaboration among learners with the teacher acting as a facilitator. The task of identifying main ideas is also authentic because learners will need to do that in various L2 settings, either academic or informal.

Objectives: Learners identify main ideas in reading excerpts.

Pre-Planning

Pre-knowledge: Students need to know what fairy tales are.
Materials needed: One handout containing the reading excerpt and one handout containing the comprehension task
Language level: Advanced
Recommended age group: Adults

Procedures

Pre-reading: The instructor introduces the topic of the reading passage, which is a discussion of fairy tales. The teacher also introduces essential vocabulary according to the level of proficiency to facilitate comprehension. In addition, the instructor pre-sets the task by discussing with the learners the task they need to complete after they read the passage (see next page).

Content for Your Handout

Select the three answer choices that express important ideas in the passage. Some sentences do not belong in the summary because they express ideas that are not presented in the passage or are minor ideas in the passage.

> *Fairy tales have proven to play an important role in children socialization.*
>
> • _____
>
> • _____
>
> • _____

a.   Social behavior is shaped by letting children deal with their fears.

b.   Fairy tales present themes that are frightening to young children.

c.   In modern society, it is often suggested that to have an easy life means to be successful.

d.   Fairy tales have been extensively studies by child psychologists.

e.   Fairy tales help children make the difficult process of maturing easier.

f.   Because of fairy tales, children internalize accepted social conduct from an early age.

During-reading: Students read this passage on the handout:

Parents and teachers have many tools at their disposal to facilitate their children's socialization, defined as the process by which humans learn the values, norms, and culture of their particular society. One of the most effective tools to bring about this process is literature. Of the various forms of literature written for children, the fairy tale has enjoyed the longest run of popularity. What is it about fairy tales that makes them an enduring agent of socialization? Child psychologist Bruno Bettelheim has explored this question in his book, *The Uses of Enchantment: The Meaning and Importance of Fairy Tales.*

According to Bettelheim, the value and appeal of fairy tales rest in the fact that they help children master the problems of growing up. Fairy tales do this by stimulating children's imagination and by allowing them to deal subconsciously with their fears.

In modern society, we stress the optimistic side of life. Humans are often portrayed as being basically good. A successful life is seen as one that is easy and free from strife. These views of the world can be confusing for children. Children know that they are not always good and that life is not always easy. The message of the fairy tales is that evil and virtue, good and bad exist in everything. Fairy tales also teach children that difficulties in life are unavoidable and must be met head on. Children see the fairy tale hero face the images of good and evil and find a way for good to triumph through cleverness and bravery.

The socialization lessons contained in fairy tales are indirect, however. According to Bettelheim, children do not identify with the good act or a bad act. Rather, they identify with the hero, who happens to be good. The hero serves as a role model for the young child. Children do not ask if they want to be good, but they ask whom they want to be like. This distinction is important because it enables children to accept socially sanctioned behavior before they are old enough to grasp the moral issues involved.

In short, the important function of fairy tales rests in allowing children to grasp the contradictions that exist in human nature and social life. Fairy tales do this in a way that is particularly suited to the developmental skills of growing children. By capturing children's imagination and allowing them to explore their unspoken fears, fairy tales help to mold social behavior.

As they are reading, the students are filling out a double-entry journal individually. Then, in pairs, they compare their answers and create a new double-entry journal they share with their classmates and receive peer and teacher feedback. In pairs again, they complete the comprehension task (handout) presented at the pre-reading stage.

Evaluation

Post-reading: Based on their filled-out handout, each group writes its selection on the board and after all choices are listed, each group defends its choice orally, with examples from the reading. After the final selection of the correct answers is completed, the learners are asked to write a summary of the reading passage incorporating the ideas they selected in the comprehension activity.

Homework: The students are asked to write a one-page summary of a fairy tale they have read.

Activity 9.3: A Press Conference

Communicative Process Reading

Rationale: In a communicative syllabus, the organization of the curriculum is based on tasks. The activities in a task-based syllabi are focused on the language and language skill needed to complete a concrete task, such as applying for a program or job, or producing a class newsletter. In this activity, the task that learners need to complete is participating in a press conference. The emphasis is placed not on grammar but on the language needed to complete the task. Language is viewed as necessary part of the process and not an end; the end is the successful conclusion of the task itself.

Objectives: Learners develop the real-world ability to answer questions on the spot, as well as to ask in-depth questions about an issue.

Pre-Planning

Pre-knowledge: The learners need to be familiar with the concept of a press conference.
Materials needed: Newspaper articles, guidelines
Language level: Beginning to advanced
Recommended age group: Young adults and older

Procedures

Pre-reading: In a previous class, the teacher surveys students' about a topic in the news. The teacher then leads a discussion that introduces the topic and includes some news articles on the topic. For each article, the teacher asks these questions:

What experience have you had with....?

What can you imagine about...?

What are three words you know about…?

The teacher writes the words students say on the board. The teacher also pre-teaches key vocabulary essential to understanding the articles. The teacher also shows a video recording of a press conference and asks the students to describe what happens. Based on students' input, the teacher writes the structure of a press conference (what's expected to happen) on the board.

During-reading: The teacher tells learners that they will participate in a press conference in the role of either a spokesperson or a reporter. Learners are divided into groups of four, one pair being the spokespersons and the other pair the reporters. Next, learners read news articles about a real-life event. The event is the same, but each group is given a different news article covering the event. In addition, the learners are given these guidelines for reporters and spokespersons.

Overall Guidelines for Reporters

You are interested in finding out as much as possible about the **who, what, when, where, and why** of the story. These are key questions that readers want answered when they read a newspaper article. For example, when they read a story about a stolen painting that was recovered and the thieves caught, the reader might be asking: Who stole it? What happened? When did it happen? When was the painting found? Where was the painting found? Where was the painting hidden? Why was the painting stolen?

As a reporter, you should:

▶ ask many questions, and try to ask follow-up questions too.
▶ repeat the question and insist on an answer if you feel that the spokesperson is not answering your question.
▶ try to get as many facts as possible.
▶ get the information as quickly as possible.

Overall Guidelines for Spokespersons

As a spokesperson, you should:

- ► be as honest as possible.
- ► stick to the facts as you see them.
- ► tell the reporter that you'll find out and get back to him or her if you don't know the answer to a question.
- ► say that you have no comment or change the subject if you wish to avoid answering a question.
- ► remember that you are the main source of information. Be confident and be in charge.
- ► not let a hostile question make you nervous.
- ► set the ground rules: there is a limited time period for questions and answers; ask reporters to raise their hands, etc.

Next, the spokespersons write a prepared statement that they will release to the press and try to prepare answers to possible difficult questions that reporters may ask them. Spokespersons have a practice session with the teacher before the event.

The learners in the role of reporters need to prepare questions to find out as much as they can about the situation. Then reporters review their questions in advance with the teacher and are given guidance on how to ask appropriate follow-up questions.

At the press conference, the spokespersons greet the press, set the rules, present their prepared statement, and then open up a 10-minute question-and-answer session. When time is up, they end the session by thanking reporters for their participation.

Evaluation

Post-reading: The teacher provides immediate feedback during the interactions with the groups (reporters and spokespersons) and then, using a self-developed rubric, evaluates language and content of the press conferences conducted in class. For best results, it is better to videotape the conferences and have a feedback session addressing possible errors using the videotaped material as a guide. An example of an evaluation rubric that be used for a variety of presentation activities is shown in Figure 9.9.

Next, the learners are asked to list three of the challenges they have had to overcome as spokespersons and reporters. The paragraph is then read to the rest of the class.

Homework: The learners are given an article and asked to write a statement that includes the main points from the perspective of a spokesperson and three questions from the perspective of a reporter.

Figure 9.9: Sample Presentation Rubric

Category	Scoring Criteria	Total Points	Score
Organization	Questions/answers appropriate for the topic and audience.	5	
	Information is presented in a logical sequence.	5	
Content	Appropriate amount of content is presented.	10	
	Questions/answers contain accurate information.	10	
	Content included is relevant to the overall message/purpose.	10	
	Points made reflect well their importance.	10	
Delivery	Speaker maintains good eye contact.	10	
	Speaker uses a clear, audible voice.	10	
	Speaker is confident.	10	
	Good language skills and pronunciation are used.	10	
	Information is well communicated .	10	
Score	**Total Points**	**100**	

Activity 9.4: Personal Information

Eclectic Reading

Rationale: Many instructors prefer using various and mixed approaches in their design of their syllabus and curriculum design. Many teachers prefer this eclectic approach because it allows them to meet various learner needs and adapt the curriculum to class-specific goals. This activity emphasizes communication with an attention to grammar. The task in the activity is authentic, but there is also a focus on explicit language structures, which makes it a good example of an eclectic language activity.

Objectives: Learners provide culturally appropriate personal information and use present tense simple.

Pre-Planning

Pre-knowledge: No pre-knowledge necessary for this activity.
Materials needed: Handouts
Language level: Beginning
Recommended age group: Young adults and older

Procedures

Pre-reading: The teacher introduces the notion of personal information and discusses with the learners what type of information can and cannot be included. The teacher also introduces essential vocabulary (*ESL, community college, single, jog, ride*) to facilitate the comprehension of the passage.

During-reading: The learners read this passage from your handout:

> Tina Brown is 34 years old, and she is single. She lives in Miami, Florida. She teaches ESL at a community college and likes her job. She works Monday to Friday from 9:00 AM to 4:00 PM. On the weekend, she visits her boyfriend. His name is Andy, and he is 35 years old. Tina and Andy like to go to the movies. They also like to jog and ride bicycles.

In pairs, students complete the Venn diagram, which is on a second handout (see next page). A Venn diagram uses overlapping circles to visually represent relationships between two sets of information. The spaces that do not overlap contain unique details of the two sets, while the space where the circles overlap contains information that is common for the two sets.

Students write the details that tell how Tina and Andy are different in the outer circles and how the Tina and Andy are alike where the circles overlap.

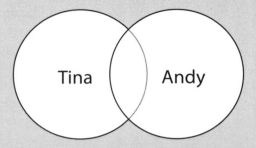

After they complete the activity, the teacher writes their answers on the board and provides feedback on vocabulary and syntax.

After that, the learners underline all the verbs in the story. The teacher asks them if they notice any changes when the third-person singular is used. A rule for the present tense simple is written (or re-written if the learners already covered this grammar point in their classes) on the board. The teacher then gives the learners the third handout and asks the students to complete this activity individually.

Content for Your Handout
Use one of the verbs in the list to complete the sentences:

teach   go   jog   work   like

Tina _____ her job.

Tina and Andy ____ to the movies often.

She___ every Thursday.

They___ on the weekends.

Tina doesn't _____ on Saturday.

Evaluation

Post-reading: The teacher writes the answers to the grammar task on the board and students check their answers. Then, learners write a list of what is appropriate and what is not appropriate to ask someone in their home country/culture.

Homework: Ask students to write a short paragraph that includes their personal information (their first/last name, their birthday and place of birth, where they are from, their address, what languages they speak, and how long they have been in the United States).

Assessing Reading Comprehension

Reading comprehension is typically measured with the help of comprehension questions based on a reading passage. Classroom-based and large-scale tests use questions that measure reading for basic comprehension, making connections, and reading to learn new information. Some examples for each category are given.

Reading for Basic Comprehension

Read the excerpt.

One of the most important historical landmarks in Washington, DC, is represented by the White House. It is virtually the most famous and celebrated site in the capital city and . . . .

1. The word *virtually* (second line in the passage) is closest in meaning to:

    A.   almost

    B.   forever

    C.   infinitely

    D.   substantial

Read the excerpt.

One of the most profoundly original composers in history, Frederic Chopin was born in Zelazowa Wola, a small city near Warsaw, Poland, on February 22, 1810. He first studied the piano at the Warsaw School of Music and was quite proficient on that instrument by his early teens. He played his first public concert at age 7 and was a published composer at 15. By the late 1820s, Chopin had won a great reputation as a piano virtuoso and composer of piano pieces. He toured Europe, giving concert performances for delighted audiences and critics. In 1831, he arrived in Paris for a concert. Suddenly, he fell in love with the city and decided to make it his new home. Until his death in 1849, he never returned to Warsaw.

1. According to the passage, when did Chopin decide to establish himself in Paris?

    A.   in 1810

    B.   in 1820

    C.   in 1831

    D.   in 1849

Reading to Make Connections

Read the excerpt.

Energy is necessary for doing all the things that go into being alive. First, sources of energy change from time to time. If a particular source of energy stops, it will probably determine the fate of various organisms dependent on it. Second, supplies of energy are normally limited.

1. Where can the following sentence be added to the passage? **However, energy is not available all the time to all organisms.**

Read the excerpt.

Any quantitative measure that describes a characteristic of a population is called a parameter. Parameters are constants that are peculiar to a given population. A quantitative measure that describes a characteristic of a sample is called a statistic. For instance, the proportion of Democrats among all voters in the United States is a parameter. However, if we interview 1,000 people among all the voters in the United States, then the proportion of Democrats in this sample is a statistic.

1. Why does the author discuss the proportion of Democrats in the passage?

    A. To provide an example of a statistic
    B. To illustrate the notion of a parameter
    C. To make links between two concepts
    D. To exemplify the demographics of the United States

Reading to Learn New Information

Read the excerpt.

Anthropologist Margaret Mead conducted a study of cultural variation among several small societies in New Guinea. Her purpose in the study was to determine whether differences in basic temperament result from inherited characteristics or from cultural influences. To find out, Mead made firsthand observations of the shared behaviors of several New Guinea societies. Two of the societies she studied were the Arapesh and the Mundugumor. Both groups lived in the northern part of what is now the nation of Papua New Guinea. Mead found out that although the two societies lived only about 100 miles apart and shared many social characteristics, their cultures were vastly different.

The Arapesh were gentle, warm, receptive, non-aggressive, and trusting people. Their society was one of complete cooperation. They lived in close-knit villages consisting of clans, which are families with a common ancestor. The women brought in the firewood and water, prepared the daily meals, carried the goods from place to place, and weeded the gardens. The Arapesh men cleared and fenced the land, built and repaired the houses, carried pigs and heavy loads, hunted, and cooked ceremonial food. Both men and women made ornaments and took care of the children. The fathers were very much involved in child care. For example, if the mother's work was more pressing, the father would mind the children while the mother completed the task.

The children grew up in a very loving and friendly social environment. The babies were always tended to when they cried, and they spent much of their time being held by someone. Children were often encouraged to join in the activities of the elders and discouraged from displaying any aggression toward each other. When they felt aggression, they were taught to express it in a way that would not harm others, such as by hitting a palm tree with a stick or throwing stones on the ground. They are taught consideration and respect for the feelings and property of others.

Unlike the Arapesh, the Mundugumor were an aggressive group of people. Men and women were violent, competitive, and jealous. They were ready to recognize and avenge any insult. They delighted in showing off and fighting. Open hostilities among all members of the same sex forced the Mundugumor to scatter their residences throughout the bush. Brothers did not speak to one another and were ashamed to sit together. There was great hostility between fathers and sons, between sisters, and between mothers and daughters.

The only ties between members of the same sex were through members of the opposite sex. These occur through a form of social organization called the rope. One rope consisted of the father, his daughters, his daughters' sons, his daughters' sons' daughters, and so on. Another rope consisted of the mother, her sons, her sons' daughters, and so on. When a person died, property was passed down the line according to the rope. For example, daughters inherited their father's property, while sons inherited their mother's property.

The child-rearing practices of the Mundugumor were different from those of the Arapesh. Infants were carried in a rigid basket that gave no direct contact with the mother. When the mother worked outdoors, she left the child hanging in the basket in the house. The mother fed the child when she was ready. Children were not picked up and comforted and faced many prohibitions. When they violated these prohibitions, they were slapped. Also, children tended to push parents apart rather than unite them. The father wanted a daughter that could be traded for a wife. The mother, on the other hand, wanted a son to work with her and be her heir.

1. The passage talked about two groups, the Arapesh and the Mundugumor. Using the table, please match five sentences from the list of seven possible choices to the groups that they describe best.

Groups	Sentences
The Arapesh	• _____ • _____ • _____
The Mundugumor	• _____ • _____

    A.   Family members viewed cooperation highly.
    B.   The men took care of the family dwellings.
    C.   The children were deprived of direct contact with their mothers.
    D.   The children did not contribute to the unity of the family unit.
    E.   The men were skilled merchants.
    F.   The women took care of most of the household chores.
    G.   The women cooked the food for important celebrations.

In addition to reading comprehension tests where learners are asked to respond to multiple choice questions, L2 instructors may also use cloze tests. **Cloze** tests are reading activities that require learners to fill in missing words in reading passages. The selection of missing words can be done using a fixed-ration or mechanical deletion procedure (typically every seventh word, +/- two) or a selective one, where instructors leave out nouns, verbs, or any other grammatical or syntactic features. When grading cloze assessments, L2 instructors may accept or not accept sensible alternatives to missing words. If they do not accept it, they use an exact replacement method of scoring. Conversely, if they accept an alternative word that makes sense in the context of the reading passage, they use an acceptable alternative method.

An example of a cloze test that uses a fixed-ration deletion is shown.

This is the original text.

Impressionism was a movement in art that developed in France during the nineteenth century. The name is derived from the title of Monet's painting called *Impressions, Sunrise.* Their paintings are unique from many perspectives and created a revolution in the world of arts. Because they tried to capture what the eyes see at a single glance, the Impressionist painters placed a great emphasis on light in its changing qualities. They were interested in visually recording reality in terms of passing. That is why the non-permanents effects of light and color can be distinguished in their paintings. Their ideas of capturing reality thorough impressions work influenced not only the art world but also helped create Impressionistic currents in music and literature.

Cloze Test (mechanical; every 7th word):

Impressionism was a movement in art _____ developed in France during the nineteenth _____. The name is derived from the _____ of Monet's painting called *Impressions, Sunrise.* _____ paintings are unique from many perspectives _____ created a revolution in the world _____ arts. Because they tried to capture _____ the eyes see at a single _____, the Impressionist painters placed a great _____ on light in its changing qualities. _____ were interested in visually recording reality _____ terms of passing. That is why _____ non-permanents effects of light and color _____ be distinguished in their paintings. Their _____ of capturing reality thorough impressions work _____ not only the art world but _____ helped create Impressionistic currents in music _____ literature.

Both multiple choice types of comprehension questions and cloze tests measure reading comprehension in a second language. The difference between the two is that cloze tests are much easier and faster to create. However, one difficulty with cloze instruments that L2 instructors may encounter comes from score interpretation. For example, if an L2 learner missed one-third of the words in a cloze test, does that mean he or she is low proficient in reading? What does that score tell us about the difficulty of the reading passage? Based on previous research, Nation (2009) has reported that an independent L2 reading level, where the reading comprehension is achieved with no assistance needed, is linked to a 90 percent score for a reading comprehension multiple choice test and a score above 53 percent on the cloze test. For an instructional level where L2 reading comprehension is achieved with a teacher's assistance, the scores are 75 percent for a multiple choice test and between 44 percent and 53 percent for a cloze test. The third level of reading difficulty, the frustration level, where L2 reading comprehension cannot be achieved even with assistance, corresponds to a score below 75 percent on a multiple choice test and a score below 44 percent on a cloze test.

This chapter looked at the characteristics of reading and explored various types of reading processes and performances. On the pedagogical side, it also suggested what L2 instructors should consider when designing reading activities. It is important that L2 instructors keep in mind that reading activities always include an assessment of reading comprehension skills but that assessment should not be the only goal of these activities. Reading offers many opportunities for acquiring a language when L2 instructors include post-reading activities in which new vocabulary and language structures are repeatedly and meaningfully practiced.

Summarizing Statements

1. L2 reading is done for enjoyment, to locate specific information, or to learn new information. These purposes are typically reflected in teaching and assessment of reading comprehension in a second language.

2. When reading, L2 learners employ bottom-up (from part to whole) and top-down (from whole to part) processes.

3. L2 reading instructors should include top-down and bottom-up strategies in their activities, which generally follow a general format with three components: pre-reading, during-reading, and post-reading.

4. When selecting content for their reading activities, L2 teachers should concentrate on texts that contain high-frequency vocabulary items and address the sub-skills of L2 reading directly.

5. L2 reading teachers need to remember that L2 readers are able to comprehend L2 text without additional help only if 95 to 98 percent of the words in a text are already familiar (Hu & Nation, 2000).

REFLECTION AND APPLICATION

1. This chapter has identified a number of advantages of written discourse over spoken discourse. Can you think of some disadvantages?

2. One of the most used tests of measuring English proficiency is the TOEFL®. The test's website (www.ets.org.toefl) includes the posted sample questions for the Reading section and identifies the type of reading purposes (basic comprehension, making connections, and reading to learn new information) associated with each question in the sample.

3. Using the examples of activities provided in the chapter and this excerpt, create a grammar-based reading activity focusing on modal usage.

   When it was first invented in 1975, the personal computer had more than 2,000 transistors on a chip. The personal computers today have more than 7 million transistors on a chip and, in another decade, that computing power will have magnified exponentially. In the race to keep up with the evolution of what has become the primary tool in so many enterprises, future workers will be forced to be ever more mobile, adaptive, and conscious of the need to continually upgrade their competencies.

   As employees become more self-reliant, so they will become increasingly aware of their value as individuals. The one-company man or woman, who in the past expected to occupy a position doing almost the same thing for three or four decades, is evolving into a multi-skilled highly responsible individual who can wear many hats, depending on the project at hand. This person might be a core worker retained at the company headquarters in a vital role in return for a personally tailored package of incentives and benefits. However, the better the remuneration, the more competencies that employee will have to possess in terms of the company business.

   That worker might be an accountant with very solid knowledge of human resource management or an information technology expert who can manage the internet potential of the company's business. In the case of such highly skilled employees, the company will see and treat them as talent to be retained, but loyalty cannot be any longer presumed, as it was in the not so distant past. In the age of workplace individualism, good workers can and will change their jobs frequently if their professional skills are in very high demand.

REFERENCES

Abbott, M. L. (2006). ESL reading strategies: Differences in Arabic and Mandarin speaker test performance. *Language Learning, 56*(4), 633–670.

ACTFL. (2012). *ACTFL proficiency guidelines.* Retrieved from www.actfl.org

August, D., & Shanahan, T. (Eds.). (2006). *Developing literacy on second-language learners: Report of the National Literacy Panel on Language minority children and youth.* Mahwah, NJ: Lawrence Erlbaum.

Bear, D. R., Invernizzi, M., Templeton, S., & Johnston, F. (2004). *Words their way: Word study for phonics, vocabulary, and spelling instruction* (3rd ed.). Upper Saddle River, NJ: Pearson.

Brown, H. D. (2007). *Teaching by principles: An interactive approach to language pedagogy* (3rd ed.). New York: Longman.

Chow, B. W., McBride-Chang, C., & Burgess, S. (2005). Phonological processing skills and early reading abilities in Hong Kong Chinese kindergarteners learning to read English as a second language. *Journal of Educational Psychology, 97*(1), 81–87.

Dechant, E. (1991). *Understanding and teaching reading: An interactive model.* Hillsdale, NJ: Lawrence Erlbaum.

Grabe, W. (2009). *Reading in a second language: Moving from theory to practice.* New York: Cambridge University Press.

Grabe, W., & Stoller, F. L. (2011). *Teaching and researching reading* (2nd ed.). Harlow, U.K.: Pearson Education.

Hedgcock, J. S., & Ferris, D. R. (2009). *Teaching readers of English: Students, texts, and contexts.* New York: Routledge.

Hu, M., & Nation, I. S. P. (2000). Vocabulary density and reading comprehension. *Reading in a Foreign Language, 23,* 403–430.

Keene, E., & Zimmerman, S. (1997). *Mosaic of thought.* Portsmouth, NH: Heinemann.

Koda, K. (2007). Reading and language learning: Crosslinguistic constraints on second language reading development. In K. Koda (Ed.), *Reading and language learning* (pp. 1–44). Special issue of *Language Learning, Supplement, 57.*

Lockwood, R. B. (2014). *Flip it! Strategies for ESL classroom.* Ann Arbor: University of Michigan Press.

Lockwood, R. B., & Sippell, K. (2012). *Four point reading and writing: Intro to English for academic purposes.* Ann Arbor: University of Michigan Press.

Muljani, D., Koda, K., & Moates, D. (1998). The development of word recognition in a second language. *Applied Psycholinguistics, 19,* 99–113.

Nation, I. S. P. (2009). *Teaching ESL/EFL reading and writing.* New York: Routledge.

Readance, J., Moore, D., & Rickelman, R. (2000). *Prereading activities for content area reading and learning* (3rd. ed). Newark, DE: International Reading Association.

Vacca, R., Vacca, J., & Mrza, M. (2013). *Content area reading: Literacy and learning across the curriculum.* New York: Pearson.

Chapter 10 ▲

Writing Activities and Assessment Techniques

This chapter discusses the skills needed for writing, from micro-skills to macro-skills, and then details the writing process for language learners. Next, the genres of writing are presented with ways that these genres are taught in the ESL and EFL classrooms. The chapter includes sample activities and focuses on the topic of error correction and the various approaches to assessing writing.

Writing in the Language Classroom

Like speaking, writing is a productive skill that allows the language learner to communicate ideas using language represented through graphic symbols. Considered the more difficult of language skills to acquire, writing is a system that has to be learned and is not simply acquired (Yule, 2014). The goal for the language learner is often related to three different genres of writing—social, academic, and professional communication. Socially, the language learner wants to be able to share information with friends, issue or respond to invitations, and ask for information or respond to conversational prompts. Academically, students need to develop different styles of writing depending on the purpose of the writing assignment, which can vary from paragraphs to essays (including persuasive, informative, or comparative styles) to a variety of research genres (research paper, thesis/dissertation, writing for publication). In the professional world, the ability to write resumes, cover letters, business letters, and emails can be critical to promotion and success.

The goal of the writing instructor is to provide a foundation for the language learner using the principles of linguistics and SLA principles (Nassaji, 2012; Reynolds, 2005) and the appropriate rhetorical mode (Silva & Reichelt, 1994). Students must develop the micro-skills of writing—such as knowing the alphabet (orthography), the meaning of words and phrases (semantics), and the sentence structure (syntax) of English—in order to communicate effectively. In addition, students must utilize macro-skills—such as understanding acceptable forms of English rhetoric (e.g., classification essay or definition essay) while taking into account the audience. It is the L2 writing instructor's job to help students develop this diversity of skills necessary to writing in another language (Ferris, 2007; Tracy, Reid, & Graham, 2009).

Micro-Skills and Macro-Skills in Writing

Students need to master micro- and macro-skills to effectively communicate. Most language learners develop micro-skills first and then, with time and practice, develop the macro-skills necessary to be proficient writers.

When it comes to **micro-skills,** the writer is focused on the foundational processes of words, sentences, and localized meaning in the language, as shown in Table 10.1.

Macro-skills focus on conveying overall meaning, the purpose of the writing, and the audience (Brown & Abeywickrama, 2010). Table 10.2 details some of the macro-skills of writing.

Writing as a Process

The activity of writing is an ongoing process for the writer who is constantly thinking, learning, discovering, reviewing, and revising throughout the course of writing. Through this process, writers develop language, ideas, and the ability to communicate their knowledge on any topic. Less confident writers sometimes become overly worried about the grammatical and mechanical aspects of writing (spelling, vocabulary, structure, or punctuation); instructors often need to remind writers that it's just as important to develop the broader aspects of writing such as ensuring cohesion of ideas, keeping the audience in mind, and making a strong argument. Reminding students to perform other parts of the writing process such as outlining, editing, and proofing can help them focus on both aspects of writing.

Just as with the other skills, writing skills in the L2 classroom are developed through a process of pre-writing, while-writing, and post-writing. Pre-writing tasks can include:

▶ reading the directions for the assignment and/or writing prompt
▶ considering the deadline for the project
▶ asking for clarification or doing research to ensure understanding of what is required (length, etc.)
▶ brainstorming ideas about the subject
▶ determining what knowledge is needed to meet the expectations of the assignment
▶ creating an outline or another pre-planning exercise

Table 10.1:   Micro-Skills in Writing

Micro-Skill/ Linguistic Foundation	Classroom Example *The writer is able to:*
Orthography and vocabulary	use the alphabet in English to create words that are spelled and used correctly.
Morphology and grammar	use the correct forms of words. This includes knowing how to create the correct form of the word (noun, verbs, case, or gender) and put it together in a grammatically correct sentence.
Semantics	express meaning through using the correct word form; use vocabulary appropriate for the situation.
Syntax	put words together in correct word order; make the main sentence constituents—such as subject, verb, and object—clear to the reader.
Punctuation	use the correct punctuation conventions.
Cohesive devices	utilize enumeration words, such as *first, second,* or *third,* or contrast words such as *nevertheless* or *whereas* that help readers to follow along easily and make the writing coherent.

Table 10.2:   Macro-Skills in Writing

Macro-Skill/ Writing Foundation	Classroom Example *The writer is able to:*
Rhetorical forms	use rhetorical forms and conventions of written discourse, such as making clear what is a stated fact and what is stated opinion.
Communicative functions	meet the stated purpose and form of the piece of writing; for example, the writer clearly answers the prompt that requires both comparing and contrasting of ideas in the written answer.
Meaningful transitions	articulate main and supporting ideas and clearly make connections between different ideas.
Cultural conventions	follow the appropriate cultural rhetorical style, such as the common U.S. style of direct expression of ideas, and at the same time be able to correctly use culture-specific references, if any, within the text.
Audience	to take into account the style appropriate to audience (such as a teacher, a friend, or a boss) who will read the text and judge the appropriate tone and language level for the text.
Writing strategy	use diverse writing strategies such as pre-writing, post-writing, editing, and peer feedback.

During-writing tasks can include:

- ▶ thinking about how to address the purpose, tone, and audience of the work in one's writing
- ▶ writing freely but focusing on the overall message
- ▶ writing freely, as much as possible, without concern for mechanics or message
- ▶ completing an initial self-review of the work to ensure it meets the guidelines of the assignment.

Post-writing tasks can include:

- ▶ reviewing the prompt and guidelines for the assignment
- ▶ proofreading and editing the grammatical and mechanical aspects of the writing, such as spelling, punctuation, and sentence structure
- ▶ improving word usage and upgrading vocabulary
- ▶ ensuring the main ideas and supporting ideas are clear
- ▶ deleting distracting or unrelated information
- ▶ rearranging sentences for clarity
- ▶ reading the text silently or out loud to ensure it flows smoothly and editing as necessary
- ▶ asking a friend or classmate to offer peer feedback on the writing
- ▶ preparing the text according to the set guidelines or purpose.

Writing in L1 and L2: Similarities and Differences

Writing in a L2 can be a complex process. The teaching of L2 combines composition, rhetoric, and language learning (Kroll, 2004). When looking at writing through the lens of composition and rhetoric, it is clear that the writing process has many similarities for both L1 and L2 writers. Both groups of writers create drafts; produce content; choose appropriate vocabulary and phrasing; revise their ideas; edit the text for errors; and, finally, produce a final draft. As Casanave (2004) points out, there are also many questions that writing researchers continue to explore that are similar for both L1 and L2 composition. For example, should writers be more concerned with fluency or accuracy? Is writing concerned with the process, the product, or both? What are the best methods of providing feedback to developing writers? Is error correction effective in producing better writers? These are questions that composition teachers and ESL/EFL writing teachers explore and consider when they prepare their Writing classrooms.

There are also differences, though, between L1 and L2 writing, and research has shown that there are questions specific to teaching L2 writing. In a review of the research regarding L1 versus L2 composition, including 72 studies of ESL, EFL, L1, and L2 writing, Silva (1993) identified a number of areas where there were differences. In looking at how writers compose, Silva found similar composing patterns between L1 and L2 writers, but research also indicated that L2 writers had a much more difficult time composing their writing and were less effective in their methods than L1 writers. L2 writers also did less planning and overall reviewing than L1 writers, leading to less accuracy and fluency in the final product. Transcribing (or producing written texts) was found to be less fluent and productive for L2 composers, and narrative structure differed depending on the culture and language background of the student. More current studies in Composition have also addressed the need to look at the differences in effective writing among Generation 1.5 (or U.S.-educated) students (those from another language background who have grown up in an English-speaking country, either arriving early into the country or later when they are older), L2 writers (whose first language is not English), and international students (who are in an English-speaking country temporarily) (Ferris, 2009). Other studies focus on corpus research, which has demonstrated that L2 academic writers struggle with the typical vocabulary and phrasing used in the L1 writing and that achieving native-like proficiency in using these writing conventions is very difficult (Perez-Llantada, 2014).

For L2 writing instructors, being aware of the similarities and differences in the writing process for their learners is crucial to developing an effective writing classroom. L2 teachers need to look at student performance in the writing classroom from the perspective of composition but also keep in mind the unique challenges for L2 writers.

Designing a Writing Activity

Students' Performance in Writing Classes

In the classroom, the final writing product is determined in advance by the purpose of the writing assignment or prompt. Brown and Abeywickrama (2010) articulated four types of writing assignments that foster different types of writing skills.

In an **imitative** task, the writer focuses on the fundamentals of writing, such as letters, words, punctuation, and short sentences. Here the focus is on mastering the basics of the English language; higher-level meaning is of little concern. An imitative task would be one where the L2 learner fills in the correct verb form in a sentence or makes punctuation corrections to given sentences. These tasks tend to be more common with lower-level language learners but can be adapted to all levels of learners. In the L2 writing classroom, an imitative task to foster correct punctuation is a correction task. In a correction task, learners are given a text in English that has errors in punctuation. The learner must correct the errors that are found in the text. An example is provided.

> *Find the 5 errors in punctuation in this text.*
>
> They say that dogs are a persons best friend, they are loyal friendly and fun. Dogs love to go for walks, and play fetch with a stick. They can even protect you from harm.
> Here are the corrections:
> They say that dogs are a person's best friend. They are loyal, friendly, and fun. Dogs love to go for walks and play fetch with a stick. They can even protect you from harm.

This type of task is very common in the L2 Writing classroom and can be easily adapted to varying levels of students and to target different language forms. For example, learners could correct misspellings in text, incorrect verb forms, scrambled sentences (e.g., *eat to like I eggs*), or even improve sentences using more sophisticated vocabulary.

In an **intensive** task, the language learner is required to produce more independent language, even though the task is still in a controlled environment like with an imitative task. L2 learners may listen to a short story that is dictated to them and try to re-create the text from clues and memory. They may also focus on grammatical structures with intensive tasks, such as changing statements into questions or changing sentences from active voice to passive voice. In the Writing classroom, an example of an intensive task is a combining task. In a combining writing task, the teacher gives the L2 learners two to four simple sentences that can be summarized into one sentence using more complex sentence structures such as clauses and phrases. An example is provided.

> *Summarize these three simple sentences into one sentence. You can add any words that do not change the meaning of the three sentences.*
>
> Trees are beautiful. They have colorful leaves. Trees give us shade.
> Example answer: Trees are beautiful because they have colorful leaves and give us shade from the sun.

While teachers control the focus and scope of intensive writing tasks, learners have more opportunity to use creative language than with imitative tasks. For the Writing classroom, these types of tasks are important for developing L2 writers who need to gain confidence in using English.

In **responsive** tasks, language learners work on the discourse level, writing more deeply and focusing on meaning and context within and between sentences and paragraphs. Examples of responsive tasks include reading a short story and writing a response to the reading or interpreting a series of pictures for meaning and story. These are more common with intermediate and advanced students. In the Writing classroom, a responsive task in a Business English classroom might be to respond to a complaint after the learners have studied this type of scenario. Here is an example task:

You have received this complaint in an email. Please respond in a professional manner to the person complaining and try to resolve the matter with the consumer.

To: Samsong "Company
Re: Computer monitor
Hello, I bought your computer monitor version XS-455B and after only 6 weeks I am already having problems. The picture is very fuzzy, and there are dark green spots that appear on the screen. I tried to take it back to the store, but they would note take it vack and told me the warranty had expired. I need help with this because I need this monitor for my home business.

Model answer: A model answer would apologize for the problem, offer a solution to the problem, and offer the customers some type of bonus to keep them happy.

Responsive tasks in the Writing class are particularly useful when the teacher wants to target certain writing styles and forms, such as those used in Business English or Academic English. The teacher still sets the focus and scope for the task, but the L2 writer has more freedom than in the intensive task to use varying forms of English and to practice paragraph- and essay-level language.

In **extensive** tasks, L2 learners utilize micro-skills, macro-skills, and all the processes necessary for writing for any stated purpose. The learners produce research papers, comprehensive essays, or even major research projects. At this advanced level, learners are focused on creating meaningful works and have mastered the foundations of writing in the language for all rhetorical styles. In the advanced L2 Writing classroom where most extensive tasks take place, the teacher may place the scope on the writing task, but the learner has almost complete control over the language used for and in the task. An example of an extensive task is a research paper in an academic English setting. The teacher in this task would set the scope of the task, such as asking learners to turn in drafts, setting the number of pages (5–8) for the paper, or giving students a rubric for how the paper would be evaluated. Learners in an advanced Writing class in an Academic English setting may be allowed to choose their topic based on their potential school major (e.g., engineering, biology, education) or determine how many resources they would use to write the paper. Extensive writing tasks focus on advanced language use and the expectation that learners may soon be leaving the L2 Writing classroom for writing in the college classroom with native speakers of the language.

Types of Academic Writing

For L2 writers who will be taught in the United States, there are several rhetorical styles (or modes) that need to be mastered. The first step is to ensure that students can recognize the style that is required based on the prompt or task and then choose the correct language and conventions that are specific to it. Table 10.3 details some of the more common styles and the types of tasks learners might complete in the classroom.

Writing Classroom Practices

Because writing involves knowledge of many aspects of language, the L2 Writing classroom is an eclectic place that requires instruction in a wide variety of skills. The Writing class may also include reading, as extensive reading and research is important for students to see models of good writing and develop their own writing skill (Hyland, 2010). L2 writing has long been considered distinct from L1 writing in many ways because of cultural, individual, and language acquisition issues (see Ferris, 2009; Hinkel, 2013; and Silva, 1993 for more details). Therefore, writing activities common to the L2 classroom address issues that are often unique to L2 writers. Some examples of these activities include:

▶ Summarizing: L2 learners read various levels of texts and summarize the information into a distinct text.

▶ Paraphrasing: L2 learners read text and then paraphrase the material into their own words. This can be very import for ESL/EFL students as they may have different ideas as to what constitutes copying, plagiarizing, and summarizing.

▶ Sourcing: L2 learners learn to reference the material that they read, using an acceptable form of sourcing material such as APA (American Psychological Association, now in its sixth edition), MLA, or other way to reference material.

▶ Synthesizing: L2 learners read or listen to material that they must then synthesize into its main points in an organized manner.

Tables 10.4, 10.5, and 10.6 detail types of language-based activities, addressing micro- and macro-skills that a writing instructor may include at different levels in ESL or EFL writing.

Table 10.3:   Common Rhetorical Essay Modes

Rhetorical Style	Purpose	L2 Learner Activity
Definition	To explain a word or concept in factual terms	Given being the word *love,* learners define what the word means to them in their own words. Students create and illustrate a picture or cartoon-style story to further detail how love is defined in different contexts such as with family, friends, pets, or partners.
Expository	To explore ideas, present general information, explain a process, or synthesize ideas	Students create a timeline with 10 steps that explains the process of how to start a blog online. Students can share the steps with a partner to see if they have added enough detail and if their partner can accomplish the task based on the written directions.
Illustrate an example	To provide detail or examples that help to explain an idea or concept	Students complete online research to find 3 different types of transportation available in the city. They create a mixed media summary, which includes pictures, timetables, and online resources to describe how people can get around the city.
Classification	To catalog or sort things in a logical way	Given 20 different kinds of fish, students classify them into their appropriate categories and describe the characteristics that put them there.
Comparison and contrast	To detail the similarities and differences between ideas	In response to this writing prompt, students write a three-paragraph essay: *Explain the similarities and differences between owning a cat and owning a dog. Be sure to finish with which animal you would prefer to own and why.*
Analytical	To carefully examine a concept and sometimes convince the reader of the correct or best conclusion	Given a choice between living in the country or living in the city, student partners must choose one place to live and write a one-paragraph analytical text convincing their partner to move there. The other partner completes the same. They then trade essays to see which paragraph is more convincing and detailed.
Descriptive	To give a detailed description of a particular person, place, or thing so the reader can easily imagine the object	Students write 10 words that describe their home and then create a one-paragraph description using those words.
Narrative, personal	To describe or relate personal events and experiences in the author's own words	In a 7-sentence paragraph, students explain their decision to study English.
Cause and/or effect	To explain the causes for and/or the effects of someone or something	The prompt *What effect will the Santa Ana winds have on the California weather this month?* asks students to explain the concepts of weather planning in an essay.

Table 10.4:   Lower-Level Student Writing Activities

Micro-Skill	Activity	Macro-Skill	Activity
Vocabulary	Organizing by grouping: Arrange a list of words into categories; look for similarities and how to describe those similarities.	**Rhetorical style**	Distinguish between Fact and Opinion: Students write 6 sentences about nature; 3 sentences should be facts and 3 sentences should be opinions.
Grammar	Editing skills: Given a paragraph with a series of article errors, find and correct the errors.	**Communicative functions**	Writing Business Letters: Following the given model, students write a 5-sentence letter complaining about a defective product.
Punctuation	Correct punctuation: Given a paragraph lacking any punctuation (capitals, periods, or commas), add in all appropriate punctuation.	**Meaningful transitions**	Supporting Main Ideas: Given the main ideas on World Geography, students write 3 supporting sentences under each topic.

Table 10.5:   Intermediate-Level Student Writing Activities

Micro-Skill	Activity	Macro-Skill	Activity
Semantics	Future tense: Students write about their plans for a future job and focus on using the correct verb forms for the topic.	**Cultural conventions**	5-paragraph essay: Using the 5-paragraph essay model, respond to this prompt: *Growing numbers of people are choosing not to get vaccinated because of fears about health issues. Others believe that vaccinations protect individuals and society. Do you think everyone should be required to have vaccinations or not? Support your opinion with the readings we have done on this topic.*
Cohesive devices	Giving directions prompt: *Your friend has asked you how to get to your house from school. Using number styles (first, second, third), email directions to your friend. You can also include a Google map to support your details.*	**Audience**	Apologizing: Students write two emails— one email is to a professor about turning in a late paper, and one is to a friend for missing a dinner date. Students focus on using appropriate language for each situation.
Syntax	Adding an idea: Using coordinating or subordinating conjunctions, students combine sentences to make more complex sentences. Students use the blank lines to create their own sentences with conjunctions.	**Writing strategy**	Writing as a process: This essay assignment has three parts. Using the general topic of scientific discoveries, students create an outline for their essay and then write the essay using the outline. When they are done, students work with a partner to peer-review each other's papers and then edit their papers before turning it in.

Table 10.6:   Higher-Level Student Writing Activities

Micro-Skill	Activity	Macro-Skill	Activity
Vocabulary	Library Research: Using the strategies discussed at the library research session, students find one journal article related to their potential field of study. Students read the article and find 15 unfamiliar words in the article and use each one in a sentence.	**Rhetorical forms**	Classification Forms: Given the topic of culture, students write an essay about the topic using one of these rhetorical modes: argument, cause-and-effect, classification, or compare and contrast.
Semantics	Emails: Students write an email to a professor, asking her or him advice about their potential college degree of choice. Describe the qualifications and ask at least 5 questions about the program.	**Communicative functions**	The art of persuasion: Students write a letter to their boss asking for a raise. Students focus on professional and appropriate language for the purpose of their letters.
Syntax	Power Phrases: After writing the first draft of a research paper, students print it out and bring it to class. As a class, share sentences in order to add more powerful and appropriate language to the paper.	**Writing strategy**	Peer Feedback: Students share their writing with a partner. They write 5 items (such as grammar, spelling, structure, vocabulary, or overall meaning) for which they would like the peer to provide feedback. Students use that peer feedback to improve their essays.

Writing tasks in the L2 classroom can be divided into integrated and independent tasks.

Integrated tasks in the language classroom require that L2 learners use more than one language skill to accomplish a task. In an integrated writing activity, students complete a writing task that mirrors real-world circumstances involving more than one language skill. This is not just true for writing. For example, L2 learners might need to listen to instructions on how to check out a book at the library, take notes, and then follow those notes when they get to the library. The learners must use good listening skills; excellent note-taking skills; and then possibly ask for help, orally, once they get to the library. As in most language tasks, there is an element of integration of different skills required for any task, so L2 learners may need to listen, read, write, and speak to accomplish a task. For example, in an academic setting, students may need to listen to a lecture, read about that topic, write about that topic, and then present it to others in an oral speech. The L2 writing teacher can use integrated tasks in the Writing classroom to prepare students for these future real-world writing tasks (see Ferris, 2009, for a further discussion of academic language and literacy for L2 students). Integrated writing tasks are also listed at the end of this chapter.

When students complete an **independent task,** they are often responding to a prompt of some kind, such as a question, a topic, or a reading. This is common on high-stakes tests. Such a task typically has established guidelines regarding length and criteria for evaluation. An example of an independent writing task would be when the teacher asks the students to respond to this prompt: "Write a one-paragraph essay about one of your family members. Be sure to explain your relationship with this person, and describe him or her in detail. Follow the guidelines set forth in our criteria. You must: (1) name the family member in your main sentence; (2) describe your relationship to this family member; (3) describe this person using at least three different details; (4) conclude your paragraph by summing up your feelings about this family member." L2 learners do not depend on other languages skills, such as reading or listening, in order to accomplish independent writing tasks. In an L2 Writing class, independent writing tasks are useful for distinguishing writing skills alone.

Now, let's look at integrated and independent writing skill activities using our four syllabi approaches.

Writing Activities for the Classroom

The writing activities presented in this section address various levels of writing proficiency and are structured as writing activities students complete after class as homework, with the exception of Activity 10.3, which is designed to be done in the classroom. These activities do not, therefore, follow the same structure as those in Chapters 7–9 and 11–12. Based on the theoretical foundations presented in the first chapters of the book, the activities are arranged according to the syllabi presented in Chapter 6.

─────────────── **Activity 10.1: Written Reports** ───────────────

Grammar-Based Writing

Rationale: This **integrated** writing activity is focused around the structure of higher-level thinking skills. It is important for students to see the connection between thinking skills and writing proficiency, so this activity focuses on reading, writing, and higher-order thinking skills.

Objectives: Students demonstrate their language skills by reading authentic material, connecting it to their own experience, and sharing information with an authentic audience through writing a report on what they have read.

Pre-Planning

Pre-knowledge: None
Materials needed: Students choose from a number of sources for text material. They can use books; books-on-tape for listening practice; or a newspaper series of articles, blogs, websites, short stories, or college newspapers according to their level and needs. Students become partners in this effort to choose a text, learning how to judge their own abilities to read authentic materials outside of the classroom.
Language level: Intermediate and higher
Recommended age group: Age 12+

Procedures

Help students select sources of text material of interest to them to increase motivation in the project. For example, pre-select certain magazines, websites, books, or library materials to help students begin their search for appropriate material. So students do not feel overwhelmed by authentic text that is beyond their current reading level, learners should pre-read the text. If after 20 percent of the text is read, students have little or no understanding, then they should choose an alternative text for the project.

Connect the written reports to current study topics in the classroom. For example, if it is a Business English course, steer students toward texts that complement current curricular goals (e.g., business articles, letters, memos, plans, end-of-year financial reports).

Consider the sample questions listed (see Table 10.7) as those that students must answer in their report. Revise questions to meet the specific goals of the project. Encourage students to read the text with a focus on grammatical structures that they can incorporate into their own writing.

The criteria for evaluation of the project should focus on grammar and writing. Table 10.7 uses Bloom's taxonomy to guide the types of tasks that learners accomplish as they prepare their report. It has some recommended keywords that can be adapted into the sample questions for students. These keywords are important because they are common to what is required in writing tasks at all levels of writing.

Evaluation

For evaluation purposes, there are a number of options for the written reports. Using an authentic audience for evaluation can increase motivation and effort, since students will know that their work will be shared with others. Students can:

- ► turn in the report. This is not an authentic audience, and students will focus on pleasing you, rather than thinking about how to make the report of the best quality.

- ► report to the class; this can be exciting or very time-consuming and dull. A long class of students reporting on a piece of text that other students may not have read is not effective.

Table 10.7:   Some Questions for the Text Report

Level of Thinking	Keywords	Sample Questions for Students to Answer for Their Written Report
Knowledge	*arrange, define, duplicate, label, list, memorize, name, order, recognize, recall, repeat, relate, reproduce, state*	1. List the text that you are using, including the title, author, and where you found the text. 2. State the reasons that you chose this text to report on today. 3. Define 5 new words that you found in the text. Where did you find these definitions?
Comprehension	*classify, describe, discuss, explain, express, identify, indicate, locate, recognize, report, restate, review, select, translate*	1. Identify 3 main points of the text and the details that support these main points. 2. Describe any pictures, graphs, or tables that helped you to understand the text. 3. Discuss the main point of the text. Did you discover some new information that you did not know before? If so, what was it?
Analysis	*analyze, appraise, calculate, categorize, compare, contrast, criticize, differentiate, discriminate, distinguish, examine, experiment, question, test*	1. Categorize this type of text. What was the purpose of this text? Why was it written? Who was the intended audience? 2. Compare this piece of text with a classmate's text report—what similarities and differences do you see in the style, information, and audience of the text? 3. Question the information contained in the text—are there questions you still have about the topic after reading the text?
Synthesis	*arrange, assemble, collect, compose, construct, create, design, develop, formulate, manage, organize, plan, prepare, propose, set up, write*	1. Write a summary of the text in your own words. 2. Construct a graph that displays the information that you found in the text. 3. Design a multimedia presentation of your text report. Find visuals, audio, or audiovisual material to support the ideas found in the text.
Evaluation	*appraise, argue, assess, attach, choose, compare, defend, estimate, evaluate, judge, predict, rate, score, select, support, value*	1. Judge the value of this text—what new information did you learn? 2. Select 3 other pieces of text that are similar in some way to this text—in the information provided, the style of the text, or the genre. 3. Evaluate the validity of this text. Can you confirm the facts or ideas presented through other means or are the ideas mostly opinion? Determine what is fact or opinion in your text.

► Create multimedia presentations limited to one important aspect of the report will keep the students interested and challenge the presenter. Afterward, students can take turns asking the presenter questions. This will keep the students focused on the presenter. The presenter must be prepared to answer questions about the report.

► report to the school or campus. Students can share their reports with other classes, send in book reviews to the campus newsletter or paper, or even post their projects in the hallway. Students can email their reports to an e-pal at the school or outside the school. Because the audience is larger than just the class, the students will feel pride in sharing their work.

► post their reviews on the internet. If students have reviewed books, ask them to write reviews of that book to post on any of the booksellers' websites, such as www.bn.com. Students can also post these reviews to a school or class website. The important aspect is that students share their work with a greater audience and feel that their project has a greater impact than just a grade in the gradebook.

► create an oral presentation that reflects both the textual and visual aspects of their projects. Students can share their presentations and then judge each other's work based on criteria that they create themselves. This challenges students to do a quality job and gives them ownership of the final project.

Activity 10.2: Book Review

Communicative Product Writing

Rationale: A communicative product syllabus is based on situational or notional/functional approaches to student learning. The syllabus has targeted, communicative language and vocabulary to use within specific topical situations. This integrated writing activity focuses on reading a book and writing a review using evaluation-style writing genres.

Objectives: In small groups, students choose from a group of books that the teacher has pre-selected as appropriate for their level (see Chapter 9 for a detailed discussion of selecting reading material for the L2 classroom). Oral negotiation, grammar, and writing skills are all needed.

Pre-planning

Pre-knowledge: Students should have some exposure to the language needed to write a critical review of a book. Depending on the age and level, students can read what others have written or look at samples of book reviews.
Materials needed: Pre-selected books and a rubric for the assignment
Language level: Intermediate to advanced
Recommended age group: Age 10 to adults

Procedures

This is an **integrated** writing task that involves reading and writing. Provide students with choices for books. Allow them time to look briefly at the books and choose one that is of interest to them. It works best if groups of students can choose the same book as then they can share their different ideas about the book review in the end.

As students complete this first step, they should then:

1. Preview the book and write some basic information about author, title, type of book (fiction, non-fiction), and some guesses about the book's content.

2. Start to share ideas about the book (if working in groups), and anticipate some ideas they might read about in the book. Orally they should each share why they chose the book they chose. Are there different opinions about what the book will be about?

3. Analyze the chapter titles or visuals.

4. Discuss and create a plan of action for reviewing the book.

5. Go over and discuss the rubric for the assignment.

6. Read the book. Students should be given an appropriate amount of time to read based on their level and the size of the book. Children can read the book during class so that you can help them with difficult vocabulary. Adults can take from 3-7 days to read the book.

7. Write the book review at home in draft form.

8. Bring in their drafts to share with a partner during a peer-response activity. If they have read the same book, this can be helpful for determining if they have understood the text. This is also a classroom opportunity for students to work in small groups and for the instructor to determine if students did not understand any aspects of the reading.

Evaluation

Here is a sample rubric for a beginning- to intermediate-level course for adults:

Book Review Components

What Should Be Included in Your Report	Points
Include the title, author, date of publication, number of pages, whether it is fiction or non-fiction, and the overall topic.	*10*
Summarize the book in 1 paragraph	*10*
Write 3–5 reasons that you liked the book if you can. Include specific examples from the book (e.g., "I really liked the main character because she was kind and helpful to everyone").	*20*
Write 3–5 reasons that you did not like the book if you can. Include specific examples from the book (e.g., "I thought the author did not give enough detail about where the book took place").	*20*
Tell if you would recommend this book. Who should read this book if you recommend it? If you do not recommend it, why do you think it is not a good read?	*10*
Use excellent English. Pay attention to grammar, spelling, sentence structure and the content listed in this rubric.	*20*
Peer feedback	*10*
Total	*100*

Activity 10.3: Filling Out Customs Forms

Communicative Process Writing

Rationale: In communicative syllabus, the organization of the curriculum is based on tasks. The task-based activities are focused on the language and language skill needed to complete a concrete task, such as applying for a program or job. One written activity focused on process is the Customs Forms **independent writing task.** This writing task is a responsive task that is best used with students who are planning to travel to another country or have experience travelling to other countries.

Objectives: Students learn the meaning of words presented on the customs form and learn how to fill out the form through imitation.

Pre-Planning

Pre-knowledge: None
Materials needed: Computers and internet connection if possible. You will need a customs form and a made-up passport number.
Language level: Low-intermediate to advanced
Recommended age group: Older teens and adults

Procedures

Warm-up: Show a YouTube video about arriving or flying on an airplane or use any visual to get students motivated and thinking about the forms you need to complete when travelling.
Explanation: Explain that everyone must fill out immigration forms to enter the United States. Students should know to be honest and fill out everything or they could be stopped by a customs official.
Pre-teach vocabulary: Put these vocabulary words from the U.S. Customs Form on the board to start:

> *Family Name, Address/Destination, Passport, Issued, Residence/Resident, Prior,*
> *No., Primary, Proximity, Livestock*

Ask students to guess at the words, and write the definition for each term on the board. Ask students to write these definitions on their own paper. Then, let students look over the U.S. Customs Form and highlight words or phrased they do not understand. Ask students if there are further words they do not understand and add any words with their definitions to the board.

Model reading and writing: If you can project the form onto the board, or write the categories in advance on the board, start writing your own information on the board (nothing personal that you do not want to share). Read out loud the information while writing on the board. Ask students to write on their form and move around the classroom to review their progress. **Tell students that they do not have to share any personal information that they do not want to share.**

Pair activity: To ensure students have filled out the entire form, ask them to pair up and assess each other's writing. Again, if students do not seem comfortable, they do not have to share their forms.

Evaluation

Review the listed vocabulary one more time. You can use a game, such as dividing the class into teams. When you read a definition of one of the vocabulary words, the first team to guess the vocabulary word gets a point.

Collect the forms for individual review. Be prepared to repeat the lesson or complete the form at another lesson if you cannot get to the end of the form.

Activity 10.4: Community Events

Eclectic Writing

Rationale: Many instructors prefer using various and mixed approaches in their design of their syllabus and curriculum design. In an eclectic approach to the language classroom, the syllabus may contain a variety of activities, such as giving directions based on a map, but may also include language-specific goals, such as the introducing the past tense, within the same framework. Teachers like this eclectic approach because it allows them to meet various learner needs and adapt the curriculum to class-specific goals.

Objectives: Students attend an event in the community, absorb critical information, and write about their experiences in a personal manner. Instead of attending an event, students can also write about events that they are already part of their normal routines, such as cultural events, movies, shopping excursions, sporting events, school events, events for their children, or even a trip to the grocery store. The main objective is for students to have the opportunity to write about an authentic life experience in their own words, even if they are at a very beginning level of writing. Requiring students to attend and write about community events accomplishes many goals for the classroom.

1. Students become engaged with their community, experiencing the setting in which their education is taking place.

2. Students can choose activities they are interested in attending or can be exposed to different events, opening their eyes to new experiences.

3. Students can attend in a group or alone, whichever they prefer. Students who need support will have such support if they attend with other students, while more confident students can work on their own. This project can help students develop closer relationships in class as they engage in social activities together.

4. Students will develop their listening and writing skills in a difficult situation. They will need to focus on main ideas in an atmosphere saturated with English or, if they are an EFL student, they will need to think about the event in their first language and then be able to translate that knowledge into their L2.

5. Students have the opportunity to use other markers to help them with understanding—visual markers, reading material, body language, or interactions within the group. Learning to use a variety of cues to listen for information helps students develop their overall listening skills, which enhances the writing skill of conveying important information.

Pre-Planning

Pre-knowledge: This is dependent on the level of the student and the event.
Materials needed: A schedule of various local community events
Language level: High-beginning to advanced
Recommended age group: All

Choose the event: Using the internet, local newspaper, social contacts, or community announcement boards, find a local event that is open to the public. Students should be able to attend and explain in advance their interest in the event. Or, if you are using events students already attend, have them discuss in class the events they have planned for the coming weeks.

Procedures

Pre-writing: Before the event, prepare some questions about it. Brainstorm ideas in class about what students might see, hear, and learn there. Think of some new vocabulary that students might hear, and ask them to look up those words. Students can predict, orally and in writing, what they expect from the event.

Students can attend:

- ► school events, such as concerts or trips to the library
- ► sporting events
- ► artistic performances
- ► musical concerts at schools
- ► lectures on various topics at the library, local school, or community center
- ► demonstrations by professionals in fields such as law enforcement, community safety, environmental issues, or city personnel
- ► farmer's markets
- ► any event that they normally attend or that you arrange, such as going to the grocery store or shopping in a market

During the event: Students listen, take notes if they want or can, and observe at the event. They note their surroundings and the other people attending the event. They listen carefully to what is said and try to remember or note as much information as possible. Students can use clues, such as visuals, body language, or support materials to help them in understanding all aspects of the event.
Post-writing: Students create a brief paragraph or report on what they learned. Beginning students may be able to write just some vocabulary or simple sentences to describe the event. Intermediate students can write paragraphs or report-style writing samples in their own words. Advanced students should be able to write descriptive and/or factual essays that pertain to the event.

Evaluation

Collaboration and presentation: If they are able, students can share the highlights of the event with the class. They can read their final report and provide a simple recommendation about the event of "thumbs up" or "thumbs down" for beginning students or a more complex recommendation for advanced students.

Final report: Students turn in a final written paper about the event. Beginning students can write as few as ten sentences about the event using simple *I liked* and *I didn't like* sentences, while more advanced students can produce essay-length writings. The teacher can determine, based on level, age, and need, what fits best with the writing curriculum in the class.

Feedback and Error Correction on Student Writing

There are diverse opinions as to the place of feedback within the writing process and what approaches are most effective (Hartshorn et al., 2010). How much feedback to give, how specific should that feedback be, how to get students to pay attention to that feedback, and how to ensure writing feedback is effective and not detrimental are all critical questions for teaching writing in the language classrooms. Ferris (2011) makes clear a number of issues in this discussion. She first defines errors as "morphological, syntactic, and lexical forms that deviate from rules of the target language, violating the expectations of literate adult native speakers" (p. 3). While teachers may spend an inordinate amount of time looking for, correcting, and trying to decrease errors in student writing, Ferris recommends looking at the issue in a more balanced way.

The first point to keep in mind is that learning a second language is a challenging process and errors are a natural part of this process. Errors, in this case, can be a positive reflection of the learner attempting to use the language. Expecting native-like proficiency in writing during early language development stages is not realistic. Second, with the diversity of ESL and EFL learners today, teachers must keep in mind that errors may be different depending on the background of the student. International students, for example, might have studied English formally for many years and might be more used to structure and direct correction. Immigrant students who have lived in the United States since they were very young (sometimes referred to as Generation 1.5 immigrants) may often write what they hear, but their errors could be very different than more recent immigrants who might struggle with cultural issues. In all cases, it is important that the teacher keep in mind that any approach to error correction in the ESL/EFL writing classroom should take into account the diversity of students' backgrounds.

Third, and perhaps most important, Ferris (2011) makes the case that error correction is an important part of the L2 classroom. Some reasons she gives are:

► Error correction gives students the opportunity to correct their own errors and become better editors of their own work.

► Research has shown that learners do benefit from targeted error correction and that their writing becomes more accurate and shows improvement over time.

► Both teachers and students want to make error correction a part of the classroom. Research has shown that language learners expect and desire error correction from their teachers and that teachers are committed to some type of formal writing feedback for their students.

► Students must demonstrate accurate writing in the real world. Regardless of how error correction takes place in the classroom, the overarching goal is for language learners to be able to write well in tasks that they undertake in the real world.

Each L2 teacher must make a decision about how to approach error correction. It is critical that the teacher be fair, consistent, and open about how and why writing will be corrected. By sharing with students that errors are an important part of the language learning process, teachers can help to de-stigmatize errors in language. Further, teachers can still provide targeted error correction without overwhelming students by returning papers with a "sea of red," pointing out each and every error. To keep students motivated, it is also important to focus on the positives as much as the negatives in every piece of writing for which students receive correction.

Providing feedback to students about their writing is different from individualized error correction. Both styles of assessment have a purpose and approach; teachers need to identify which style is best fitted to the goals of that particular task in the classroom and identify any factors that may affect the effectiveness of that feedback (see Bitchener & Ferris, 2012; Jinyan, 2009).

Assessing Writing

Three types of scoring writing are discussed: holistic, analytic, and objective. Each type has its own characteristics and feedback purposes.

Holistic scoring uses a single scale for different levels of writing performance with only a single score awarded to each individual. This is the most common method of scoring writing for standardized testing because it can be done quickly and should have strong inter-rater reliability with understood standards. It has disadvantages for a classroom teacher because it does not give the writer or the reader any specific feedback on what problems need to be addressed. As a result, it is not a recommended scoring method for writing tests in which instructors are encouraging students to identify strengths and weaknesses, and improve their writing.

To have quality results in a holistic scoring situation (see Figure 10.1) requires at least two readers for each paper, intensive training for all readers on the rubric, and consideration of the inter-rater reliability among scorers.

Figure 10.1:   Example of Holistic Scoring

Holistic scoring is a method by which trained readers evaluate a piece of writing for its overall quality. The holistic scoring in the standardized writing assessment used in Florida Public Schools, for example, requires readers to evaluate the work as a whole, while considering four elements: focus, organization, support, and conventions. This method is sometimes called *focused holistic scoring*. In this type of scoring, readers are trained not to become overly concerned with any one aspect of writing but to look at a response as a whole (Florida Department of Education, n.d.).

Focus

Focus refers to how clearly the paper presents and maintains a main idea, theme, or unifying point.

Organization

Organization refers to the structure or plan of development (beginning, middle, and end) and whether the points logically relate to one another. Organization refers to (1) the use of transitional devices and (2) the evidence of a connection between sentences.

Support

Support refers to the quality of the details used to explain, clarify, or define. The quality of support depends on word choice, specificity, depth, credibility, and thoroughness.

Conventions

Conventions refer to punctuation, capitalization, spelling, and variation in sentence used in the paper. These conventions are basic writing skills. The Florida Writes! rubric further interprets the four major areas of consideration into levels of achievement. The rubric used to score papers starting in spring 1995 on the Florida Writes! test is presented and is based on a seven-point scale from unscorable (0) to 6. Each level contains a sample of what is expected to reach that score.

6 Points

The writing is focused, purposeful, and reflects insight into the writing situation. The paper conveys a sense of completeness and wholeness with adherence to the main idea, and its organizational pattern provides for a logical progression of ideas. The support is substantial, specific, relevant, concrete, and/or illustrative.

5 Points

The writing focuses on the topic, and its organizational pattern provides for a progression of ideas, although some lapses may occur. The paper conveys a sense of completeness or wholeness.

4 Points

The writing is generally focused on the topic but may include extraneous or loosely related material. An organizational pattern is apparent, although some lapses may occur. The paper exhibits some sense of completeness or wholeness.

3 Points

The writing is generally focused on the topic but may include extraneous or loosely related material. An organizational pattern has been attempted, but the paper may lack a sense of completeness or wholeness.

2 Points

The writing is related to the topic but include extraneous or loosely related material. Little evidence of an organizational pattern may be demonstrated, and the paper may lack a sense of completeness or wholeness. Development of support is inadequate or illogical. Word choice is limited, inappropriate or vague.

1 Point

The writing may only minimally address the topic. The paper is a fragmentary or incoherent listing of related ideas or sentences or both.

Unscorable

The paper is unscorable because

- ▶ the response is not related to what the prompt requested the student to do.
- ▶ the response is simply a rewording of the prompt.
- ▶ the response is a copy of a published work.
- ▶ the student refused to write.
- ▶ the response is illegible.
- ▶ the response is incomprehensible (words are arranged in such a way that no meaning is conveyed).
- ▶ the response contains an insufficient amount of writing to determine if the student was attempting to address the prompt.
- ▶ the writing folder is blank.

While holistic scoring can be a great tool if it is implemented appropriately, it is a tool best used for large groups or when placing or assessing students, as an overall score may give you the information you need. As a teacher in the classroom, though, this type of score may not create the kind of feedback struggling L2 writers are looking for in their writing feedback. For a writer looking for more specific feedback, the Analytic Scoring Method provides more information.

Analytic scoring guides are designed to rate papers on established criteria. Whereas holistic scoring assigns a single score that represents a weighing of all the different factors addressed by the scoring guide in one score, an analytic score might assign a high score to one factor, such as organization, and a lower score to another, such as mechanics (grammar and spelling). Analytic scoring takes much longer to accomplish on the part of the teacher, but it provides richer feedback and is helpful when determining issues for individual writers.

An Example of Analytic Scoring

Let's take a look at an example of an Analytic Scoring Guide developed for an upper-level ESOL class by John R. Edlund (Essay Scoring Guide, English 096, n.d.). He sets up this scoring guide to address specific issues of writing that he considers vital in order for a student to move to an upper grade. When students receive their writing sample back, the instructor will have not only given the students their scores but also provided the areas where the students lost points or did not meet the criteria of the writing task. Students are assigned scores within each category, demonstrating at what level they are writing for each of the seven categories. This type of scoring gives both the teacher and learner more specific feedback on set writing skills that the teacher sets in advance, so the teacher can diagnose the areas where students need to improve. It also gives the L2 learners positive feedback so they can see their strengths, not just their weaknesses. It certainly is more time-consuming than holistic scoring, and more difficult for more than one reader to agree on, if that is the case, because the interpretation of the rubric is very specific and can be subjective. You can be as specific as you want to be in scoring this type of writing, and it can even involve underlining grammar mistakes or making corrections. That type of specific scoring is more in line with objective scoring, which is discussed next.

The Analytic Scoring Guide in Figure 10.2 has seven categories: thesis, organization, development, word choice, sentence structure, documentation, and grammar/mechanics.

Figure 10.2: Analytic Scoring Guide

90–100: Essays in this range demonstrate consistently superior writing ability. The writer is fluent and clearly ready for English 104 (the next level).

- ▶ The essay has a strong thesis, consistently addresses the question or topic, and demonstrates a clear sense of audience and purpose.
- ▶ The essay engages the reader and is easy to follow, with effective opening paragraphs, clear transitions, effective paragraph divisions, and a good conclusion.
- ▶ All points are relevant, and supported with examples, facts, or logical arguments.
- ▶ Word choices are correct and appropriate for academic writing.
- ▶ Sentence structure is fluent, varied, and effective.
- ▶ When appropriate, the writer effectively and purposefully quotes and paraphrases materials from other texts without extensive and unnecessary summarizing. Sources are accurately documented when necessary.
- ▶ Although the essay may have a few minor flaws, the writer avoids errors in mechanics, grammar, and usage.

80–89: Essays in this range demonstrate strong writing ability. The writer is clearly ready for English 104.

- ▶ The essay has a clear thesis or main idea and consistently addresses the question or topic, although it may develop some aspects of the topic more effectively than others.
- ▶ The essay is easy to follow, has a good introduction, effective paragraph divisions, and a conclusion.
- ▶ Points are relevant, well developed, and well supported.
- ▶ Word choices are accurate and appropriate.
- ▶ Sentence structure is varied and effective.
- ▶ When appropriate, the writer quotes and paraphrases materials from other texts without extensive and unnecessary summarizing. Sources are accurately documented when necessary.
- ▶ The essay is largely free of serious errors in mechanics, grammar, and usage.

70–79: Essays in this range demonstrate adequate writing ability. The writer is ready for English 104.

► The essay has a thesis or main idea, is on topic and has a focus but may slight or omit some aspects of the topic.

► The essay has a sense of beginning, middle, and end, and reasonable paragraph divisions.

► Most points are relevant and supported. Ineffective repetition of facts, ideas, words, or phrases may appear but should not overwhelm rhetorical effectiveness.

► Word choices may be informal or conversational on occasion but are acceptable.

► Sentence structure is correct, for the most part, but may be repetitive or awkward at times.

► When appropriate, the writer refers to other texts and sources, without extensive and unnecessary summarizing, and documents them.

► There may be minor errors in mechanics, grammar, usage, and sentence structure, but the writing problems will not be serious or frequent enough to distract or confuse the reader. Furthermore, it is clear that the writer has demonstrated an ability to correct these problems through revision.

65–69: Essays in this range demonstrate weak writing ability. Such essays may be largely similar to those in the 70–79 category but with more problems. The writer is not yet ready for English 104.

► The essay is unfocused or off topic.

► The essay may have a sense of beginning, middle, and end but may begin and end abruptly or vaguely. There are paragraph divisions but not necessarily in the appropriate places.

► Some points may be undeveloped or unsupported. Supporting arguments may be illogical.

► Word choices may be informal or typical of oral language. Ineffective repetition of facts, ideas, words, or phrases may hinder rhetorical effectiveness.

► Sentence structure is often correct but may be repetitive or awkward and may exhibit chunking—that is, sentences that are composed of two or more phrases that don't fit together grammatically.

► The writer may refer to other texts and sources on occasion and may document them, but not always accurately or appropriately. Long summaries and other inappropriate uses of text may appear.

► Grammatical errors may distract and confuse the reader.

0–64: Essays in this range demonstrate inadequate writing ability. The essay is marred by at least one of the following problems but probably several in combination. The writer is clearly not ready for English 104.

- ▶ The essay is unfocused or off topic.
- ▶ Organizational structure is lacking or ineffective. Paragraph divisions may be non-existent or inappropriate.
- ▶ Points are unsupported or undeveloped, or consist largely of simplistic generalizations.
- ▶ Text includes largely oral, informal, or inappropriate word choice and ineffective repetition of facts, ideas, words, or phrases.
- ▶ Text includes repeated inattention or confusion regarding sentence boundaries. Some sentences may be difficult to read or understand.
- ▶ Text includes copying or other use of texts and sources without documentation and/or unnecessary or ineffective summarizing of texts.
- ▶ There are errors in grammar, usage, and mechanics that are frequent and serious enough to distract or confuse the reader. It is also clear that the writer has not demonstrated an ability to correct these problems through revision.

Objective scoring uses a rubric that not only identifies which types of errors will be marked but also weights those errors according to their impact. Some errors may have little impact on the overall writing meaning (i.e., small spelling errors that don't confuse the reader), while others actually confuse the meaning and content of the writing. The former would be weighted less and the latter would be weighted more. You don't see as much objective scoring in writing today because it is time-consuming and tends to focus on the negatives rather than the positives. This type of scoring is not really appropriate for beginning writers because students could end up with negative scores on their writing, which is hardly encouraging. One of the advantages of this type of scoring is that it provides specific, guided, and thorough feedback on a piece of writing, which for the upper levels of L2 learners can be very helpful as students move from language classes to mainstream or university classes where they will be graded according to a more stringent scale. One example of an objective scoring guide is shown in Figure 10.3.

While there is much research how effective certain forms of error correction works with students, there is one consensus you will find with your L2 learners—they want feedback on their writing. By keeping your feedback clear and focused, you can provide wanted feedback. For example, you can let students know you are focusing on certain vocabulary or grammar usage, (e.g., the correct use of articles *a, an, the,* null), or a particular writing style when they write. Then the feedback they receive is focused and clear, and does not overwhelm them by correcting every aspect of writing all at once.

Figure 10.3: Writing Prompts Objective Scoring Guide

Student Name	Type of Writing Product
Date	Corresponding Atlas Reading Segment

3 — The description is met.
2 — The description accurate, but not fully developed.
1 — The description attempted, but inaccurate.
0 — The description is not attempted.

Score Earned	Desired Weight for Item	Adjusted Score	Description of Item in Final Writing Product [Teachers may choose which of these descriptors to use and what weight to give to each one.]
	X	=	The final product reflects the task described in the corresponding prompt.
	X	=	The final product contains main and supporting ideas from the corresponding reading and the student's own ideas, which blend together to meet the prompt's objective.
	X	=	The final product demonstrates continuity in the development of paragraphs based on the type of product.
	X	=	The final product is free of distracting grammatical and spelling errors.
	X	=	The final product is organized in a neat and appropriate manner given the type of writing product.
	X	=	The student provided a graphic organizer, outline, or notes.

Total Points Earned_____Total Points Possible_____Percentage_____
COMMENTS:

Peer Response in the Writing Classroom

Peer response refers to a process where students read and respond to each other's work. Active participation in peer feedback can bring multiple benefits to both the reader and the writer. Some students may not be very familiar with the idea of peer review, and cultural and psychological issues can either assist or impede this process of peer response. As a result, it is critical to carefully determine if peer feedback will work well in each classroom setting and whether it may require you to train students (Reid, 2008; Rollinson, 2005). For example, with regard to age, gender, and language knowledge, there are cultural customs that may prevent younger students from feeling free to offer advice or criticism to older students, and the same can go for female students providing feedback to male students. If students are still in a lower interlanguage stage, they may not be able to effectively correct errors or may even make mistakes in their error correction with other students. This means that it is critical for the L2 teacher to determine if and when learners are ready for peer feedback, to train students in what they will be doing, and to oversee that the process is effective with that particular group of students. Some learners may feel too insecure to participate fully in this process, while other learners will be more confident and prepared in their responses.

Peer response can also be a great opportunity for students to share their cultural perspectives with their classmates. The more students talk to their classmates in a smaller group setting, the more confident they will become in sharing their views with the entire class. More important, by seeing how other students think and write about the same topic, L2 learners will begin to look at their own writing from a different perspective. In other words, by critiquing their peers' work, students will learn various aspects of academic writing—both content and writing issues—and will be able to strengthen their own arguments and edit their own work more effectively. So, utilizing peer assessment creates the opportunity for students to get comments on their early drafts from their classmates and incorporate more diverse perspectives in their work.

This chapter discussed writing from the perspective of skills, process, product, and activity practices. Writing involves different levels of skill, including micro-skills, such as grammar knowledge, and macro-skills, such as writing for a particular audience. The writing process in the language classroom includes pre-writing, during-writing, and post-writing tasks. The writing product is just as important as the writing process, so the diverse products and styles used in the writing classroom were detailed. Four writing activities meant to stimulate writing skill at all levels of language were shared. Because error correction and evaluation of writing is challenging for the L2 instructor, the issues related to how evaluation can be accomplished varies according to the curricular goals.

Summarizing Statements

1. The goal for the Writing classroom is for L2 learners to develop writing skills in all areas of life including social, academic, and professional.

2. Developing both micro- and macro-skills are critical for writers if they want to become truly proficient during any level of language learning.

3. The final product in the writing process is represented by the type of writing that is being attempted, such as extensive writing, and the genre of that particular piece, such as narrative.

4. When it comes to error correction, although there still may be discussion as to what type of error correction is most effective, in the end it is critical that L2 learners receive quality feedback for their written work.

5. For language instructors, it is important that they identify which assessment approach (e.g., holistic, analytic, or objective) is best fitted to the goals of a particular piece of writing.

REFLECTION AND APPLICATION

1. One way of creating ESL/EFL writing activities is by dividing assignments into pre-writing, during-writing, and post-writing tasks. Take a minute to review what kinds of activities are listed in this chapter. Then, in a small group, work together to create three writing assignments. Be sure to include pre-writing, during-writing, and post-writing activities for each activity. Why do you think dividing writing into these different tasks can help L2 learners develop their overall writing skill?

2. Make a list of all the types of writing that you do in your own life, such as writing emails, papers, notes, or Facebook postings. Now, think about your ESL/EFL classroom and how you might structure activities to help students write for all those different scenarios. Choose one scenario and create a writing activity geared toward helping students develop their writing skill for that particular writing task.

3. This chapter explored three different ways to assess ESL writing, including holistic, analytic, and objective scoring methods. As a class, discuss which method would be appropriate in each of the following scenarios or if none of these methods would be appropriate. Be prepared to explain why you think the method you chose is appropriate and what information you would hope to gather as a teacher using this method.

   a. All third-grade ESOL students are writing a one-paragraph essay for a standardized test given by the state.

   b. Beginner EFL students are writing an introduction letter to the teacher.

   c. Advanced ESL students in an EAP are writing a research paper at the end of the course..

   d. Intermediate ESL students in an IEP are writing their first essay of the class term.

REFERENCES

Bitchener, J., & Ferris, D. (2012). *Written corrective feedback in second language acquisition and writing.* New York: Routledge.

Brown, H. D., & Abeywickrama, P. (2010). *Language assessment: Principles and classroom practices.* White Plains, NY: Pearson Longman.

Casanave, C. (2004). *Controversies in second language writing: Dilemmas and decisions in research and instruction.* Ann Arbor: University of Michigan Press.

Edlund, J.R. (n.d.). *Essay scoring guide: English Ø96.* Retrieved from www.cpp.edu

Ferris, D. (2007). Preparing teachers to respond to student writing. *Journal of Second Language Writing, 16*(3), 165–193.

Ferris, D. (2009). *Teaching college writing to diverse student populations.* Ann Arbor: University of Michigan Press.

Ferris, D. (2011). *Treatment of error in second language student writing* (2nd ed.). Ann Arbor: University of Michigan Press.

Florida Department of Education. (n.d.). Retrieved from www.fldoe.org

Hartshorn, K. J., Evans N. W., Merrill, P. F., Sudweeks, R. R., Strong-Krause, D., & Anderson, N. J. (2010). Effects of dynamic corrective feedback on ESL writing accuracy. *TESOL Quarterly, 44*(1), 84–109.

Hinkel, E. (2013). *Teaching academic ESL writing: Practical techniques in vocabulary and grammar.* London: Routledge.

Hyland, K. (2010). *Teaching and researching: Writing.* London: Routledge.

Jinyan, H. (2009). Factors affecting the assessment of ESL students' writing. *International Journal of Applied Educational Studies, 5*(1), 1–17.

Kroll, B. (Ed.). (2004). *Exploring the dynamics of second language writing.* Cambridge, U.K.: Cambridge University Press.

Nassaji, H. (2012). The relationship between SLA research and language pedagogy: Teachers' perspectives. *Language Teaching Research, 16*(3), 337–365.

Perez-Llantada, C. (2014, June). Formulaic language in L1 and L2 expert academic writing: Convergent and divergent usage. *Journal of English for Academic Purposes, 14,* 84–94.

Reid, E. (2008). Mentoring peer mentors: Mentor education and support in the composition program. *Composition Studies, 36*(2), 51–79.

Reynolds, D. W. (2005). Linguistic correlates of second language literacy development: Evidence from middle-grade learner essays. *Journal of Second Language Writing, 14*(1), 19–45.

Rollinson, P. (2005). Using peer feedback in the ESL writing class. *ELT Journal, 59*(1), 23–30.

Silva, T. (1993). Toward an understanding of the distinct nature of L2 writing. *TESOL Quarterly, 27*(4), 657–677.

Silva, T., & Reichelt, M. (1994). Writing instruction for ESL graduate students: Examining issues and raising questions. *ELT Journal, 48*(3), 197.

Tracy, B., Reid, R., & Graham, S. (2009). Teaching young students strategies for planning and drafting stories: The impact of self-regulated strategy development. *Journal of Educational Research, 102*(5), 323–332.

Yule, G. (2014). *The study of language* (5th ed.). Cambridge, U.K.: Cambridge University Press.

Chapter 11 ▲

Grammar Activities and Assessment Techniques

This chapter looks at grammar in language curriculum from a historical viewpoint, defines the grammar skill, and adds the perspective of a tri-dimensional model of grammar structures proposed by Larsen-Freeman (2003). It then details the process of designing grammar teaching and assessment activities, providing examples for both.

Grammar and L2 Teaching: A Historical Perspective

Previous chapters looked at the role of grammar in L2 teaching. For many centuries, grammar was at the core of L2 pedagogy. To know another language was equivalent to both knowing and articulating its grammar rules. The emphasis on grammar was reflected in many traditional grammar-based approaches, such as grammar translation and the audiolingual method. In spite of their differences, these methods were based on the principle that learning the grammatical structure of another language should be at the center of language teaching and be allocated the most amount of time in the language classroom.

However, many learners who were taught an L2 using grammar-based approaches realized that they were unable to communicate in the target language when they came in contact with a native speaker. Those L2 learners had a vast inventory of grammar rules and a deep knowledge of how those rules applied to language, but they found it very difficult to use those forms in free oral production (Ellis, Basturkmen, & Loewen, 2002). This recognition that knowing a language goes beyond knowing its grammar rules moved the L2 teaching pendulum to the other extreme, with the focus changing from language forms to language meaning. In L2 pedagogy, grammar-based approaches were replaced with communicative approaches. The role of Krashen's model of SLA was pivotal to the adoption and worldwide acceptance of communicative approaches.

His distinction between acquisition as an unconscious and implicit process and learning as a conscious and explicit one provided the theoretical foundation for a focus-on-meaning teaching approach in language classrooms, with the virtual elimination of explicit grammar instruction.

After decades of using communicative approaches in the classroom, L2 teachers became dissatisfied with this new approach because there was not enough emphasis on the correction of pronunciation or grammar errors. Moreover, many L2 learners failed to fully acquire many aspects of the target language available to which they were exposed in the classroom (Nassaji & Fotos, 2011). Therefore, the analysis of the effectiveness of communicative approaches in promoting all aspects of language learning (e.g., accuracy) has moved the pendulum in the direction of including grammar in L2 classrooms. This move has not meant a return to Grammar Translation, but, rather, has taken the shape of what it is known as **focus on form (FonF)** instruction.

Focus on form is a type of grammar instruction that directs L2 learners' attention to language forms in the context of meaningful communication.

Focus on form is different from **focus on forms,** which represents how grammar is traditionally taught. Focus on Forms is based on the assumption that language is a discrete series of grammatical forms that will be acquired in a prescribed sequence.

One example of a FonF activity is a task in which students compare two universities. After reading a description of the two universities provided by the teacher, students discuss their characteristics and record the information on task sheets. Then, they are instructed to write sentences comparing the universities according to the features they have described (e.g., *University A has more undergraduate majors than University B*). Students are not explicitly taught comparative structures at any point during the task, but they have to use comparative forms to complete it. Afterward, their instructor teaches a lesson on comparatives, and students rewrite incorrect sentences, complete more production exercises, and read stories that contain many instances of the comparative form.

Grammar as a Skill

According to Purpura (2004), grammatical ability or skill is defined as the production of grammatical knowledge in a meaningful and accurate way. It is a combination of grammatical knowledge and strategic competence. Grammatical knowledge is a set of grammatical forms and meanings, readily accessible in language use. For example, when learners see the *–ed* at the end of a verb, they recognize this grammatical form as the marker for the simple past tense. They also recognize the meaning attached to this form, which is an action that happened in the past. Strategic competence is defined as a set of metacognitive (evaluating, planning) and cognitive (clarifying, connecting) strategies. Figure 11.1 illustrates the components of grammatical ability.

As is the case with other language skills, grammatical ability is assessed in formal (language proficiency tests) and informal (provision of correction in class) ways. Grammatical performance, as illustrated in Figure 11.2, is the observable expression of grammatical ability in situations where language is used.

Figure 11.1: Grammatical Ability

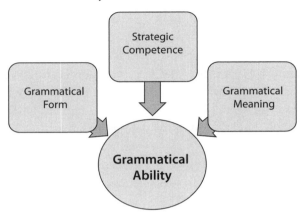

Figure 11.2: Grammatical Performance

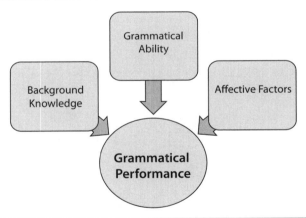

However, as shown in Figure 11.2, other factors contribute to an accurate display of grammatical ability, including background knowledge and affective factors. Suppose we consider a 5th grade student in Bulgaria is at high level of proficiency in spoken English. He started learning English in kindergarten and, over the years, has interacted with several native speakers of English who have been employed by his school to teach English classes. As a result, he uses conversational English well and virtually error-free. However, one day, his English teacher asks him to participate in a class activity where he has to study a map and then give directions based on it. He is not familiar with using or reading maps as he has lived all his life in the same city. As a result, he gets confused and makes grammar errors in his oral response. Because of nervousness (affective factors) and unfamiliarity with map usage (background knowledge), he is unable to show his true grammatical ability.

Teaching Grammar Structures: A Tri-Dimensional Model

Earlier chapters have illustrated that, traditionally, grammar has been viewed as a set of rules to be memorized by L2 learners with the ultimate purpose of improving their L2 proficiency. For many L2 learners, knowing the grammar rules well had meant knowing the language well. However, a solid knowledge of L2 grammar rules does not automatically equal solid L2 proficiency. Because of this gap between knowledge of grammar and its successful use, there has been a change in the way L2 teachers perceive grammar instruction. Figure 11.1 identified grammatical ability as having three components: form, meaning, and strategic competence. Grammar is no longer seen as a set of rules or forms that have to be studied and memorized by L2 learners. Rather, it is a language skill, just like listening, speaking, reading, or writing. From simply studying grammar, we have moved to practicing grammar in use.

Grammatical structures have gone through the same transformation. From the simple presentation of rules, many grammar classes are teaching L2 learners how to use the grammatical structure they are studying. Presenting a model that goes beyond form, Larsen-Freeman (2003) created a **tri-dimensional model of grammar structures** by adding two more dimensions: meaning and use, as shown in Figure 11.3. For example, let's suppose that an L2 learner says this sentence to a friend: *He must help her with this assignment.* The statement is correct from a grammatical standpoint but a bit unnatural because it sounds strong and formal when the intention of being strong and formal was not there. This implies that, when studying L2 grammar, L2 learners should take all three dimensions into account if they want to avoid making mistakes from a sociolinguistic or appropriateness perspective.

Figure 11.3: A Tri-Dimensional Model of Grammatical Structures

World leaders **must take** action to stop
the loss of innocent lives.

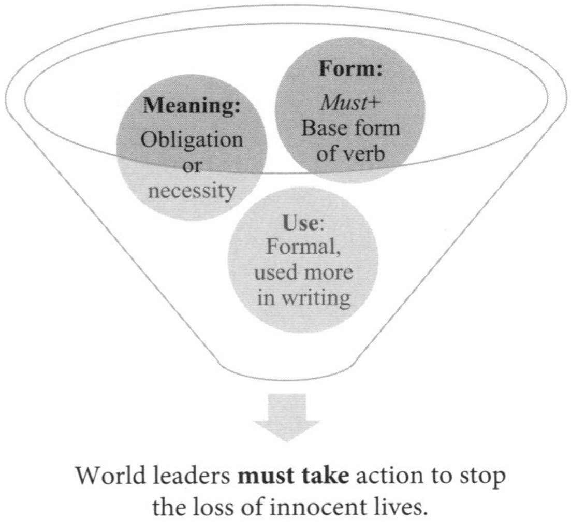

Grammar in the Classroom

Grammar is the systematic glue that holds everything together (Folse, 2009). Grammar can be part of Listening, Speaking, Reading, or Writing courses, or it can be taught as a stand-alone class. For both formats, L2 teachers may present new grammar structures either explicitly or implicitly.

The purposes of **explicit grammar teaching** are to introduce a new grammar structure in a direct manner, to provide guided instruction for understanding the new structure, and to allow learners to master the new grammar structure through practice. In an explicit presentation, L2 teachers begin by telling students what the grammar structure in focus is. Then, they give ample explanations focusing on form, meaning, and usage, along with modeling the process of how to use the grammar structure. The last step of an explicit presentation involves L2 teachers guiding students with hands-on application and practice of the grammar structure in various language situations.

To exemplify these steps, in an explicit presentation, an L2 teacher starts by stating the grammar focus: "Today we are going to learn about regular simple past tense." Teachers can write examples of the structure on the board or refer students to a grammar chart or box in the textbook. For example:

> *I walked to school yesterday.*
>
> *You walked to school yesterday.*
>
> *She walked to school yesterday.*
>
> *We walked to school yesterday.*
>
> *You walked to school yesterday.*
>
> *They walked to school yesterday.*

The L2 teacher models the structure by reading the sentences on the board or in the textbook and then explains the form, meaning, and use. Next, the L2 teacher moves to practice. One activity that can be used to practice past tense is called Last Time. L2 students sit in a circle with a set of action flashcards (*play, cook, watch,* and so on) in the middle. One student picks up a card and makes a sentence using the structure, *The last time I ___ was ___.* Some examples they can come up with are: *The last time I played soccer was last summer, The last time I watched TV was yesterday evening,* or *The last time I cooked was two days ago.* If the sentence is grammatically correct, the student keeps the card. If it is not, the card is returned to the set. The next student picks up a card and the activity continues until all the cards have been claimed. The student with the most cards wins.

Explicit grammar teaching is teacher centered in the beginning and gradually moves toward more student independence. In terms of advantages, some L2 learners might prefer a more structured approach where grammar rules are stated clearly. However, explicit teaching relies a lot on rule memorization and doesn't offer many opportunities for communicative and contextualized learning.

Explicit grammar teaching is not the only way to teach grammar. Grammar can also be presented implicitly. The L2 teacher may start with examples that contain the target grammar structure. Grammar rules are then inferred from the examples presented. The purposes of **implicit** (or deductive) **grammar teaching** are to move from a teacher-centered to a more student-centered introduction of new grammar structures, to emphasize the teaching of grammar with examples and not with memorization, and to allow students to create their own systems for understanding rules instead of relying on rote learning.

In an implicit grammar presentation, the L2 teacher typically begins by introducing the target structure in a meaningful context using examples and avoiding grammar explanations. The presentation context could be based on a visual such as a photo or an illustration in the textbook, or on the teacher's or students' own experiences. For example, the L2 teacher could bring a photo that shows the downtown area of a city now and 20 years ago and then ask students to compare the two using *is* and *was* to differentiate between the present and the past forms of the verb *to be*.

After the L2 learners are aware of the difference between present and past forms of *be* and state the rule, the L2 teacher could employ an activity to check whether the students understand the grammar rule. An example of an activity is: The teacher brings two pictures. The first, labeled **Before,** shows a man dressed as a waiter; the other, labeled **Now,** shows the same man dressed as a doctor. The teacher makes statements like these and the students say yes or no.

Teacher: He is a waiter. (No)

Teacher: He was a waiter. (Yes)

Teacher: He was a doctor. (No)

Teacher: He is a doctor. (Yes)

Next, the teacher asks the students to write statements based on the picture. For example, *He is a doctor now. He was a waiter before.*

Similar to explicit grammar teaching, the implicit approach has both advantages and disadvantages. In terms of advantages, implicit grammar teaching offers more context for L2 learning and is more authentic. Nevertheless, it may seem less structured than a more explicit approach at times. In addition, L2 learners may have a hard time inferring the grammar rules in the implicit approach.

According to Savage, Bitterlin, and Price (2010), three learner variables can influence L2 teachers' decision whether to teach grammar explicitly or implicitly. The first variable is **language level.** Lower-level learners may not know enough English to be able to understand the explanation. An explicit presentation that relies on use of grammatical terminology is probably less effective with those learners. The second variable is **previous formal L2 learning experiences.** Learners with limited formal or classroom-based experiences may not have a deep knowledge of grammatical terms (e.g., verb tense, adverb, or clause). On the other hand, L2 learners who have studied English in their countries through Grammar Translation may think that they are not learning English if they are exposed to a more implicit teaching. As a result, they may become demotivated if they are not given a formal explanation of a new grammar pattern. The third variable is represented by **learner goals for studying English.** Some L2 learners' main goal is survival in a new environment or finding a job. These learners want to be able to communicate in English, but they do not necessarily want or need to know grammar rules. An implicit presentation may be more appropriate for these students. However, L2 learners with academic goals or those who have jobs requiring writing skills need to learn grammar more explicitly than learners with non-academic goals. For those L2 learners, an explicit approach is recommended.

The Purposes of Grammar in the Language Classroom

In many educational environments and language institutes, L2 grammar is taught as a stand-alone class. Other language schools infuse grammar in their classes and do not have a separate L2 Grammar class. Some L2 teachers present grammar explicitly, while others prefer a more implicit presentation. Regardless of the approach taken, grammar has a well-defined place in language classrooms. Savage et al. (2010) have identified three purposes of grammar: as an enabling skill, a motivator, and a resource for learners' self-correction.

As an enabling skill, the accurate application of grammar knowledge allows the development of competence in listening, speaking, reading, and writing in the L2. When an incorrect application of grammar rules occurs, communication may be broken. For example, one typical error L2 learners make is the incorrect interpretation of present perfect. In many instances, when responding to a *How long have you. . .* type of question, L2 learners may use either the simple present or past tense, as in *I am married for two years* or *I worked there for five years.* When processing this response, listeners wonder whether the respondent is still married or working at the same place. Correct application of grammar rules, therefore, enables learners to be effective communicators.

The presence of a solid grammar component in language programs may increase motivation for many L2 learners. There are students who have learned a second language in their home country and identify grammar knowledge as paramount for the improvement of their language proficiency. For these students, the inclusion of direct or indirect grammar teaching in L2 classes may increase their motivation for attending those courses. Grammar can act as a motivator for other categories of students. For example, there are L2 learners who acquired language in a more naturalistic way, through interactions with native speakers or exposure to pop culture. Because their accuracy is many times less than adequate, they recognize the importance of having a good command of L2 structural organization. These students are very interested in improving their L2 accuracy, so the inclusion of a grammar component in their language program has the potential to motivate them to attend L2 classes.

Grammar teaching can also help L2 learners develop the important skill of correcting their own errors in speaking or writing. This ability is crucial for L2 learners, especially in situations where they cannot take advantage of teacher-generated corrective feedback. The development of self-monitoring skills leads to independence and self-sufficiency, which is what teachers want to occur when their L2 learners leave the classroom—the ability to improve their language proficiency on their own using the skills they have acquired in class.

Designing a Grammar Activity

When teaching grammar, either as a separate skill or included in the other language skills, L2 teachers often wonder about what approach they should use in grammar instruction. The beginning of this chapter discussed how the grammar pendulum has swung widely from a very grammar-focused approach to a grammar-free orientation that has CLT. Table 11.1 looks at these two methods and their inclusion or exclusion in grammar instruction.

For L2 instructors, the best course of action would be a combination of effective elements selected from different methodologies. Grammar Translation represents the Focus on Forms approach, where the assumption is that language can be learned by acquiring a series of grammatical forms. Contrastively, CLT is more focused on meaning, where learners are seen as able to analyze grammar structures inductively and create their own grammatical system. FonF takes the positive aspects of the two approaches and proposes a new pedagogy where the learner's

Table 11.1: Comparing Grammar Translation and Communicative Language Teaching

Method	Characteristics
Grammar Translation	Grammar is taught explicitly. Special emphasis is placed on grammar forms. There is little communicative practice. Reading and translation are the two most important class activities.
Communicative Language Teaching	Focus on communication is at the expense of grammar. Emphasis is on meaningful interaction. Contextualized materials are used. Accuracy may suffer as a result of the emphasis placed on fluency.

attention is directed to grammatical forms in the context of meaningful communication (Long, 1991; Nassaji & Fotos, 2011). In addition to FonF, grammar teachers need to design activities that include form, meaning, and use as well as utilize the learner's listening, speaking, reading, and writing skills.

The Structure of Grammar Activities

Compared to the other four skills presented in this book, which included a pre-, during-, and post-type of sequence, grammar activities follow a slightly different order. First, the grammar instructor presents the target grammar structure in a meaningful context. Next, the instructor provides learners with an activity where they practice the form, meaning, and use of the target grammar structure. The last step is an activity where the teacher assesses and diagnoses learners' active understanding and application of meaning, form, and use of the target grammar structure. Sometimes, the instructor may prefer a more inductive form of teaching. In that case, the explicit listing of the form and rules associated with a specific grammatical structure can be done as an activity performed by students at the end of class. An example of a grammar activity associated with the present and past forms of verbs is shown in Figure 11.4.

Content Selection in Grammar Classes

When selecting what should be included in their grammar classes, L2 instructors could first look at the sub-skills of grammar. For example, Virginia's Department of Education provides a list of **grammar sub-skills** ("English Standards of Learning," 2010) arranged in the order of instructional emphasis, from the most repeatedly emphasized structures to the least repeatedly emphasized ones:

► punctuation (commas to indicate interrupters, conjunctions, hyphens to divide words at the end of a line, capitalization of proper nouns and the pronoun *I*, apostrophes, quotation marks with dialogue)

► singular and plural forms for nouns and pronouns

► past and present verb tense

► subject-verb and noun-pronoun agreement

► singular/plural possessives

► adjective and adverb comparisons

► consistent verb tense use across paragraphs

► modifiers, standard coordination, and subordination in complete sentences

► knowledge of the eight parts of speech and their functions in sentences

► use of comparative and superlative degrees in adverbs and adjectives

Figure 11.4:   The Structure of a Grammar Activity

Step 1: Present grammar structure in a meaningful context

The instructor draws a timeline:

```
  2009         Now
-----X------------X-----------
Student      English teacher
```

The instructor uses the timeline to create sentences about life experiences, such as:

> *I am an English teacher now. I was a student before.*

The instructor writes these sentences on the board.

Step 2: Practice meaning, form, and use.

Then, the instructor asks students about their experiences. For example, the instructor can ask:

> *What is your job now? What was your job before? What was your job in 2013?*

In addition, the instructor adds new dates on the timeline and asks students if each date added is now or before.

Step 3: Assess/diagnose understanding of meaning, form, and use.

Students listen to a short passage where a student named Tony talks about various events in his life. Students are asked to write N (Now) or B (Before) next to each item in the handout (or this can be done on the board or OHP).

Listening Passage:

> *Hi. My name is Tony. I was a banker not too long ago, but I've decided to change careers. I am a lawyer now. When I was a banker, I wasn't very happy, but I am very happy now. I was rich, but I didn't feel my life had a purpose. I am a lawyer now, and I help people with money problems get back on their feet.*

The handout given to students includes this list:

Banker
Lawyer
Happy
Not happy
Rich
No purpose
Help people

Finally, as a homework assignment, students are asked to write a paragraph about present and past personal circumstances.

In addition to including the sub-skills of grammar in their teaching and assessment, L2 teachers need to keep in mind that the best materials are authentic materials. Authentic materials allow learners to identify the most commonly used grammatical structures in speaking and writing. Moreover, authentic materials reveal that grammatical structures used in written and spoken discourse may differ radically. In adult conversational ESL classes, the past perfect tense is seldom used (Lane & Lange, 1999). In spoken English, we say *I talked to him before I went out* instead of *I had talked to him before I went out.* For L2 learners who need academic English, L2 instructors should select materials that emphasize the structures that are common and frequent in written English. Conversely, if learners need to gain fluency in speaking and are not interested in the written aspect of English, grammar materials should be selected from radio and TV sources, which provice some of the best examples of authentic materials.

Frequency is another important criterion in selection of grammar materials. **Lexical frequency** involves cases where words are used with certain grammatical structures. **Form frequency** involves cases where some grammar forms that express a function are more commonly used than others that fulfill the same purpose. For example, in terms of lexical frequency in speaking, the verb *know* accounts for 25 percent of the simple intransitive verb examples in Switchboard, as in Example 1. Switchboard is a corpus, or collection, of telephone conversations between strangers collected in the early 1990s. The second most common verb form, *mean*, as in Example 2, accounts for another 6 percent of the data. Other discourse-related structures, such as in Example 3, account for lesser percentages of the data (Roland, Dick, & Elman, 2007).

Example 1:   a. I don't know. (Switchboard)

b. You know, hobbies. (Switchboard)

Example 2:   I mean, I've never seen two cats so close. (Switchboard)

Example 3:   I see. (Switchboard)

Form frequency can take many aspects. Biber and Conrad (2010) looked at the data analyses in **corpus linguistics** (a method of linguistic study that uses a collection of natural or authentic texts known as corpus) and found several noteworthy frequency-related facts. One finding is that the progressive aspect is more common in conversation than in writing. However, grammar teachers should be careful because that does not mean that they should focus exclusively on progressive tenses, especially present progressive. The simple aspect verb phrases are more than 20 times as common as progressives in conversation. Moreover, in addition to being less frequent, the progressive aspect is used for special effects, usually focusing on the fact that an event is in progress or about to take place, as in *What are they doing?*

Another aspect of frequency is discussed by Savage et al. (2010) in their analysis of frequency of use of grammatical structures when they express the same language function. For example, future time can be expressed as:

> *I am going to go to concert this Saturday. (be + going to + VERB)*
>
> *I'll go to a concert this Saturday. (will + VERB)*
>
> *I'm going to a concert this Saturday (be + VERB + -ing)*

Their recommendation for grammar teachers is to teach the first structure first (*be + going to + VERB*) because it is the most common way to express future time according to corpus-based research. The second structure (*will + VERB*) should be taught in the context of expressing future intention, while the third one, very similar in structure to present continuous (*be + VERB + -ing*) should be introduced only after L2 learners have learned to use it to express actions happening now.

To sum up, L2 instructors should rely on authentic materials when selecting content for grammar class. These materials could either supplement or even replace L2 grammar textbooks. In terms of the focus, they should use research findings from corpus linguistics and pay special attention to frequency.

Students' Performance in Grammar Classes

L2 learners may participate in activities that focus only on one grammatical structure or in multi-form activities that promote overall accuracy. L2 performance in grammar-based activities generally target either one grammar item or multiple grammar items.

An example of a one-grammar item that uses speaking as a vehicle for grammar instruction and practice is shown. The target grammar structure is the present tense continuous.

Teacher: What is she doing? (pointing to a picture of a woman playing tennis)

Student A: She is playing tennis.

Teacher: What is she doing? (pointing to a picture of a woman playing soccer)

Student B: She is playing soccer.

This exercise is an example of an accuracy exercise with multiple grammar items.

Teacher:	You have one minute to answer this question: What do you miss most about your home country and why? While you speak, I will record your answer on tape and then play it back to you. If you make a grammar error in your answer, I'll stop the tape and give you a chance to self-correct.

After exploring the three elements of designing grammar activities (structure, content, and student performance), let's consider a few examples of activities. Because this book advocates combining form with meaning, the activities will all be eclectic in nature.

Grammar Activities for the Classroom

These grammar-focused activities are all examples of FonF instruction. In FonF Grammar classes, L2 learners are made aware of the grammatical forms when they occur in lessons that emphasize meaning and communication. FonF is different from both Focus on Forms, concerned only with the explicit description of grammar, and focus on meaning, concentrated only on meaning with no attention to form at all. The four activities progress from more structural practice to more communicative practice and include an eclectic activity.

Activity 11.1: *I Would If I Could*

Grammar-Based (Structure Practice)

Rationale: This activity is based on the review of real conditional clauses and the introduction of unreal conditionals in the present. The two structures are contrasted in the teacher's presentation of the two types of the conditional and in students' practice. Grammar is presented deductively, from language sample to targeted focus on grammar structures. This activity emphasizes L2 learners practicing those structures in controlled interactions.

Objectives: Review conditional clauses and practice writing unreal conditional clauses

Pre-Planning

Pre-knowledge: Students should have been introduced to real conditional clauses (*I will... if I can...*) before this grammar activity.
Materials needed: Cue cards with real and unreal situations
Language level: Intermediate
Recommended age group: Young adults to adults

Procedures

Review of grammar structure: The teacher discusses different situations to review the tenses used in real conditionals and introduces the tenses used in the present unreal conditionals (*I would…if I could…*).

Teacher: This year, I want to go to New York. If I go to New York, I will visit the Statue of Liberty. I don't think I have enough money to go to Boston. However, if I went to Boston, I would walk the Freedom Trail.

The teacher writes the two examples on the board, underlining the verb tenses used in each:

Real: If I go to New York, I will visit the Statue of Liberty.

Unreal: If I went to Boston, I would walk the Freedom Trail.

Practice: The teacher gives the students these cue cards:

Real	Unreal
Travel to Vermont/Go skiing.	*Travel to Florida/Go to the beach.*
Be late to a concert/Be seated at intermission.	*Be early to a concert/Get good seats.*
Take an early flight/Get to Los Angeles in the afternoon.	*Take a late flight/Get to Los Angeles at night.*
Eat too much sugar/ Have health problems.	*Eat a lot of fruit/Have fewer health problems.*

In pairs, students produce sentences in written form in which they practice the correct use of conditionals, such as:

If Tom eats too much sugar, he will have health problems.
However, if he ate a lot of fruit, he would have fewer health problems.

Evaluation

The teacher takes each element in the cue card and asks students to produce a sentence using the appropriate conditional clause.

Homework: The teacher asks the students to respond to these questions in writing:

What will you do if you go to college in the United States?

What would you do if your parents won ten million dollars in the lottery?

What will happen if you don't come to class tomorrow?

What would you have done if you hadn't come to study in the U.S?

What would you do if you won free air travel for a month?

────────────── **Activity 11.2: Interviewing Classmates** ──────────────

Communicative Product Grammar

Rationale: The purpose of this activity is for L2 learners to use the present and past tenses (simple aspect) accurately. Unlike the previous activity, where the language generated could be controlled with the use of cue cards, this interview-based activity increases the amount of meaningful communication by asking L2 learners to talk about their own personal experiences and opinions. The open-question interview format makes the activity less controlled in terms of what language structures could be generated by L2 learners. Therefore, the instructor needs to make sure that accurate present and past tense structures are used by L2 learners by closely monitoring their conversations and taking notes on and correcting their grammar accuracy.

Objectives: Practice the simple present and simple past through oral interviews and written recordings.

Pre-Planning

Pre-knowledge: The students need to be familiar with the present and past tense (simple)
Materials needed: Interview forms
Language level: Beginning
Recommended age level: Adults

Procedures

Review of present tense and past tense (simple aspect for both) by discussing the interview sheet.

	Name	Name	Name
1. Why did you come to this country?	1.	1.	1.
2. What did you do in your country?	2.	2.	2.
3. Where do you live in the United States?	3.	3.	3.
4. Why do you live there?	4.	4.	4.

Practice: The students work in small groups asking and answering questions. They use the interview chart provided by the instructor to record their answers. Then, using the information collected in the chart, students write sentences and paragraphs about their classmates.

Evaluation

To assess grammar accuracy, the instructor asks students to write three sentences about their classmates on the board. Under the instructor's guidance, the class discusses the accuracy of the verb tenses produced by learners. In addition, at the end of class, the instructor collects L2 learners' individually generated written materials to assess whether the two verb tenses were used correctly.

Homework: The instructor asks students to interview one person outside the classroom and write a paragraph about the person they have interviewed.

————— Activity 11.3: Birthday Party Advice —————

Communicative Process Grammar

Rationale: Similar to the previous activity, the purpose of this activity is for L2 learners to practice grammatical structures in a highly communicative environment, with an emphasis on personal experiences. The focus of this activity is to use modals *could* and *should* accurately in the context of making suggestions and giving advice. Because of varying degrees of strength associated with modals (e.g., *must* versus *should*), the activity creates opportunities for L2 learners to use modal verbs not only accurately but also in socially appropriate ways.

Objectives: Use the modals *could* and *should* accurately by making suggestions and giving advice.

Pre-Planning

Pre-knowledge: The students need to be familiar with advice columns and modal verbs.
Materials needed: A handout with the description of a problem (Dear Abby type)
Language level: Advanced
Recommended age group: Ages 15+

Procedures

The instructor reviews grammatical structures used in making suggestions and giving advice, emphasizing *could* and *should*. The instructor asks students what they *could* and *should* do in different situations to remind students about the form, meaning, and use associated with *could* and *should*. For example:

> *I can't find my phone! What should I do?*
>
> *The cable went off. What do we do?*

Practice: Students are presented with this problem, in the form of a letter written to an advice column:

Dear Abby:

I have a very good friend who likes to look good. He spends way too much money on clothes. Every time I see him he wears something new, and I don't think I've ever seen him wearing something twice. Last week, he came to me for a loan telling me he is broke. He knows he spends too much on clothes, and he asked me to help him with his spending habits. Do you have any advice for him? What could he do?

The instructor distributes the handout with the reading passage and asks L2 learners to work in small groups and discuss the problem stated. Then, they present their answers to the rest of the class as a response to the letter. The instructor writes the suggestions and advice on the boards and the class can then vote on the best suggestion and advice.

Evaluation

After student presentations, the instructor discusses the accuracy of their language and any language-related issues. While the students are talking, the instructor should move around the room and make sure they are on task. The instructor also notes grammar or vocabulary problems students might have. Students also hand in their answers for review.

Homework: Students write a response to the request for advice:

Dear Abigail,

I have been invited to my friend's family for a birthday party. The invitation said "no gifts." Should I bring a gift anyways? I thought you've always needed to bring gifts to birthday parties. Any ideas of what I should do would be much appreciated.

Signed,

Friend in Need

———— Activity 11.4: *I Can Do It!* ————

Eclectic Approach to Grammar

Rationale: Many instructors prefer using various and mixed approaches in their design of the syllabus and curriculum. This activity takes an eclectic approach to grammar because it focuses on grammar and communicative skills through discussing personal skills. This activity is perfect for students to get to know each other. This eclectic activity focuses on language used in a real-world setting and includes a strong grammatical focus.

Objectives: Identify and use the modal verbs *can, should,* and *would* appropriately.

Pre-Planning

Pre-knowledge: The students should have been introduced to the concept of modal verbs and other verb forms used in discussing personal activities.
Materials needed: Paper
Language level: Intermediate
Recommended age group: Young adults and adults

Procedures

The teacher introduces the topic and shares a skill, such as *I can fly a plane*. The teacher reminds students about the function of modal verbs and asks them about their prior knowledge of the three modals—*can, should,* and *could*. The teacher then writes the three modals on the board—*can, should, could*—with some example sentences:

What Can You Do?	can	should	could
play the piano	I **can play** *the piano.*	I **should play** *the piano every day.*	I **could play** *the piano if I took lessons.*
drive a car			
ride a bike			
play soccer			

The teacher asks students if they understand the difference between the modals and asks them to create a series of their own sentences (using each modal) that describes personal skills.

Share: The teacher asks students to partner with a student to share what the student can do. Students write what they hear so that they can share with the entire class what their partner *can, should,* and *would* like to do.

Evaluation

The teacher checks the answers the students provided during the sharing portion of the activity. The teacher should provide feedback during this time to ensure that students are using the forms correctly by writing further samples on the board.

Homework: Ask students to interview a family member or friend about what that person *can, should,* and *could* do. Ask them to write the information and bring it to class to share.

Assessing Grammar

In large-scale assessments, grammar may be tested in a separate section as in the paper-and-pencil (PBT) version of the TOEFL®. Other language tests have no grammar section, but grammar is evaluated in speaking and writing responses, as is the case with the newest version on the TOEFL iBT®. The evaluation rubric for the independent speaking tasks in the TOEFL iBT® contains a section called Language Use, which focuses on grammar and vocabulary evaluation.

Grammar instructors need to be familiar with the format of existing large-scale assessment instruments and use similar formats to familiarize their L2 learners with the type of test items commonly used in standardized tests. This does not mean that instructors cannot and should not create their own test items. Instructors should generate their own testing materials to evaluate the quality of their instruction while taking into consideration that knowledge of standardized test items is critical for many L2 learners who must take these exams for academic or job purposes.

There have been many attempts to categorize the types of test items. One categorization that is very beneficial to L2 teachers is the one created by Purpura (2004). This categorization organizes test items according to the type of response. Consequently, there are selected response, limited production, and extended production items in his classification as seen in Table 11.2.

Let's illustrate each type with an example.

Table 11.2: Types of Grammar Test Items

Type of Test Items	Examples
Selected response	multiple choice true/false matching discrimination
Limited production	cloze short-answer dictation dialogue completion
Extensive production	summaries essays role-plays stories

Selected Response Items

Multiple choice items are examples of selected response. For example, test takers are presented with an item that contains one grammatical error and are required to identify the error. One example of this type of test item is shown in Figure 11.5.

The test item could be changed by introducing two pictures and one sentence. One issue with discrimination tasks is that low-proficiency test-takers can obtain high scores by simply guessing.

Limited Production Items

One example of a limited production item is dialogue completion. Dialogue completion items are short exchanges or dialogues with either an entire turn or part of a turn deleted. L2 learners are expected to complete the exchange with an utterance that is not only grammatically accurate but also grammatically meaningful. Figure 11.6 provides an example of a dialogue completion task.

Figure 11.5:   Multiple Choice Grammar Test Item

Directions: Circle the letter corresponding to the error.

John Wayne was an <u>act</u> best <u>known</u> for his demeanor, including his <u>distinctive</u> calm voice and <u>walk</u>.
       A   B   C   D

Figure 11.6:   Dialogue Completion Test Item

Directions: Complete the conversation between two friends.

Jenna: Why are you always complaining about your parents?

Kim: That's because_____.

Jenna: Why don't you try telling them how you feel about it?

Extended Production Items

One example of an extended production item is an information-gap item. This grammar test item presents L2 learners with two or more sets of partially complete information and asks them to obtain one complete set of information through negotiated interaction and feedback. Figure 11.7 illustrates an information-gap test item.

This chapter reviewed the history and place of grammar in the second and foreign language curriculum and discussed as the purposes of including grammar in language programs. From a pedagogical perspective, it also suggested what L2 instructors should take into account when designing grammar activities and assessments. Grammar is perhaps more challenging to teach and assess than the other four language skills. The challenge stems from the fact that some L2 students may have little knowledge of their L1 grammar and do not understand grammar terminology. Conversely, some L2 learners understand their L1 grammar well and strongly believe that learning L2 grammar is simply memorizing grammatical forms. However, when L2 instructors teach and assess grammar, they teach and assess not only form but also meaning and use. Therefore, it is very important that L2 instructors understand the importance of providing L2 learners with a meaningful context when they are either teaching and assessing L2 grammar.

Figure 11.7:   Information-Gap Test Item

Directions: Work with a partner. Student A looks at the information on New York. Student B looks at information on Boston. Each needs the other person's information to prepare a report on U.S. cities. Ask each other questions from the cues and record your answers.

Information Card

Name:

Year it was settled:

Location:

Number of inhabitants:

Information Card Student B	**Information Card Student A**
Name: Boston	Name: New York City
Year it was settled: 1630	Year it was settled: 1624
Location: Massachusetts	Location: New York
Population: 625,087	Population: 8,244,910

Summarizing Statements

1. Grammar can be taught as a stand-alone class or as an enabling skill in Listening, Speaking, Reading, and Writing classes.

2. Grammar pedagogy has shifted from Focus-on-Forms to Focus-on-Form, an approach where grammatical forms are presented in the context of meaningful communication.

3. When teaching grammar structures, L2 teachers should give equal attention to form, meaning, and use.

4. Frequency should be an important criterion in the design or selection of grammar materials.

5. Grammar production is always included in the evaluation of L2 proficiency in both large-scale and classroom-based assessments.

REFLECTION AND APPLICATION

1. Is a more communicatively focused approach to teaching grammar appropriate in an EFL setting, given its constraints related to the opportunities L2 learners have when it comes to using English?

2. How do you or would you treat grammar errors in your classroom? What corrective techniques do you or would you use more often? Do you have any preference for correcting one type of error more often than other—for example, subject-verb agreement versus noun plurals?

3. As TESOL professionals, how can we create grammar activities that work with different learner proficiency levels? Create a grammar activity that can be adapted for beginning, intermediate, and advanced L2 learners. Detail those level-specific adaptations.

REFERENCES

Biber, D., & Conrad, S. (2010). *Corpus linguistics and grammar teaching.* White Plains, NY: Pearson Education.

Ellis, R., Basturkmen, H., & Loewen, S. (2002). Doing focus-on-form. *System, 30,* 419–432.

Folse, K. (2009). *Keys to teaching grammar to English language learners.* Ann Arbor: University of Michigan Press.

Lane, J., & Lange, E. (1999). *Writing clearly: An editing guide.* Boston: Heinle & Heinle.

Larsen-Freeman, D. (2003). *Teaching language: From grammar to grammaring.* Boston: Heinle/Cengage.

Long, M. (1991). Focus on form: A design feature in language teaching methodology. In K. de Bot, R. Ginsberg, & C. Kramsch (Eds.), *Foreign language research in cross-cultural perspective* (pp. 39–52). Amsterdam: John Benjamins.

Nassaji, H., & Fotos, S. (2011). *Teaching grammar in second language classrooms: Integrating form-focused instruction in communicative context.* New York: Routledge.

Purpura, J.E. (2004). *Assessing grammar.* Cambridge, U.K.: Cambridge University Press.

Roland, D., Dick, F., & Elman, J. L. (2007). Frequency of basic English grammatical structures: A corpus analysis. *Journal of Memory and Language, 57*(3), 348–379.

Savage, K. L., Bitterlin, G., & Price, D. (2010). *Grammar matters: Teaching grammar in adult ESL programs.* Cambridge, U.K.: Cambridge University Press.

Virginia Department of Education. (2010). *English standards of learning.* Retrieved from www.doe.virginia.gov/testing/sol/standards_docs/english/2010/progression_charts/grammar_skills_by_grade.pdf

Chapter 12 ▲

Culture Activities and Assessment Techniques

Previous chapters have focused on the teaching and assessment of listening, speaking, reading, writing, and grammar. However, is a solid knowledge of grammar and vocabulary, for example, sufficient for achieving a high proficiency in a second language? Research has shown that language and culture are closely related and that learning a second language implies learning a second culture. For some researchers, the view that culture and language are inseparable has led to the use of the term *sociocultural* instead of *sociolinguistic* in their discussion of communicative competence, as discussed in Chapter 3 in this book (Savignon, 2010; Savignon & Sysoyev, 2005). Consequently, we cannot separate the two without losing the significance of either language or culture (Brown, 2014). In terms of the presence of culture in language classroom, Moore (2006) found that at least 80 percent of the L2 teachers in her study reported they were teaching culture for more than half of their instructional time. Undoubtedly, L2 teachers have begun to incorporate more culture in their classrooms, but is culture teaching a benefit or a detriment when it comes to its contribution to L2 acquisition? Before examining the effectiveness of integrating culture and language with the purpose of preparing L2 learners to be highly proficient, let's look first of what culture is and what its characteristics are.

Culture: Definition and Characteristics

The link between language and culture has captured the interest of many anthropologists and linguists. One of the reasons we use language is to communicate socially. All societies have developed a unique culture, which is expressed through language in most instances. Culture can be defined as a system of standards for perceiving, believing, evaluating, and acting (Goodenough,

1971). As noted by Adaskou, Britten, and Fahsi (1990), culture has many dimensions. It can have an aesthetic dimension, which encompasses the literature, film, and music of a specific group of people. This is also known as **culture with capital C.** Culture can also have a sociological dimension, known as **culture with small c,** consisting of the norms, customs, behaviors, and institutions of a country or group of people. In addition to those two dimensions, we also have the semantic dimension of culture, including the way in which a culture's conceptual system is embodied in a language. Finally, the pragmatic dimension contains the selection of language based on context appropriateness.

To characterize culture is to say that culture, very much like language, is dynamic, creative, and continuous. Culture is also learned and shared (Lessow-Hurley, 2012). Like language, culture changes over time to meet changing circumstances and environments. Like language, culture is creative; it quickly adapts to societal changes. For example, today, as a result of a more women being in the workforce, different views exist regarding the abilities of women or the perception of family structure, as compared to 100 years ago. Even though dramatic changes can take place in a relatively short period of time, the new cultural concepts or systems contain elements of previous systems or traditions; culture is without a doubt continuous. Also, like language, culture is learned and is not genetically determined. Infants born in China and adopted by American parents will learn the language and culture of their adoptive country. In spite of their physical characteristics, they will be completely unable to communicate in and understand the language and culture of their biological parents. Finally, like language, culture is shared. Because it is *par excellence* a social product, culture needs shared assumptions to function.

Language and Culture: A Fundamental Connection

The strong relationship between language and culture is revealed when examining the two constructs in interaction with each other. Through language, people express their attitudes and points of view that are understood by their interlocutors because of a shared body of knowledge about the world. In other words, language expresses cultural reality. Language also embodies cultural reality. Members of a cultural group are not limited to only expressing their experience; they create experience through language as well. They give meaning to these new experiences through verbal and non-verbal aspects of language, experiences understandable to the group the speakers belong. Because language is a system of signs that is seen as having cultural value, we can say that language symbolizes cultural reality. Members of a cultural community identify themselves through language, thus making language a symbol of their cultural identity. If their language is ridiculed or prohibited, speakers perceive that as a rejection of their social group and their culture (Kramsch, 1998).

Perhaps the most relevant explanation of the relationship between language and culture is provided by the Sapir-Whorf Hypothesis. According to this hypothesis (Whorf, 1956):

> We dissect nature along lines laid down by our native languages. The categories and types that we isolate from the world of phenomena we do not find there because they stare every observer in the face; on the contrary, the world is presented in a kaleidoscopic flux of impressions which has to be organized by our minds—and this means largely by the linguistic systems in our minds. We cut nature up, organize it into concepts, and ascribe significances as we do, largely because we are parties to an agreement to organize it in this way—an agreement that holds throughout our speech community and is codified in the patterns of our language. The agreement is, of course, an implicit and unstated one, but its terms are absolutely obligatory; we cannot talk at all except by subscribing to the organization and classification of data which the agreement decrees. (pp. 213–214)

The hypothesis consists of two parts, linguistic relativity and linguistic determinism. Linguistic relativity assumes that culture is shaped by language while linguistic determinism states that language determines thought. One example that shows that language reflects culture is provided by the nomenclature for *camel* in the Somali language. To the Somali nomads, the camel has been traditionally the most important animal. The standing of a family in the community was often measured by the number of camels it owned. Not surprisingly, there are 46 different words that describe camels in the Somali language (Hassig & Latif, 2007). Here are some examples:

aaran—young camels who are no longer sucklings

awradhale—camel that always gives birth to he-camels

baarfuran—female camel that is not used as a pack camel

baarqab—stude camel

baloolley—she-camel without calf that will or will not give milk depending on her mood

caddaysimo—unloaded pack camel; unpoisoned arrow

caggabbaruur—lion cub; young camel

daandheer—strong camel of the herd

farruud or qarruud—mature male camels; elders

garuud—old male camels; old people

Moreover, each of these terms is explained through the use of separate words. One possible explanation for this lexical richness associated with *camel* is that camel is a central feature in the Somali culture. Therefore, for this culture, it is imperative that sufficient specialized vocabulary exists to specifically describe this concept.

The Influence of Culture on L2 Teaching and Learning

So far this discussion of culture has noted the strong connections between language and culture. Learning a new language arguably means learning a new culture. For L2 instruction, the culture of the target language is important, depending on the learning context. While the importance of culture in the language classroom might not be evident in cases where English is taught as a foreign language (EFL), the importance of culture becomes extremely clear when students learn ESL. In this learning context, English is not only the language of instruction but also the language of transaction outside the classroom. In ESL contexts, students learn or perfect their English in English-speaking countries and they have very limited occasions where they can use their native language instead of using English.

In ESL contexts, most learners find positive benefits in cross-cultural living and learning experiences. However, in many cases, learner expectations stemming from their native culture might be in stark contrast with the norms and behaviors of English. Hofstede (1986, 2011) outlined these mismatches in expectations by looking at the cultural norms and work-related values of different countries. To organize the differences he found, he used six different cultural dimensions.

The first dimension, **Power-Distance**, indicated the extent to which less powerful people in a culture accepted inequality of power. The second dimension, **Individualism,** separated cultures where people look primarily after their own interest and cultures where the needs of the group were more important than the needs of the individual. The third dimension, **Uncertainty Avoidance**, dealt with a culture's tolerance for uncertainty and ambiguity, as well as people's level of comfort in situations that were new and different from usual circumstances. The fourth dimension, **Masculinity**, measured the importance a culture placed on stereotypically masculine values such as assertiveness, power, and materialism. **Long-Term Orientation**, the fifth cultural dimension, described cultures with long-term orientation as being goal-focused and ones that consider time from a linear perspective; cultures with short-term orientation were more traditional and looked at time as circular, with the past and present interconnected. The final cultural dimension, represented by **Indulgence vs. Restraint**, measured the ability of a culture to satisfy the immediate needs and desires of its members. It is important to note that this model cannot and should not be indiscriminately applied to all cultures. Hofstede indicated that the cultural dimensions were only one possible framework that could be used to interpret cultural norms. His proposed dimensions cannot predict all individual behaviors of all members of a particular culture as they do not take into account individual personalities.

Table 12.1:   Differences in Teacher-Student and Student-Student Interaction

Individualist Perspective (U.S., Great Britain, etc.)	Collectivist Perspective (Venezuela, Pakistan, etc.)
One is never too old to learn.	Young people should learn. Adults cannot accept student roles.
Students are expected to learn how to learn.	Students are expected to learn how to do.
Students will speak up in class in response to general calls by the teacher.	Students will only speak up in class when called on personally by the teacher.
Confrontation in learning situations can be beneficial, and conflicts can be brought into the open.	Formal harmony in learning situations should be always maintained.
Education is a way of improving one's economic worth and self-respect based on ability and competence.	Education is a way of gaining prestige and joining a higher status group.
Teachers are expected to be strictly impartial.	Teachers are expected to give preferential treatment to some students based on ethnic affiliation or on recommendation by an influential entity.

For the first dimension, individualism, Hofstede found that countries such as the United States and Great Britain have very strong individualistic characteristics, whereas countries such as Venezuela or Pakistan have very strong collectivistic features. When it comes to classroom interactions, Table 12.1 shows clear differences between the expectations of students and teachers from individualist cultures on one hand, and the expectations of students and teachers from collectivist cultures on the other hand.

As a result of cultural differences between educators and learners, there is strong potential for classroom conflict because of the mismatch between teacher actions and student expectations. Before exploring the benefits and challenges of teaching culture explicitly in the second language classroom, let's look at several ways culture is reflected in the L2 curriculum.

Culture in the L2 Curriculum

When we look at the curricula of IEPs, we notice that the explicit teaching of culture is not typically included in the list of courses. That does not mean that L2 culture teaching is deliberately avoided by L2 teachers because, as we have noted, the teaching of language requires the teaching of culture to some degree, especially in an ESL setting. In some instances, however, culture is used as resource for teaching other language skills. For example, an IEP may offer a Communication in American Culture course, which may be focused on speaking and listening and aim to develop L2 students' communication skills for dealing with different aspects of daily life in American culture. In this course, L2 learners may discuss readings, participate in planned and unplanned conversations in class, watch topic-related videos, or listen to radio programs. They may also be asked to perform real-world tasks outside of class. Possible culture-related topics may include emergency situations, going to restaurants, traveling, shopping, and finding housing. Because L2 learners are encouraged to consider culture as an important component of successful communication, special attention should be given to language-use variations according to how formal the situation is and who the participants are.

Learning about the target culture can be part of the curriculum as an elective. For example, an IEP or any language learning entity may offer a Topics in American Culture course where the focus of the class is discussing current events. In this course, L2 students will be exposed to and gain a better understanding of certain aspects of American history and culture. The materials used in class may include news sources that focus on U.S. news or present the news with an American perspective. In-class activities may include the use of current news accounts via videos, radio, newspaper or online articles, group discussions, and group presentations.

In rare instances, culture learning can also be part of an L2 curriculum as a required course. For example, students may take an Idioms and Topics in American Culture class, which focuses on the relationship of American culture and language. This course is built on American idioms, one of the most tangible aspects of this relationship. In this class, L2 learners may explore various aspects of American culture through reading news articles, watching news programs, taking weekly field trips to local places of interest (such as a car dealership, a factory, a hospital, a park), reporting on cultural similarities and differences, and discussing observations from daily life. Some example of course objectives may include: interpret and accurately use common American idioms; identify common customs related to shopping, driving, and traveling; and identify historical events and attitudes that have influenced American language.

We have seen several ways in which L2 culture teaching and learning is present in the L2 curriculum. But how beneficial is this inclusion in terms of English language instruction? In other words, does an explicit focus on culture positively affect the language proficiency of L2 learners in ESL or EFL contexts?

The Benefits of Teaching Culture in the ESL/EFL Classroom

As discussed, without a doubt, there is a strong and documented connection between language and culture. In spite of this clear connection, some L2 instructors may consider other aspects of the language curriculum, such as vocabulary acquisition or grammar, more important. However, L2 teachers should make an effort to explicitly include culture in their classes for several reasons. First, the inclusion of culture could potentially help ESL/EFL learners avoid common stereotypes associated with the target language. For example, in social situations, refusing an invitation is not done directly in American English. U.S.-born English speakers might say, "Sorry, I have other plans" when they want to refuse an invitation. If the L2 learner is not aware of this indirectness, it may result in misunderstanding due to differing cultural norms rather than language usage.

Learning a new language does not mean understanding the culture of that language automatically. L2 instructors teach the sub-systems of language in a very direct manner and to assume that the teaching of culture in an explicit manner is not necessary actually denies the complex relationship between culture, language learning, and communication. Moreover, when L2 learners are exposed to the culture of the target language in class, they acquire the skills that will enable them to take control over their own learning and expand the context in which the second language they are studying occurs.

Based on a thorough research of the literature in the field, Genc and Bada (2005) list several benefits of explicitly incorporating culture in language courses. First, studying culture has the potential to positively affect the motivation of learners studying English. The more motivated the students are, the more likely they will achieve a high level of English proficiency. The inclusion of culture can increase student motivation because learners enjoy culturally based activities such as singing, dancing, or researching countries or people. This leads to another benefit of adding an explicit cultural dimension to English language classrooms. Culture makes the target language real and meaningful: Language learning is not only an exploration of grammar and syntax but also of worldviews and human behaviors. Culture helps learners relate the abstract knowledge of sounds and forms of English to real people and places.

Culture in the L2 classroom has a motivating and humanizing effect on the entire language learning process. It is important to note that, in many circumstances, the native culture of English learners may be different from the culture of the language they are acquiring. English is studied as a foreign language in many countries. It is very common for English learners in those circumstances to be culture-bound individuals who might have the tendency to make unfortunate decisions regarding the cultural characteristics of the language they are learning. Therefore, it is crucial L2 instructors explicitly introduce the culture of the target language and discuss similarities and differences between the native and the foreign cultures to avoid the negative impact of stereotyping on student motivation.

In addition to increasing motivation, cultural instruction has a positive effect on increasing language proficiency. Tsou (2005) conducted a study that examined the effect of cultural instruction on EFL elementary students in Taiwan. After one semester of explicit exposure to American culture, the students who received cultural instruction in the study increased their language proficiency significantly compared to the students who did not receive the treatment. Furthermore, students in the experimental group showed increased motivation toward English language learning.

The Challenges of Teaching Culture in the L2 Classroom

The teaching of culture in foreign language classes does have its challenges. English language teachers sometimes face negative consequences as a result of explicit culture-based instruction in the classroom. Culture-centered language classrooms require students to critically examine their own native culture and perhaps change some of the cultural assumptions they already bring to the English classroom. Students who learn a new language are expected to play not only a linguistic but also a cultural role: They are demanded to not only learn the formal structures of English but also study and understand the culture of the target language. Consequently, they might suffer from culture shock, which is defined as the stress a learner experiences as a result of the differences between native and target culture (Ellis, 1985). Additionally, they might create a third culture that is an artificial combination of native and target culture and has a utility in neither (Kramsch, 1993).

Opponents of cultural instruction in English courses have also noted other negative effects experienced by students inundated with English-related cultural information. Classroom strategies designed to reduce the cultural barriers between the native and target languages may be perceived by L2 learners as attempts to invalidate their own culture. As a consequence, students might develop hostility toward the target culture in an attempt to protect their native culture. It is important to note that many ESL and EFL textbooks present a cultural perspective that is materialistic and free from religious beliefs, which is often alien to the culture of many ESL and EFL students.

Sometimes EFL, and especially ESL, classroom activities and materials have the opposite effect on English learners. Instead of defending their own culture, learners might express a certain degree of dissatisfaction about their own culture and start to consider their native culture's practices as being inferior to those of the United States or the United Kingdom. It is important for the L2 instructor to make clear that teaching L2 culture should not be perceived as eliminating or demeaning the native culture.

Designing L2 Culture-Based Activities

To ensure that culture-oriented English classes foster cultural understanding and not cultural confrontation, ESL and EFL teachers need to be very careful in their selection and presentation of cultural elements. Thanasoulas (2001) provides several guidelines to culture teaching with the purpose of ensuring that English learners will develop an accurate and empathetic understanding of cultural behaviors associated with the target culture. First, students need to develop a cultural awareness that is dynamic in nature. They need to move beyond the receptive aspect of culture learning and become highly skilled in culturally appropriate communication in the target culture.

Second, culture teaching needs to be systematic and structured; it should not be based on the assumption that language contains culture and no direct effort to discern cultural norms from linguistic messages is necessary. Third, culture learning needs to be assessed. An essential component of the culture-based curriculum, culture learning assessment will provide students with feedback and teachers with important information regarding the quality of their instruction.

The Structure of L2 Culture-Based Activities

Compared to other language skills, such as listening and speaking, where we have had a pre-, during, and post-type of sequence, culture-based activities may be more flexible in structure. Instead, there will be a pre-activity (introduction of the cultural concept and essential vocabulary) stage, followed by an activity stage, which is in turn followed by a post-activity (reflection on/application of the cultural construct discussed) stage. Here's an example, adapted from Neff and Rucynski (2013), assuming the teacher has a different cultural background than the students.

Intercultural Interview/Discussion

Pre-Activity

In groups, students are asked to develop questions they want to ask about the instructor's culture. The instructor provides them with several guidelines as to how to format their questions. Students should avoid questions that will require overly quick or simple yes/no responses, provide enough detail to make the question understood, and use illustrative examples to explain a concept or an idea.

Activity

Each student writes three questions that describe an idea the student has about the instructor's culture. For example, one common type of question relates to food: "It seems to me that people eat a lot of fast food. Can you tell me about a typical meal?" After making several of these questions individually, students share them with their group members in the next class and together choose the ones they will ask their instructor.

The instructor takes home the questions and, without answering them, makes response questions related to the same theme. The instructor might respond to the question about food by asking, "Is it more common in (name of country) for people to eat a mix of foods or only food from that country at meals? Please explain with some examples." These response questions are given to the groups in the next class session, and the original questions are returned.

The students research the information related to the response questions they received from their instructor, concentrating on facts and examples and not simply generalities and stereotypes, as one of the goals of this activity is to help students examine stereotypes about their own culture.

In class, on the interview day, students begin by asking the instructor their questions. After answering students' questions, the instructor ask students for their response questions. Although students know the questions in advance, they do not know who will be asked each question. To add spontaneity and de-emphasize overly scripted responses, the instructor will also include some follow-up questions.

Post-Activity

The students write a reflection paper in which they discuss the way this discussion has confirmed or challenged some of their perceptions regarding the other culture.

To use this activity in a context where the teacher comes from the same culture as the students, modifications need to be made. One option is to invite a guest speaker to be the interviewer or use technology (such as Skype) to set up an exchange with speakers from another culture. If the EFL teacher has lived or traveled extensively in an English-speaking country, the students could ask about the teacher's experiences and impressions of that country.

There are several specific activities for incorporating culture in English language courses. One example is using "culture capsules," which are descriptions of what is expected during communication exchanges in terms of culture. Culture capsules contrast the cultural expectations related to the target language with the cultural expectations of the native language (Medina-López-Portillo, 2014; Singhal, 1998). The teacher usually presents these capsules orally and then directs the discussion by focusing on cultural differences between the native and target culture. An example of a culture capsule examining the differences between Romanian and U.S. introductive gestures is shown.

Gestures used by Romanians when introducing themselves or others are quite similar to what is expected in the United States. One example is shaking hands with people during introductions at the beginning of meetings or informal get-togethers. Most people in the U.S. who interact with Romanians feel very comfortable with this introduction gesture. However, there are some gestures of meeting and greeting people that are different in Romania. In Romania, it is not unusual for men to kiss the hand of a woman. In other cultural contexts, such as in the United States, this gesture from a stranger who is trying to be formal and polite could be taken as flirtation by women who are not used to such a practice.

For a more effective provision of cultural information, culture capsules are often presented in clusters. They consist of three or more capsules on a related topic, followed by a classroom role-play activity that integrates the information contained in the capsules (Peck, 1998). For example, a culture cluster about the significance of grades for college students in the United States could contain a capsule about what a grade point average means, followed by a capsule about the impact of grades on awarding scholarships and by another one discussing the importance of grades in getting a better job. Table 12.2 illustrates four additional culture-oriented activities that facilitate culture acquisition in ESL or EFL classes.

Table 12.2: Four Activities for Teaching Culture in the ESL/EFL Classroom

1. Culture assimilators (Bhawuk, 2001; Fiedler, Mitchell, & Triandis, 1970; Saluveer, 2004)	Culture assimilators are short, written descriptions of an interaction between at least one person from the target culture and people from other cultures. The description is followed by four possible choices about the meaning of the behavior, action, or words of the participants in the interaction. After students choose one of the four options, the teacher leads a discussion about why particular options are appropriate or inappropriate in interpretation.
2. Cultoons (Henrichsen, 1998)	Cultoons are visual culture assimilators. Students are given a series of four pictures describing a possible misunderstanding of the target culture. Students are asked if they think the reactions of the characters in the cultoons seem appropriate or not. Students then read explanations of what was happening and why there was a misunderstanding.
3. Critical incidents/ problem solving	Critical incidents describe situations that demand that a participant in the interaction make some kind of decision. Students read the incident independently and make individual decisions about what they would do. Then the students are grouped into small groups to discuss their decisions and why they made them the way they did. All the groups discuss their decisions and the reasons behind them. Finally, the teacher leads a discussion on how students' decisions and their reasoning compare and contrast with the decisions and reasoning of members of the target culture.
4. Mini-dramas	Mini-dramas consist of brief episodes that illustrate miscommunication that occurs between language learners and native speakers of English. Students act out the parts based on the script provided by the teacher. After each act, the teacher asks students to make judgments about characters and actions in the play. Finally, students are asked to reinterpret what they have seen after taking into consideration the new cultural information they acquired.

Content Selection for L2 Culture-Based Activities

When selecting content for L2 culture-based activities, L2 instructors should ensure that the activities that result from this selection focus on interactional spoken or written communication, involve practical language knowledge, allow for personal expression and expansion of intercultural knowledge, and are achievable in one or two class sessions (Neff & Rucynski, 2013). L2 culture-based activities also require the instructor to maintain a delicate balance between the L1 culture and the target culture. Therefore, it is important to take into account these five guidelines for an ethical selection of topics and content for L2 culture-based activities (Deckert, 2004).

First, the content should include topics that further students' adjustment to the local community. L2 learners newly arrived to an English-speaking country go through culture shock, and the ESL instructor is often best able to detect what a student needs for successfully completing the cultural adjustment process. In L2 culture-based activities, the content can address the topics of contact and friendship with English speakers both in and outside the classroom. For example, addressing communicative gestures directly in a culture-based activity can spare L2 students from many embarrassing situations.

Second, the content should feature topics that relate to students' shared interests. Many students in tuition-based L2 classrooms are highly motivated. Therefore, L2 administrators and instructors should keep students focused on academic or practical interests in learning another language.

Third, the content should promote mutual respect toward others' views. In many L2 classes that are composed of young or older adults, there are many cultural differences. Although American pop culture seems to be drawing people of diverse cultures closer together, L2 learners may still have core values that may be in noticeable tension with the prevailing assumptions of U.S. society, as well as in tension with views of other language learners. Some students, in fact, come from countries that do not allow freedom of choice on matters of religious faith or political perspective. When topics such as gender roles, conflict resolution, freedom of speech, forms of acceptable entertainment, and public expression of affection are part of content, teachers should require planning that takes into account the differences in cultural perspectives. If careful planning and thoughtful replies to classroom questions still bring offense to students, L2 instructors should make amends with individual students as needed.

Fourth, content should facilitate students' adjustment to classroom methodology and should address the ethical expectations of the academic community. Many L2 students have previously studied English in teacher-centered classes that emphasize mastery of grammar points and memorization of vocabulary, skills far removed from meaningful communication. Consequently, the L2 instructor using a communicative approach must help students understand the rationale behind using this approach and the benefits to them of doing so. However, L2 instructors must not assume that the communicative approach necessitates the dismissal of students' previous learning approaches. Many L2 learners have achieved high levels of English proficiency (perhaps partly) through traditional drill and memorization in their EFL setting. Therefore, they should be encouraged to continue to use techniques and strategies they have found helpful while gradually gaining confidence in new ways of learning. Moreover, L2 learners should be exposed to prevailing typical U.S. academic notions such as of plagiarism, copyright, discriminatory expression, and personal privacy, all topics that should be included in L2 culture-based activities.

Student Performance in L2 Culture-Based Activities

Many language programs do not have L2 culture teaching as a stand-alone class in their curriculum. Instead, culture is used as a source of content for instructional activities for other language skills. For the activities with a strong L2 component, L2 learners are engaged in simultaneous language and culture learning, but language learning and skill development are still very important. Therefore, L2 learners' class performance is similar to what was discussed in previous chapters in terms of a focus on specific language skills. Students can be asked to select responses in multiple choice tasks, cloze exercises, or sentence completion tasks. They are also expected to do presentations, write essays, compile portfolios, write journals, be involved in group activities, or lead classroom discussions. There is a great deal of reflection involved in these extended production activities since L2 culture learning is an explicit component of the pedagogical process and often means a drastic re-evaluation of first culture values and norms.

Now that we have explored the three elements of designing L2 culture-based activities (structure, content, and student performance), let's see several examples of activities.

L2 Culture Activities for the Classroom

The culture-based activities provided here are predicated on the various approaches to the language syllabus (grammar-based, communicative product, communicative process, and eclectic), integrate English language skills within each activity, and emphasize how culture can be integrated into any language activity.

─────────────── **Activity 12.1: Marriage Customs** ───────────────

Grammar-Based Culture

Rationale: Grammar and vocabulary lessons that include culture-based content are essential to enforcing the language and demonstrating the importance of understanding cultural differences. They also expose the students to a variety of cultural practices and give teachers the opportunity to assess how accurately the language learners are using the grammatical structures and new vocabulary. Grammar-based culture activities demonstrate to students the importance of grammar and vocabulary, not only in the academic setting but also in understanding cultural customs as well. This activity uses grammar as its main focus and allows the student to practice the various forms of grammatical structures while understanding differences in marriage customs based on culture.

Objectives: Students ask and answer questions in English to talk about various marriage customs from different countries.

Pre-Planning

Pre-knowledge: The students are familiar with using question forms in English, including the question words and phrases such as *who, what, where, when,* and *how.*

Materials needed: One or two copies of a visual provided to encourage interest in the topic. The visuals can be a photograph, printed picture, or even a webpage displaying wedding scenes from around the world. Write these questions on the board or put them on a handout:

1. How old are people when they get married in your country?
2. Where do most weddings take place?
3. What does the bride wear?
4. What does the groom wear?
5. Who comes to the wedding?
6. What happens before the ceremony?
7. What happens during the ceremony?
8. What happens after the ceremony?

Language level: Intermediate
Recommended age group: Teens to adults

Procedures

1. Ask students to get in pairs or place them in pair groups. Students take turns asking each other about the marriage customs in their partner's country, listing answers on a sheet of paper or the handout provided. Students should also add two questions of their own to the list to ask using any of the question words.

2. After 10–15 minutes, students take turns sharing the information with the class, while the teacher lists the different customs on the board.

3. The teacher can extend the activity by asking students about other special occasions, such as holiday celebrations in their countries, using the question words and sharing that information on the board.

Evaluation

The teacher walks around during the pair work to listen for errors that can be corrected related to asking and answering questions.

Homework: Students write about a wedding or special event they attended in their country. The students answer all the basic questions about the event, including *what, where, when, how* (*how long, how old*), and *who.* This is collected and graded.

—————————— **Activity 12.2: Party Invitations** ——————————

Communicative Product Culture

Rationale: The syllabus has targeted, communicative language and vocabulary to use within specific topical situations, or targeted notions/functions within the language, such as interpersonal functions. Culture activities within the communicative product syllabus are highly motivating to students because they are targeted, functional, and help students understand how to function in another culture. In this activity, learners learn how to respond to invitations, practice targeted language forms, and develop language confidence.

Objectives: Using email, students appropriately respond to an invitation to a party from another student. Students also practice extending invitations via online tools. This activity is focused on how to respond to an invitation, what questions to ask, and what is expected from guests.

Pre-Planning

Pre-knowledge: Students are familiar with simple forms of invitation language.

Materials needed: It is preferable that students have access to a computer, the internet, and their Facebook or email account during the class. The teacher prepares a party invitation in advance with the following information and decides how the invitation is extended (Facebook, Evite, email, or printed):

> *Who:* Teacher's name
>
> *What:* End of year party
>
> *When:* Saturday, June 15, from 1:00 to 5:00 PM
>
> *Where:* 4255 South Division Drive
>
> Potluck. Bring a dish to share.
>
> Bring a swimsuit and towel!
>
> RSVP to (teacher's email, social media, or Evite invitation)

Language level: Intermediate to advanced

Recommended age group: Teens to adults

Procedures

1. The teacher should open the discussion about party invitations by explaining that most invitations are now extended through online tools and not often through mail, phone, or in-person. Ask students to share how party invitations are extended in their own countries and what are some important events for which people hold parties. The teacher should list the different occasions, such as birthday parties or barbecues, and what can be expected from the hosts and the guests.

2. Vocabulary: The teacher can pre-teach the vocabulary by writing the words on the board and asking students to define the words:

    BYOB

    potluck

    RSVP

    host

    guest

    occasion

3. If all students have a computer, the teacher can issue an invitation to students right there in class.

4. The teacher then shows some models of how students can respond to the invitation. Let students know they may ask questions of the host:

    a. Thank you for the invite! What dish can I bring? Is it OK if I don't swim?

    b. Thank you for the invitation. I will come and bring a vegetarian salad.

    c. Thanks so much for inviting me! Should I bring a dessert? Is the invitation just for students or for families also?

Evaluation

The teacher then sends the invitations using students' emails. The students should respond to the event using the same tool, in class if there is time or after class for homework.

Homework: Students respond to the teacher's invitation for evaluation. Additionally, students create their own invitations for an event that they send to each other. Students respond to at least two other students and include the teacher on all correspondence for review.

———— Activity 12.3: Introductions ————

Communicative Process Culture

Rationale: In the communicative process syllabus, the organization of the curriculum is based on tasks. The task-based syllabi activities are focused on the language and language skill needed to complete a concrete task. Students who are in a new country or will be meeting people from another country need to understand cultural differences when meeting new people. This activity is focused on the dialogue process of meeting someone new and also provides discussion time for understanding what questions are considered impolite when meeting new people. This is an inductive exercise, so students should complete the dialogues on their own and the teacher should save evaluation and assessment for after the activity.

Objectives: The objective of this activity is for students to practice simple dialogues for meeting someone new, potential topics of conversation, and taboo subjects when meeting someone from a different culture.

Pre-Planning

Pre-knowledge: Basic conversational language
Materials needed: Handout of the dialogues listed
Language level: Beginning
Recommended age group: Pre-teens to adults

Procedures

The teacher prepares the three dialogues on handouts. The teacher then pairs the students in order to fill in and practice the dialogues in pairs. The teacher walks around, listens, and helps students with questions. After the students are done, the teacher asks for volunteer pairs to model the dialogue for the class. The students then vote as a class whether the dialogue is considered polite or impolite for most cultures. The discussion focuses on what part of the dialogue is polite and what part is not, if that is the case.

Content for Your Handout

Dialogue 1

Partner 1:   Hello, my name is _____. It is nice to _____ you.
Partner 2:   Hi _____, it is nice to meet you too. Are you new in the class?
Partner 1:   Yes, I just moved here from _____.
Partner 2:   That is a beautiful _____. I would love to visit there.
Partner 1:   Thank you, you _____ visit some time.

Polite or Impolite? Circle one.

Dialogue 2

Partner 1:   Good morning, I am _____. What is your name?

Partner 2:   Hello, my name is _____. It is nice to meet you. What are you _____ at this school?

Partner 1:   I am studying _____.

Partner 2:   That is _____. Are you married?

Partner 1:   No, I _____ not _____.

Polite or Impolite? Circle one.

Dialogue 3

Partner 1:   Good afternoon Mr./Mrs. _____. I am _____ to be in your class.

Partner 2:   Hello _____, I am Mr./Mrs. _____. I'm glad you are _____. You can _____ anywhere that you would like.

Partner 1:   Do I _____ to buy the book for this _____?

Partner 2:   Yes, _____ course you do.

Polite or Impolite? Circle one.

Evaluation

The teacher moves about the room and helps students with the dialogues to informally evaluate their progress. After the role modeling and discussion, the teacher collects the dialogue handouts for individual evaluation. The teacher opens a final discussion about what topics or questions are considered impolite in many cultures, which can include questions about age, marital status, salary, or school grades.

Homework: Students should list the topics or questions that are considered impolite when meeting a new person in their country. They also write a few questions directly to the teacher about topics they are unsure about, which the teacher answers and returns to the student. For example, "Mr. Rodriguez, can I ask the teacher to be friends on Facebook?"

— Activity 12.4: World Travel —

Eclectic Approach to Culture

Rationale: Many instructors prefer using various and mixed approaches in their design of their syllabus and curriculum. In an eclectic approach to the language classroom, the syllabus may contain a diverse number of activities focused on various language skills and topics. Teachers like this eclectic approach because they can focus on more than one language skill to meet different goals. This activity focuses on cultural information about travel, and students are required to use all language skills to complete this task.

Objectives: Students will write an informative essay that demonstrates their ability to write for the purpose of conveying specific information on a given topic. Students will then use their skimming and scanning reading skills to search for main ideas within the essays written by each other and report orally on what they have read.

Pre-Planning

Pre-knowledge: Students should have been told prior to the class that they will be writing about a travel experience they have had and should be prepared to write about the details of that travel. Students should be able to write in the past tense.
Materials needed: None
Language level: Adaptable to any level
Recommended age group: Teens to adults

Procedures

1. Students write about their favorite travel experience. It includes information such as where they went, when they went, how they got there, what they saw and did, costs of the travel, recommended sightseeing, and historical or significant sites. For beginning students, the teacher can limit the essay to one paragraph focused on very specific information, such as answering these questions: *Where did you go? How did you get there? What did you see? What did you eat? What did you like? Would you recommend going there?* For more advanced students, the teacher can allow students to write freely up to three paragraphs.

2. After students have written for about 5–15 minutes, depending on their level, they pass their essay to another student. Students then read, skim, and scan the essay in order to report on the main ideas from the essay. Students can use a highlighter, circle, underline, or write notes next to the essay. The students then write a report on what they have read in the form of 30-second sound bite to share with other students. The sound bite would sound something like this: "Maria traveled to

Prague in the Czech Republic last year with her family. They visited castles, the Praha Museum, and went to a blacklight show. She also got to visit the Jewish Cemetery. She did not like the food a lot, but bought lots of glassware to take back for souvenirs."

Make sure students write their names on the essay and then ask the reviewing students write their names on their part of the report.

3. As other students listen to the oral reports, they should write the top three destinations they would like to visit and why.

Evaluation

The teacher collects the essays and follow-up reports written by the students to evaluate the second students' ability to scan for the most important information and write about the main ideas.

Homework: Students use websites to search for an area of the world they would like to visit. They write an essay about that area and include why they want to visit it. They are prepared to share that information and include a reference to where they found that information using an acceptable reference style, such as APA or MLA.

Assessing Culture

Content for Assessment

When it comes to assessing a student's awareness of culture, L2 teachers can concentrate on facts, behavior, and attitude. At the most basic level, they can assess factual knowledge. Facts of history, geography, politics, government, religion, and social institutions can be taught and tested. Beyond the facts, teachers can also teach and assess the cultural significance of the facts. L2 learners need to be aware of the cultural impact of historical or social events; otherwise the facts offer little insight into cultural understanding.

In addition to facts, L2 teachers can also measure behavior. Compared to the assessment of facts, behavior is more difficult to measure, but it can be done if students can be assessed on their appropriate performance of a particular behavior. Some examples are using the correct level of formality, greeting others appropriately, and knowing what subjects could be offensive. Verbal and non-verbal behaviors can be assessed, especially if there are opportunities to video record the interaction. Students will display that they know the written and unwritten rules of a culture through their behavior, which is very important if they want to operate successfully in another culture.

The third element of content that can be assessed is attitude, which is difficult to measure directly. Changing people's attitudes toward another culture is often done indirectly through personal contact and relationships. There are many questions associated with the assessment of attitude. Is it mandatory that a student form a positive attitude about the target culture? Can teachers even control that? What if the attitude toward the target culture remains negative? Is it ethical to assess someone's attitude?

How to Assess Cultural Awareness

One way to assess a target culture's contemporary life, cultural heritage, art, society, and civilization is to ask questions based on factual knowledge (e.g., define vocabulary) or ask students to explain facts about a broad topic that they have studied (e.g., talk about senior citizens in the United States). Another way to assess cultural knowledge is to ask students to compare cultures (e.g., U.S. culture with home culture). Regarding the format, it is easier to grade an objective test (multiple choice, true/false, matching), which often has a higher reliability than an essay test, but an objective test may not be as valid because students do not actually show their understanding or cultural insight in a multiple choice quiz. Table 12.3 details several techniques of measuring culture learning in a valid and meaningful manner (Byram & Morgan, 1994; Schulz, 2007; Wang & Kulich, 2015).

Just like language proficiency levels previously discussed in this book, culture proficiency levels that go hand in hand with language competence can be identified. Therefore, L2 teachers can recognize a beginning, intermediate, and advanced levels of cultural competence. Beginning students have to have factual information of the language and some understanding of social life or institutions. Students at the intermediate level are not paying attention to strictly linguistic information. They are looking at written and oral communication not only for linguistic understanding but also for cultural information. Advanced students display a critical dimension of understanding that is not focused solely on language and takes culture into account. This type of competence comes from living in the target country and truly understanding the norms of the culture.

Table 12.3:   Techniques for Assessing Culture

Format	Task
Oral assessment	Students are given role-plays of conflict to enact. Later, they are interviewed about the role-play. Both the behavior (in the target language) and the interview (in the native language, if possible) provide information about the students' cultural understanding.
Written assessment	Students are given role-play exercises to write out (e.g., write a letter as if you had to resolve this situation), and cultural knowledge is assessed in both the target and native language if possible. The written exercise elicits comparisons of both cultures to get at the differences between the two. Students are assessed on their ability to go beyond stereotype and describe variations in culture.
Mediation	This is another role-play situation in which students have to mediate between two people of different cultures and broker a solution between the two. To do this, students must have knowledge of the two cultural points of view. One example of role-play here would be to persuade a French foreign exchange student to wear a British school uniform.
Interview with a native speaker	Students write questions to elicit information from a native speaker. The evaluators should be looking for questions that elicit information about cultural or regional identity, questions that go beyond asking for factual information about someone's home town or their family. They should also evaluate how well a student actually listens and reacts to the native speaker.
Evaluation interview	Sometimes students can be assessed simply by interviewing them and assessing the areas of personal attitudes, cultural awareness, and deeper cultural understanding through interviews.

Given the benefits of cultural instruction, this chapter emphasizes that the teaching of culture should be directly and explicitly included in English language classes. English language teachers should strive to link key cultural items with every aspect of English they teach. L2 learners can achieve high degrees of proficiency in English and be successful in speaking a second language only when cultural issues are a natural part of instruction. However, the teaching of culture should take into account the native culture of English learners and should not be done in a way that promotes cultural confrontation or the dominance of one culture over another. The teaching of L2 culture should provide learners with opportunities to explore and appreciate not only the culture of the target language but also their own culture. Learning another culture should enrich and not diminish English learners' cultural perspective.

Summarizing Statements

1. Defined as a system of standards, culture is dynamic, creative, continuous, learned, and shared (Lessow-Hurley, 2012).

2. Because of the strong connection between language and culture, it is virtually impossible to teach culture-free L2 classes.

3. Including culture in the L2 curriculum can potentially reduce stereotyping, increase motivation, and improve L2 proficiency.

4. The teaching of culture is not without challenges, such as culture shock or perceived attempts of invalidating L1 culture.

5. When L2 instructors decide to include culture in their curriculum, they need to do it systematically with the purpose of developing a cultural awareness that moves beyond the receptive aspect of culture learning (Thanasoulas, 2001).

REFLECTION AND APPLICATION

1. How would you incorporate culture in your ESL or EFL classroom? Do you think that the teaching context would influence your pedagogical decision?

2. Look at Table 12.3, and create one classroom activity based on the activities listed.

3. Review the assessment techniques from Table 12.4 individually or in groups. Can you think of other assessment techniques for evaluating cultural learning in the classroom?

REFERENCES

Adaskou, K., Britten, D., & Fahsi, B. (1990). Design decisions on the cultural content of a secondary English course for Morrocco. *ELT Journal, 44*(1), 3–10.

Bhawuk, D.P.S. (2001). Evolution of culture assimilators. Toward theory-based assimilators. *International Journal of Intercultural Relations, 25*, 141–163.

Brown, H. D. (2014). *Principles of language learning and teaching* (6th ed.). White Plains, NY: Pearson.

Byram, M., & Morgan, C. (1994). *Teaching-and-learning language-and-culture.* Clevedon, U.K.: Multilingual Matters.

Deckert, G. (2004). Guidelines for the selection of topical content in ESL programs. *TESL Canada Journal, 4,* 73–86.

Ellis, R. (1985). *Understanding second language acquisition.* Oxford, U.K.: Oxford University Press.

Fiedler, F., Mitchell, T.R., & Triandis, H.C. (1970). *The culture assimilator: An approach to cross-cultural training.* (Technical Report.) Springfield, VA: Clearinghouse for Federal Scientific and Technical Information,

Genc, B., & Bada, E. (2005). Culture in language learning and teaching. *The Reading Matrix, 5*(1), 73–83.

Goodenough, W. (1971). *Culture, language, and society.* Reading, MA: Addsion-Wesley.

Hassig, S.M., & Latif, Z. A. (2007). *Somalia.* (2nd ed.) Tarryton, NY: Marshall Cavendish.

Henrichsen, L. E. (1998). *Understanding culture and helping students understand culture.* Retrieved from http://linguistics.byu.edu/classes/ling577lh/culture.html

Hofstede, G. (1986). Cultural differences in teaching and learning. *International Journal of Intercultural Relations, 10,* 301–320.

Hofstede, G. (2011). Dimensionalizing cultures: The Hofstede model in context. *Online Readings in Psychology and Culture, 2*(1), 1–26. doi:http://dx.doi.org/10.9707/2307-0919.1014

Kramsch, C. (1993). *Context and culture in language teaching.* Oxford, U.K.: Oxford University Press.

Kramsch, C. (1998). *Language and culture.* Oxford, U.K.: Oxford University Press.

Lessow-Hurley, J. (2012). *The foundations of dual language instruction* (6th edition). New York: Pearson.

Medina-López-Portillo, A. (2014). Preparing TESOL students for the ESOL classroom: A cross-cultural project in intercultural communication. *TESOL Journal, 5,* 330–352.

Moore, Z. (2006). Technology and teaching culture: What Spanish teachers do. *Foreign Language Annals, 39,* 579–594.

Neff, P., & Rucynski, J. (2013). Tasks for integrating language and culture teaching. *English Teaching Forum, 2,* 12–23.

Peck, D. (1998). *Teaching culture: Beyond language.* New Haven, CT: New Haven Teachers Institute.

Saluveer, E. (2004). *Teaching culture in English classes.* Unpublished master's thesis, University of Tartu, Estonia.

Savignon, S. J. (2010). Communicative language teaching. In M. Berns (Ed.), *Concise encyclopedia of applied linguistics* (pp. 254–261) Boston: Elsevier.

Savignon, S. J., & Sysoyev, P. V. (2005). Cultures and comparisons: Strategies for learners. *Foreign Language Annals, 38,* 357–365.

Schulz, R. A. (2007). The challenge of assessing cultural understanding in the context of foreign language instruction. *Foreign Language Annals, 40,* 9–26.

Singhal, M. (1998). Teaching culture in the foreign language classroom. *Thai TESOL Bulletin, 11*(1), 9–19.

Thanasoulas, D. (2001). The importance of teaching culture in the foreign language classroom. *Radical Pedagogy, 3*(3). Retrieved from http://radicalpedagogy.icaap.org/content/issue3_3/7-thanasoulas.html

Tsou, W. (2005). The effects of cultural instruction on foreign language learning. *RELC, 36*(1), 39–57.

Whorf, B. (1956). *Language, thought & reality.* Cambridge: MIT Press.

Wang, Y.A., & Kulich, S.J. (2015). Does context count? Developing and assessing intercultural competence through an interview- and model-based domestic course design in China. *International Journal of Intercultural Relations.* doi:10.1016/j.ijintrel.2015.03.013

PART IV

Contemporary Trends in TESOL Course Design

This section examines the influence of globalization and technology on the TESOL curriculum and language course design. This section is a necessary addition for two reasons. First, because English is taught worldwide either as a second language or as a foreign language, L2 teachers need to examine the current trends in English teaching not only from a U.S. perspective but also from an international one. Second, technology has had a tremendous and undeniable influence in the field of language teaching. More and more, TESOL course design classes focus on how to incorporate synchronous or asynchronous technologies in language teaching courses.

The first chapter in the section, Chapter 13, provides a comprehensive look at TESOL in Europe and the United States and discusses two curricular instruments: the Common European Framework of Reference for Languages (CEFR) and the TESOL PreK–12 English Language Proficiency Standards. The following chapter, Chapter 14, continues this global focus by presenting the history and current state of EFL in two countries with extensive EFL programs, China and South Korea. Finally, Chapter 15 details how technology has transformed the teaching of ESL and EFL in the modern L2 classroom.

Chapter 13
▲

Curriculum Trends in English Language Teaching in Europe and North America

This chapter starts with a discussion of globalization and its influence on economic, political, cultural, and educational systems. It then provides a detailed analysis of two important curricular documents that have had guided L2 teaching and assessment in Europe and the United States: the Common European Framework of Reference for Languages (abbreviated as CEFR) and the TESOL PreK–12 English Language Proficiency Standards. The chapter ends with an exploration of the interplay between global and local forces in shaping L2 curriculum worldwide to determine whether a global English language curriculum exists.

Globalization: The Dominant Influence of Today's National and International Contexts

Before analyzing global trends in teaching English as a second or foreign language curriculum development, it is important to define and discuss the term *globalization*, which has been operationalized in different ways. From one perspective, it refers to the emergence of supranational institutions whose deciding powers not only surpass national borders but also shape and constrain the policy options for any particular nation state (McGinn, 1997). Another view emphasizes the overwhelming impact of global economic processes such as production, consumption, trade, capital flow, and monetary interdependence (Burbules & Torres, 2000). Another perspective considers globalization part of the rise of neoliberalism (shift of control from the public sector to the private) as a hegemonic political discourse (Apple, 2000). A different perspective defines globalization as the emergence of new global cultural forms, media, and technologies of communication, all of which shape the relations of affiliation, identity, and interaction within and across local cultural settings (Luke & Luke, 2000).

To define globalization is to include all these perspectives and points of view under one unifying proposition. Therefore, globalization could be seen as the product of the emergence of a global economy, an expansion of transnational linkages between economic units, the development of supranational institutions, an intensification of transnational communications, and the creation of new regional and military orders (Morrow & Torres, 2000).

Characteristics of globalization can be traced in economic, political, cultural, and educational trends of contemporary societies. In **economic** terms, globalization is characterized by an increase in international advertising and consumption patterns, and by a reduction of barriers to encourage a free circulation of goods, workers, and investments across international borders (Burbules & Torres, 2000). Stromquist and Monkman (2000) note that the dynamics of globalization have emphasized the importance of the market and transnational corporations in the economic decision process, with repercussions in the political arena. A characteristic of contemporary markets is their clustering in regional blocks with the purpose of attaining benefits of scale, coordinating production, and targeting specific populations. Europe, North America, and East Asia are three examples of such blocks that have emerged and that are preparing themselves for increasing competition.

In **political** terms, globalization influences not only economic decision-making processes, but political ones as well. Blackmore (2000) warns that the international market now disciplines the state, whereas previously, the welfare state disciplined the market within its national boundaries. The notion of the citizen as a unified and unifying concept characterized by precise roles, obligations, and status is changed.

In **cultural** terms, globalization brings considerable complexity through the interaction between the global and the local. On one end, there are ways in which globalization pushes for more standardization and cultural homogeneity. On the other end, there are ways in which globalization brings more fragmentation through the rise of locally oriented movements, opposing standardization, and homogeneity (Barber, 1995). However, there is a third theoretical alternative in which the global and the local do not find themselves in an irreconcilable position. This perspective views cultural homogeneity and cultural heterogeneity as appearing simultaneously in the cultural landscape in what Arnove and Torres (1999) identify as "the glocal."

In **educational** terms, there is a growing understanding that the neoliberal version of globalization, particularly as implemented (and ideologically defended) by bilateral, multilateral, and international organizations, is reflected in an educational agenda that privileges, if not directly imposes, particular policies for evaluation, financing, assessment, standards, teacher training, instruction, and testing. Pure market mechanisms are utilized to regulate education exchanges and other policies that seek to reduce state sponsorship and financing and to impose management and efficiency models borrowed from the business sector as a framework for decision-making.

It is important to note that globalization affects all nation-states in all in many ways—political, economic, cultural, and educational. Davies and Guppy (1997) identify two broad concepts of globalization with direct influences on educational systems. First, economic globalization promotes market competition and global capital by encouraging a convergence of institutional agreements among nations and their educational systems. One consequence of this convergence is the standardization of knowledge systems in all industrialized states. Nation states organize and distribute knowledge through formal education. Therefore, across the developed nations, there is a tendency for schools systems to converge. In the case of less developed states, Inkeles and Sirowy (1984) note that change toward this common structure may result from taking structures and practices from more developed nations. This borrowing is possible because the less developed nations belong to various networks of influence that are vehicles for ideas and social forms. Representatives of international organizations, which encourage all educational systems to accept common international standards, distribute these greater global pressures, which at times take the shape of educational reform movements.

Global rationalization is the second conception of globalization identified by Davies and Guppy (1997). While not unrelated to economic imperatives, global rationalization emphasizes the idea of a global cultural system. This stress on rationality and standardization illustrates a second general force toward convergence in existing societies. While not implying that all nations move toward a worldwide uniform structure of education, this view on globalization suggests that schools systems will adopt broadly similar forms because of increasing global rationality.

Has this stress on standardization had a visible influence on English language curriculum, with a possible result of a global curriculum? This question can be answered by looking at two important curriculum documents for English language teaching: the Common European Framework of Reference for Languages (CEFR) and the TESOL PreK–12 English Language Proficiency Standards.

The Common European Framework of Reference for Languages (CEFR)

The Common European Framework of Reference for Languages has been created by the Council of Europe and recommended for use in November 2001. Essential for course and test designers, textbook writers, teachers, and teacher trainers, it is a practical tool for setting standards and evaluating outcomes of language teaching and learning. The foundation of this important curricular document has been the Threshold Level concept, which started in 1971, when Trim (1978) initiated a series of projects, known as the Council of Europe Languages Projects. Initially, these projects examined the needs of adult learners, who were seen as needing to be able to express themselves in terms of certain notions and functions. The description of the notions and functions were published in 1975 and extended in the book *Threshold Level English* (Van Ek & Alexander, 1980). The threshold levels for the projects were not a syllabus or methodology per se, but a statement of content for a course design. It was recommended that language teaching should center on the learner, not the teacher; be relevant to the learner's life; and be communicative.

CEFR represents a common basis for the development of language syllabi, curriculum guidelines, assessment, and textbooks across Europe. It addresses the questions of what language learners have to do in order to use a language for communication, as well as what knowledge and skills they have to develop. In addition, CEFR covers the cultural context in which language is set and defines levels of proficiency. By overcoming the barriers to communication among professionals working in the field of modern languages due to the different educational systems in Europe, CEFR represents a critical tool for educational administrators, course designers, teachers, and teacher trainers to reflect on their current practice to ensure they meet the real needs of the learners (Council of Europe, 2001).

Regarding language acquisition, learning, and teaching theories, the position of CEFR is neutral. One dominant characteristic of CEFR is that it strives to be open, dynamic, and non-dogmatic. For that reason, the Framework does not endorse any theoretical framework on language acquisition and its relation to language learning. Additionally, it does not exemplify any one particular approach to language teaching to the exclusion of all others. It encourages all those involved in language teaching and learning to state explicitly and transparently their own theoretical foundation and practical procedures.

Two major principles can be identified in the organization of CEFR. The first principle is the language learners' levels of competency. As seen in Figure 13.1, language learners are categorized as Basic, Independent, and Proficient. The Basic User category has two levels, Breakthrough and Waystage; the Independent User includes the Threshold and Vantage levels; while the Proficient User category consists of the Effective Operational Proficiency and Mastery levels. The Threshold level is the central element that aims to identify the minimal linguistic means that are necessary for a learner to deal independently with the more predictable transactional and interactional situations of daily life as a visitor or temporary resident.

According to Figure 13.1, the Basic User category comprises two levels of proficiency. To understand how the levels function, it is necessary to explore the way in which the levels have been operationalized through CEFR. This is a description of the global characteristics of a learner at the Breakthrough level:

Can understand and use familiar everyday expressions and very basic phrases aimed at the satisfaction of needs of a concrete type. Can introduce him/herself and others and can ask and answer questions about personal details such as where he/she lives, people he/she knows and things he/she has. Can interact in a simple way provided the other person talks slowly and clearly and is prepared to help.

A learner at the Waystage level can be described as:

Can understand sentences and frequently used expressions related to areas of most immediate relevance (e.g., very basic personal and family information, shopping, local geography, employment). Can communicate in simple and routine tasks requiring a simple and direct exchange of information on familiar and routine matters. Can describe in simple terms aspects of his/her background, immediate environment and matters in areas of immediate need.

The second organizing principle of CEFR is language skills. There are four identified language skills, which work in conjunction with the levels of proficiency previously discussed. The

---

Figure 13.1:   CEFR Categories of Language Learners

A. Basic User
A1: Breakthrough
A2: Waystage

B. Independent User
B1: Threshold
B2: Vantage

C. Proficient User
C1: Effective Operational Proficiency
C2: Mastery

---

four skills are Listening, Speaking (Spoken Interaction and Spoken Production), Reading, and Writing. For each language skill, CEFR recommends instructional activities and provides rubrics for evaluation and assessment.

For example, for written production, the following are samples of activities: completing forms and questionnaires; writing articles for magazines, newspapers, newsletters, etc.; producing posters for display; writing reports, memoranda, etc.; making notes for future reference; taking down messages from dictation, etc.; creative and imaginative writing; writing personal or business letters, etc. Illustrative rubrics are provided for overall written production, creative writing, and reports and essays. The rubric for overall written production is exemplified as:

Breakthrough: Can write simple isolated phrases and sentences.

Waystage: Can write simple phrases and sentences linked with simple connectors.

Threshold: Can write straightforward connected texts on a range of familiar subjects within his field of interest, by linking a series of shorter discrete elements into a linear sequence.

Vantage: Can write clear, detailed texts on a variety of subjects related to his/her field of interest, synthesizing and evaluating information and arguments from a number of sources.

Effective Operational Proficiency: Can write clear, well-structured texts of complex subjects, underlining the relevant salient issues, expanding and supporting points of view at some length with subsidiary points, reasons and relevant examples, and rounding off with an appropriate conclusion.

Mastery: Can write clear, smoothly flowing, complex texts in an appropriate and effective style and a logical structure which helps the reader to find significant points.

This brief analysis at the parameters of CEFR reveals that this curriculum document employs a skill-based, communicative, notional-functional approach. Naturally, the next question is whether this curriculum development approach is singular and isolated or whether it is part of a global trend in English language curriculum design. Are the TESOL PreK–12 English Language Proficiency standards similar with CEFR's parameters, or are they vastly different?

TESOL PreK–12 English Language Proficiency Standards in the United States

Focusing on the importance of the relationship language-academic content, the International TESOL association has created a new set of language proficiency standards for English learners (ELs) enrolled in preK–12 schools in the United States. These new standards recognize the fact that content area instruction is an integral part of language development. These new standards are a response to the provisions of the federal law No Child Left Behind Act of 2001, which required states to develop language proficiency standards grounded in state academic content standards (TESOL, 2006).

> Standard 1: ELLs communicate for **social, intercultural,** and **instructional** purposes within the school setting.
>
> Standard 2–5: ELLs communicate information, ideas, and concepts necessary for academic success in the area of **language arts (S2), mathematics (S3), science (S4),** and **social studies (S5).**

How are these standards operationalized? The organizing matrix for each standard, as seen in Figure 13.2, contains five levels of language proficiency, four language domains, grade-level clusters, content topics, and samples of performance indicators.

Figure 13.2: Organizational Matrix for TESOL PreK–12 Standards

Grade Level 1–3		
Standard 3: ELs communicate information, ideas, and concepts necessary for academic success in the area of science.		
Language Domain	**Content Topic**	**Level 1 Starting**
Reading	Life cycle Water cycle Organisms and environments	Match pictures with labels (e.g., caterpillars/butterflies)

Similar to CEFR, the matrix for each standard contains several language proficiency levels. In CEFR, there are six language proficiency levels, whereas in the TESOL Standards, there are five. At **Level 1, Starting,** ELs have little or no understanding of English, and most of the time, they respond non-verbally to simple commands or questions. At **Level 2**, **Emerging,** ELs are beginning to understand phrases and short sentences. They can convey limited information in routine situations by using memorized chunks of language. ELs at this level begin to use general academic vocabulary and familiar expressions used in everyday communication. ELs at **Level 3, Developing,** have a more developed vocabulary and start to understand more complex speech. They use English spontaneously, using simple sentences that are both comprehensible and appropriate but frequently marked by grammatical errors. They understand not only general academic vocabulary but also specialized vocabulary. They still have some problems understanding and producing complex structures and academic language. At **Level 4, Expanding,** ELs have language skills that are adequate for everyday communication demands, but they still make occasional structural and lexical errors. They are proficient in communicating in new or unfamiliar settings but have some difficulty with complex language structures and abstract academic concepts. Even though ELs at **Level 5**, **Bridging,** are not fully proficient in English, they can express themselves fluently and accurately on a wide range of social and academic topics in a variety of contexts. They need very minimal language support to function in English based instructional environments.

Similar to CEFR, there are four language domains in the TESOL Standards: listening, speaking, reading, and writing. Another aspect the links the two curriculum documents is the provision of rubrics that can be used for teaching and assessment. In the case of TESOL Standards, the rubrics contain performance indicators. These performance indicators are examples of measurable language behaviors ELs are expected to demonstrate as they engage in classroom activities. Sample performance indicators are made of three elements: content, language function, and support/strategy. An example of a performance indicator for science is shown.

Describe (language function) how *systems, chains, or cycles operate (content-specific information)* from diagrams or graphic organizers (support/strategy)

For a better understanding of the structure of the new TESOL PreK–12 Standards, Table 13.1 shows the matrix for PreK–12 TESOL Standard 1.

Table 13.1: PreK–K Matrix for TESOL Standard 1

Topics Grade: PreK–K	Classroom	Family	Rules and Games	Social Behavior
Language Domains	**Reading**	**Writing**	**Listening**	**Speaking**
Level 1, Starting	Match words with pictures on words walls, bulletin boards, etc.	Draw family members.	Identify objects from pictures or realia as directed orally.	Practice simple polite expressions, such as *please* and *thank you*.
Level 2, Emerging	Identify letters in the names of classroom objects in pictures or text.	Label photos or drawing of family members or friends using letters or scribble writings.	Follow one-step oral directions in groups in games and activities.	Make polite requests of teachers or classmates.
Level 3, Developing	Match names of familiar objects with pictures or realia.	Write descriptions of family members using drawings, letters, scribble writings, or words with invented spelling.	Follow multiple-step oral directions with partners in activities and games.	Role play conversations with adults using polite language.
Level 4, Expanding	Identify words and phrases that are school related, such as *entrance*, *exit*, etc.	Write stories of family experiences using drawings, letters, scribble writings, or words and phrases with invented spelling.	Demonstrate rules explained by the teacher in activities and games.	Offer apologies, give compliments, etc., in small-group environments.
Level 5, Bridging	Build meaning from picture books with text.	Write notes to family members using words and phrases with invented spelling.	Respond to commands while engaged in activities and games.	Adapt language appropriate to familiar audiences.

English Language Curriculum: Uniformity or Fragmentation?

The examination of CEFR and TESOL PreK–12 Standards reveals that there are several identifiable global trends in curriculum development approaches for teaching English. The first trend revolves around the fact that language learning is seen from a competency perspective. For example, in the case of CEFR, a language learner at the Waystage level can describe in simple terms the immediate environment (Council of Europe, 2001). Similarly, according to the TESOL PreK–12 Standards, PreK–K English learners at the Emerging level should "make polite requests of teachers or classmates" (TESOL, 2006). In the current English language teaching context, learners are often required to successfully demonstrate they have acquired the necessary knowledge at the end of an instructional cycle. Worldwide, there is a stronger link between assessment and instruction and a more defined emphasis on assessment as a central component of teacher accountability and learner evaluation.

The second identifiable trend deals with the nature of the curriculum. The approach adopted for both curriculum documents is notional-functional, with a strong communicative component. There is a very visible departure from the more typical syllabus that focused on grammar and structure, perhaps responding to the tendency in the English language teaching field to strongly promote the communicative approach, which essentially allows for very little grammar instruction. In addition, both curricula are organized by levels of proficiency, which are well defined in terms of competency. According to these two curriculum documents, language competency measures what the learners know, what the learners can demonstrate they can do, and the skills teachers can assess after formal instruction is completed. Last, but not least, both curricula are structured by language skills, or domains: reading, writing, listening, and speaking.

To sum up, a global curriculum for English language teaching is not a distant concept, but rather a very strong presence in today's ESL/EFL field. This global curriculum is driven by standards and accountability, is skills based, and is notional-functional and communicative. However, this does not mean that the global influences are the only forces at work when nation states revisit or reform their language curricula. One good example of the interaction of the global forces with the local context is represented by the new EFL curriculum in Romania. The new curriculum was explicitly designed to follow the CEFR. However, because of the very strong prevalence of the structural grammar-based curriculum before the reform, the reformed EFL curriculum continues this tradition of strong reliance on explicit grammar. For example, in the new Romanian EFL curriculum for Grades 3 to 9, grammar and vocabulary are presented as crucial elements for building communicative competence. This is possibly a result of the influence exerted by the pre-existing local EFL context before the educational reform of the late 1990s (Mihai, 2003–2004).

This chapter began with a detailed discussion of globalization, defining it and looking at the way it has influenced economic, political, cultural, and educational systems. Then two important curricular documents in Europe and North America—CEFR and TESOL PreK–12 English Language Proficiency Standards—were analyzed. This analysis took into account the tremendous influence globalization has exerted on the directions the two documents took but did not discard the role of local contexts in shaping long-term educational decisions.

In conclusion, it is important to acknowledge that the ELT global curriculum is a reality, but it is a reality that does not automatically imply the negation of the local context. Clearly, the identifiable general characteristics of this worldwide curriculum are present in many of the today's national curricula for English teaching. However, the influence of the local context results in a very important modification: These new global trends are adapted to fit the needs of the local environment and are not and will not be adopted by national educational systems unconditionally.

Summarizing Statements

1. Globalization has deeply influenced not only economies, cultures, and political systems but also educational environments.

2. CEFR and TESOL PreK–12 English Language Proficiency Standards have been influenced by CLT approaches, resulting in a linear skills-based curriculum with an emphasis on competencies.

3. In both Europe and North America, standards and accountability play a huge role.

4. Local context still plays a role especially in places where grammar-based approaches were the mode of instruction in the past.

5. The presence of a global English language teaching curriculum is a reality but does not indicate unqualified uniformity in curriculum design and implementation.

REFLECTION AND APPLICATION

1. Find the CEFR document online and look for the listening skill rubrics in Chapter 4. Design a listening activity based on the C1 description for overall listening comprehension (see Figure 13.1).

2. Using the information presented in Table 13.1, design an activity for Level 3 Speaking.

3. What are some similarities and differences between CEFR and the TESOL K–12 standards?

REFERENCES

Apple, M. W. (2000). Between neoliberalism and neoconservatism: Education and conservatism in a global context. In N.C. Burbules & C.A. Torres (Eds.), *Globalization and education: Critical perspectives* (pp. 57–78). London: Routledge.

Arnove, R., & Torres, C. A. (Eds.). (1999). *Comparative education: The dialectic of the global and the local*. Lanham, MD: Rowman & Littlefield.

Barber, B.R. (1995). *Jihad vs McWorld*. New York: Times Books.

Blackmore, J. (2000). Hanging onto the edge: An Australian case study of women, universities, and globalization. In N.P. Stromquist & K. Monkman (Eds.), *Globalization and education: Integration and contestation across cultures* (pp. 285–304). Lanham, MD: Rowman & Littlefield.

Burbules, N.C., & Torres, C.A. (2000). Globalization and education: An introduction. In N.C. Burbules & C.A. Torres (Eds.), *Globalization and education: Critical perspectives* (pp. 1–26). London: Routledge.

Council of Europe. (2001). *Common European Framework of Reference for Languages: Learning, teaching, assessment*. Cambridge, U.K.: Cambridge University Press.

Davies, S., & Guppy, N. (1997). Globalization and education reforms in Anglo-American democracies. *Comparative Education Review, 41*(4), 435–459.

Inkeles, A., & Sirowy, L. (1984). Convergent and divergent trends in national educational systems. In A. Inkeles & L. Sirowy (Eds.), *Current issues and research in macrosociology*. Leiden, The Netherlands: E.J. Brill.

Luke, A., & Luke, C. (2000). A situated perspective on cultural globalization. In N.C. Burbules & C.A. Torres (Eds.)., *Globalization and education: Critical perspectives*. London: Routledge.

McGinn, N. F. (1997). Supranational organizations and their impact on nation-states and the modern school. In W.K. Cummings & N.F. McGinn (Eds.), *International handbook of education and development: Preparing schools, students, and nations for the twenty-first century* (pp. 539–555). New York: Pergamon.

Mihai, F.M. (2003–2004). The teaching and learning of English as a Foreign Language (EFL) in Romania after 1989: A comprehensive analysis. *Analele stiintifice ale Universitatii "Al. I. Cuza" din Iasi. Serie noua. Limbi si literaturi straine* [Al. I. Cuza Scientific Annals. New series. Foreign Languages and Literatures], *VI–VII*, 214–236.

Morrow, R.A., & Torres, C.A. (2000). The state, globalization, and educational policy. In N.C. Burbules & C.A. Torres (Eds.), *Globalization and education: Critical perspectives* (pp. 27–56). London: Routledge.

Stromquist, N.P., & Monkman, K. (2000). Defining globalization and assessing its implications on knowledge and education. In N.P. Stromquist & K. Monkman (Eds.), *Globalization and education: Integration and contestation across cultures* (pp. 1–20). Lanham, MD: Rowman & Littlefield.

TESOL. (2006). *PreK–12 English language proficiency standards. Augmentation of the world-class instructional design and assessment (WIDA) consortium English language proficiency standards*. Alexandria, VA: TESOL.

Trim, J. L. M. (1978). *Some possible lines of development of an overall structure for a European unit credit scheme for foreign language learning by adults*. Brussels: Council of Europe.

Van Ek, J. A., & Alexander, L. G. (1980). *Threshold level English: In a European unit/credit system for modern language learning by adults*. New York: Pergamon Press.

Chapter 14
▲

Teaching Practices in Asia: A Focus on China and South Korea

This chapter presents the history and current state of EFL in two countries with expansive educational programs in this area, China and South Korea. In addition to providing a brief history, this chapter explores insights from current teachers as to the best practices in those countries with regard to EFL pedagogy, curriculum, and the systematic approach to SLA. The two countries we have selected are representative of many long-standing English learning programs in Asia. Each offers perspectives that new EFL instructors should be aware of.

English Language Teaching in China

The Development and Current State of ELT in China

English language teaching (ELT) has been a booming industry in China. More than 200 million Chinese primary and secondary school students are taking regular English course, and millions of adults are studying English in universities and other institutes (Wu, 2001). Benefiting from the support of Chinese national educational policy and Chinese citizens' appetite for learning the lingua franca of the 21st century, ELT has become a billion-dollar industry for the Chinese economy.

Absent for many decades in the 20th century, ELT came back to the Chinese education system after the Reform and Open Policy in late 1970s. In the teaching syllabi of 1977, 1982, and 1993, EFL was introduced to junior middle school (Jin & Cortazzi, 2002). In some urban elementary schools, English was introduced as early as in third grade. In 2001, the Chinese Department of

Education required English courses to be offered in elementary schools (Liu & Liu, 2008). Today, most Chinese students start to learn English from third grade in elementary school (age 9).

English is one of the essential subjects in Chinese middle school and high school. English is taught around seven class hours per week, and English scores are a large portion of the scores in high school and college entrance examinations (about one-fourth of the total scores). To increase their English scores, students will not only take English classes at school but also spend money and time to hire experienced EFL teachers as private tutors or attend extra English classes provided by their schools or English teaching institutes.

At the college level, Chinese students of all majors need to take another two years of EFL classes for four class hours per week. English Corners and English Clubs for oral English practice are teeming with students every week. Moreover, some Chinese universities open selective English courses for their junior and senior students who are not English majors to meet their needs of further English study.

In addition to the public education system, private English teaching centers are also quickly developing. Such ELT institutes, such as Xing Dong Fang and EF, are well designed to provide courses of different levels, from kindergarten to occupational specialty. These educational institutes usually put together their own textbooks and teaching materials. They have very efficient pedagogical strategies to help their students achieve their learning objects in a short time.

Clearly, ELT is a very important part of the Chinese education system. From elementary school to college, every student will have received at least 12 years of EFL education. Many of them even start learning English as early as in kindergarten and continue to learn this foreign language after graduation from colleges. The scale and number of people of EFL education in China has become a unique phenomenon.

The Need of ELT in China

Admittedly, the development of the Chinese economy and the cultural communication in the globalization age require a certain amount of multilingual speakers, and English is the most widely used global language. However, most English learners in China study English not to communicate in the language but to obtain higher scores on exams. The most popular instructors are those who know the format of English exams well and are experienced in exam strategies.

China has been carrying on a "nine-year compulsory education" for many years. The government makes sure that every person gets educated from elementary to middle school. However, after middle school, the investment in and access to higher education is limited. Therefore, passing the high school and college entrance examinations is critical. The competition to get into higher education is fierce. As mentioned before, English takes a great part in these examinations. To maximize the fairness and objectivity of these high-stakes examinations, these examinations focused only on reading and writing abilities for a long time. Listening comprehension was introduced into exams in the late 1990s, with the development of the economy as well as technology. Speaking is still not tested in these high-stakes entrance examinations.

At the college-level ELT, students and teachers do not feel the pressure of examinations as much as at the secondary level. Because they have special listening and speaking classes to train their communicative competence, most native English–speaking instructors are needed at this level. However, all students who are not English majors still have to pass an English language test—College English Test 4 (CET 4). Some universities also require their students to pass CET 6. Although the Chinese government does not require it, many colleges and universities make passing CET 4 a necessary condition to get an undergraduate diploma and bachelor's degree. In their job description, some recruitment agencies also require applicants to provide their CET 4 or CET 6 scores. Consequently, to get their degree and a better job, some Chinese college students spend more time on English than on their major.

English also takes an important role in graduate education. In the written portion of the graduate entrance examination of all majors except English, English takes one-fifth of the total score. Students will not be admitted if their English level does not pass a certain grade set by the government. Once admitted, Chinese graduate students will continue to take English for one year in their graduate studies at the master's and PhD levels.

In some industries, such as medicine and statistics, where tests are required to get promotions, English exams play an important part. People study by themselves or attend special training classes for the exams.

Another increasing need for ELT is attributed to the dramatic increase in studying abroad. As Chinese people have become better off in the past 20 years, more can afford to pursue higher education in Western countries. Since resources for higher education are limited in China, many people are willing to invest their money to help ensure that their children do not face the pressure of competitive high-stakes examinations. For these people, English competence is not only important for examinations such as TOEFL®, IELTS®, SAT®, or GRE®, but also a practical need because they will have to use English in their daily life. To prepare for life abroad, students work on improving their listening and speaking ability in English, as well as their knowledge of Western cultures.

Other than the need to pass examinations and to study abroad, higher English proficiency is needed to get promotions and a better salary, especially in the commercial area. In companies doing international business, those who speak fluent English are indispensable. The need for professional communication directly motivates the reform of ELT in the Chinese education system from an examination orientation to one of communicative competence.

The Educational Resources and Teaching Methods of ELT in China

One of the most important features of ELT in China is the imbalance of educational resources among different districts. The best teachers, universities, and facilities are all concentrated in the east provinces and in the largest cities such as Beijing, Shanghai, Guangzhou, and Shenzhen. In these areas, children receive excellent ELT from the very beginning. There are expensive bilingual/international kindergartens or elementary schools where students not only receive extensive English education but also have great opportunities to interact with native English–speaking peers. Most native English–speaking teachers will also go to the east provinces, capital cities, and urban areas. At the same time, a large number of qualified English teachers are needed in the west provinces and rural areas. After the Chinese government's requirement of teaching EFL courses in elementary schools, the situation has become more alarming due to the low pay, poor facility, and hardship experienced by primary education teachers in the western part of China and in rural areas (Liu, 2009; Liu & Liu, 2008).

For many years, China's central government was the only authority for designing and implementing assessments, especially in primary and secondary education. Therefore, the whole Chinese educational system used the same textbooks published by People's Education Publishing House for all academic subjects, including English. These textbooks of the 1980s generation are still vivid in the minds of many. There are movies and different parodies about the characters in the English language textbook after they are grown up. In the beginning of the 21st century, the central government began to authorize provincial governments to design their own college entrance exams. The provincial governments also have the right to publish their own textbooks.

Currently, Chinese students from different provinces learn English from different textbooks under the guidance of a general curriculum generated by the central government. The content and style of English textbooks in secondary schools are similar to the classic U.K.-published textbooks *New Concept English* (by L. G. Alexander) and *Essential English* (by C. E. Eckersley). The texts start with daily conversations and then continue with short passages; the characters in the textbooks have continuous stories. Although the new textbooks contain more classroom activities than the textbooks used decades ago, students still spend most of their time in class on listening, reading, and grammar because of the pressure of examinations.

At the college level, textbooks are more diverse. The best universities usually use teaching materials compiled by their own professors. The textbooks for English majors focus more on cultural knowledge and communicative skills. The college English course for all majors often use simpler textbooks provided by foreign language education publishers. Because of the increasing portion of the listening part in CET 4 and CET 6 as well as the communication needs of college students, most colleges and universities have English listening, speaking, and culture classes in addition to comprehensive English courses.

In the era of the internet, students have more access to authentic learning materials. Native English speakers are sometimes amazed by Chinese young people's current information about American TV series, movies, and pop music. Many college students are not satisfied by just speaking fluent English but also want a native-like accent. Outside textbooks have become a crucial part of ELT in the 21st century.

Problems and Solutions

ELT in China has achieved a lot during the past three decades, but there are still several issues that need to be addressed. The primary problem of ELT is the pressure of examinations. Extensive input and exposure to the target language is critical in learning foreign languages. Focusing on examination narrows the input and, therefore, affects the comprehensive competence of Chinese students in English. Motivation is another crucial factor that may influence the learning of foreign languages. The pressure of examinations could potentially hinder Chinese students' integrative motivation. Too much pressure could also be harmful to their interest in English and motivation to study this foreign language (Chen, 2008).

Scholars of ELT also express their concern about introducing English courses in elementary schools (Chen, 2008; Dong, 2003; Liu & Liu, 2008). Chen (2008) has stated that English is still a foreign language in China and, for most Chinese students, the only exposure to the language is the limited English class. Chen (2008) further explains that young children are not cognitively mature to learn the vocabulary and sentence structure in a traditional classroom environment. Without a language-rich and an age-appropriate environment, the rate of success of English proficiency for young children has not been high.

The lack of qualified teachers is another factor that negatively influences the success of ELT in elementary schools. Many Chinese EFL teachers were not English majors and have pronunciation and grammar problems (Liu & Liu, 2008). According to a survey conducted by Dong (2003), many elementary students lost all interest in English in their first year of study.

Another problem is specialized training of EFL instructors. Many secondary- and college-level Chinese EFL instructors have excellent English proficiency, and some even earn their degree in an English-speaking country. However, a large portion of them do not receive professional TESOL training. For many less experienced teachers, they need to gather teaching experience on their own or learn teaching skills from other experienced peers. To solve these problems, schools will usually provide brief training sessions on educational issues (not specifically in TESOL) to new teachers and assign them experienced instructors to guide them in the first one or two years of teaching practice. Provincial Departments of Education have also started to invest in programs of TESOL training with the universities and have begun to bring in TESOL specialists from English-speaking countries.

English Language Teaching in South Korea

The Development and Current State of ELT in South Korea

South Korea has been undergoing a transformation of its educational system since 1948, cultivated by a strong public demand for education. This "education fever" (*kyo yu yeol*) has helped create one of the most literate and prosperous industrialized nations in the world (Seth, 2012). Today, "education is seen as the most powerful means to achieve upward social mobility and economic prosperity, and many Korean parents believe that they can help their children succeed by emphasizing, and even imposing, education for their children" (Park, 2009, pp. 50–51). Korean parents invest significant amounts of time and money in private education, sometimes starting their children as young as age three in an EFL education.

The focus on attaining language proficiency in English, whether it is on a standardized or any other English-ability test such as the TOEFL®, TOEIC®, or the Korean National English Ability

Test (NEAT®), is considered a shortcut to get into a prestigious college and land a good job. For example, the Korean version of the Scholastic Aptitude Test (KSAT), which students must take to enter a Korean university, is so competitive that the washback (the influence an exam has on the way in which students are taught) seriously impacts the Korean high school curriculum, particularly for the English section (Inn-Chull, 2008). Competitiveness in developing English skills is continuing to grow rapidly in South Korea. Many believe that the earlier students get familiar with English, the more fluency they will develop in English, which will give them a head start when entering school.

This high motivation of students' parents or students themselves to learn English is one of the reasons EFL is so successful in South Korea. South Korea is a small country and, culturally, is quick to respond to the results. Private institutions apply a variety of methods according to what students' parents or the students consider critical for their success. This is more noticeable in high-end institutions that are expensive and respond to rapid consumer demand (Jeon, 2012). Consequently, English is not just about education but also about a successful business model. The many private English institutions across the nation, particularly in large cities such as Seoul, Busan, Incheon, and Daegu, are continually offering up new models for more efficient learning and test preparation.

Pedagogical and Assessment Practices

Parents in South Korea are highly focused on educational achievement, and students in this country tend to study English for fluency starting at very young ages. For older students (from tenth grade on), studying academic English, focused on reading and grammar in preparation for college entrance exams, is more important. Students study English (*yeongeokyoyuk*) in public school, continue their English studies after school in what is known as cram schools (*hagwon*), receive private tutoring (*kwaoe*), attend English camps in summer and winter (*yeongeocamp*), and attend language institutions abroad (*haewoeyonsu*). Some estimate that more than half of the consumer money spent on education in South Korea is focused on English education, up to 20 trillion won ($20 billion) annually (Park, 2009).

Because of the strong focus on exam readiness for older students, much of the English curriculum focuses on the reading and writing needed for the KSAT. As the government prepares to implement the new NEAT® exam, though, which has a more balanced focus on reading, writing, listening, and speaking, South Korean students will find a change in curriculum in public and private schools as the washback from the test affects teaching. Because NEAT® requires students to better prepare for fluency in all language skills, a more communicative approach to the language will be needed throughout the curriculum of English from young students to adults.

An example of a literature-based lesson using the book *Holes* as a basis for the lesson is provided on page 296. Note the very specific directions for teacher conduct and the focus on critical thinking and creativity. This is a break from the past in South Korea, where the educational system was strongly focused on rote memorization (Park, 2009).

Lesson Title: Chapters 20–22 from *Holes* by Louis Sachar

Class: 10th grade of CAFL
Duration: 50 minutes
Materials: *Holes*, PPT, video clips, worksheet
Goal: Students will comprehend the text and promote the ability to think critically and creatively.

Objectives

⇒ Students will be able to recall and explain what they learned in the last class.
⇒ Students will be able to summarize the story (from ch 20 to ch 22).
⇒ Students will be able to describe the characters in the story and empathize with them.

Time (minutes)	Procedures Followed	
1	**1. Greeting and checking attendance** (not calling roll, just checking by their seats)	
	Teacher (T)	**Students** (Ss)
	2. Review for the last class	

3	- Comprehensive check (for the last class)
	- Task a few questions to check Ss' comprehension
	    A. Who did Stanley get a letter from?
	    B. Describe the accident.
	    C. Anything new we found about Zero?
		- Ss raise their hands and when picked and give their answers to each question.

	3. Summary of the today's chapters (20–22)	
13	- T provides PPT slides including each chapter's summary. The summaries will include some blanks (most keywords). T reads the summaries out loud. - T points out some specific parts of sentences to	- Ss read along the summary to themselves, filling the blanks by answering them out loud.
6	think about and asks related questions.	- Ss freely express their opinions.
	4. Character comprehensive activity	
13	- T distributes worksheets for writing self-introductions of each character. The worksheet includes the questions to think about, related to each character. T gives a detailed instruction in Korean.	- Ss, divided into groups of four or five, listen to T's instructions carefully.
	- T walks around the classroom and helps Ss and gives advice.	- Ss cooperate to create a story and designate one who will present.
	- T gets Ss' attention and asks them to present their story, each team talking turns. T can ask follow-up questions based on the Ss' stories to other students at the end of each team's presentation.	- Ss volunteer to share the story they come up with; when the presenter shares their story, the rest of the Ss listen carefully. Ss are ready to answer T's questions and share their opinions.
	5. Wrap-up	
4	- T summarizes what they did in the class. - Farewells and notice about the next class.	- Ss listen and think about what they did in the class. - Greeting.

Teacher Training

Korea has Education departments in almost all four-year universities where students major in various disciplines, including Korean, Math, English, or Physics. After graduating, students can take the state teacher recruitment test to be hired as a teacher in secondary schools, which includes middle and high schools. To be an elementary school teacher, students go to universities of education, of which there are now about 11 in South Korea. The competition rate to be an elementary school teacher is fairly high, with about two applicants for every slot at the university. Korean students who major in English Literature (not part of Education departments) and who want to be English teachers must get a graduate degree in Education, which takes two and a half years (five semesters) after graduating from college.

Becoming a secondary school teacher in South Korea by merely taking the State Recruitment Test is very difficult. If applicants pass the exam, they can go to public secondary school to teach. If graduates do not want to take the exam, they can look for a teaching position in private schools where the principals or the chairs of the school boards can hire a teacher through several steps of testing that they create according to their school's needs (e.g., Step 1—examining personal history or career paper of the applicants; Step 2—paper-based test; Step 3—demonstration class to see how well the applicants teach; Step 4—interview with the principal, vice principal, and senior teachers; and Step 5—final interview with the chairman of the board and other executives).

Therefore, it can be quite competitive to be a teacher in South Korea, which means applicants must be highly qualified for the position. For students who want to be English teachers, a study abroad experience (e.g., degrees in English-speaking countries) is increasingly important, because it could potentially increase their fluency and cultural understanding of the English language and their repertoire of efficient and practical teaching methods through a wide range of teaching experiences. When it comes to the preference for non-native or native English speakers in public and private schools, the concern of South Korean parents is high. Today, it is more common to believe that native English speakers are not always better than non-native speakers, and they want native speakers who also have a background in TESOL or teaching experience.

Challenges and Solutions

One of the challenges within the South Korean English system is its focus on standardized test scores. English has been a part of its elementary curriculum since 1977, and yet schools still struggle with the amount of time spent on English instruction and the quality of the instruction (Inn-Chull, 2008). This has fomented the extensive after-school programs in the private sector, where students can spend up to 15 hours outside of school studying English, Chinese, Japanese, or other academic-focused topics. The focus for these programs is on improving test scores, which is the gateway to a university education and other opportunities for Korean students. While the system is moving toward more fluency in languages, this focus on test-taking and content skills has had negative consequences for overall language acquisition for all students and in areas such as creative thinking and communicative language skills.

This system has also created an incredibly expansive private sector of schools (*hagwons*) throughout South Korea. In essence, these private schools foster a system where the families with the most means can access private educational services that improve a student's chance to pass critical exams, such as the KSAT, NEAT®, or TOEFL®, with families spending billions of dollars per year (Jeon, 2012; Mihyon, 2012). This system also puts pressure on the students, who attend these private institutes for hours after school, on weekends, and during school breaks. Despite the expense and time spent on an English education outside public schools, there is still concern that South Korean students, on average, do not do as well as other countries on standardized tests such as the TOEFL® (Park, 2009).

The government is taking steps to address this inequity in English education with the NEAT® and changes to the English curriculum in public schools. Increasing standards for teachers of English, focusing more on communicative and creative skills, and testing fluency on the NEAT® are all ways the system is moving toward a more effective approach to English education. New teachers in Korea will find that, because all Korean children have to take English, they will find students at various levels of English proficiency in their classes. It will take some time to see how effective this new approach to SLA is with regard to language fluency and test scores, as the system undergoes some significant changes.

This chapter discussed two countries in Asia with extensive systems of EFL, China and South Korea. The focus was on how EFL has developed in these countries and the current state of those systems as they look today. Both countries have systematic, country-wide approaches to curriculum and instruction, and both invest significant amounts of resources to enhance English language acquisition. The chapter concluded with the challenges those systems are facing in their current form, along with contemporary improvements that these countries are implementing to enrich their overall EFL programs, both public and private.

Summarizing Statements

1. China is one of the most populated countries in the world with an extensive system of English instruction, which is compulsory from elementary school to college.

2. China invests billions of dollars in its EFL system and yet struggles to retain the instructional and curricular resources to maintain that system.

3. South Korea has an extensive public and private system of English language instruction throughout the country.

4. The curriculum and instructional practices in South Korea are fueled by a focus on high-stakes standardized testing and a global approach to success.

5. Families in South Korea invest a significant amount of money in preparing students for success in English and education overall.

REFLECTION AND APPLICATION

1. After reading the chapter on these two countries, did you see some similarities and differences between EFL approaches in China and South Korea? Compare and contrast practices from these countries with your own country (or another with which you are familiar). As a class, share your thoughts on ESL and EFL practices around the world and how they are similar and different.

2. Outside class, do some research online about EFL educational policies around the world. Choose 3–4 different countries to write about and share what you find with the class. As an EFL teacher going overseas or as an ESL teacher with students from different countries in your class, how could different policies and practices affect your classroom dynamic?

3. Reflect on what was discussed regarding the impact standardized testing has had on EFL curriculum in these two countries. What knowledge do you have about standardized testing and its impact on ESL/EFL curriculum in your current teaching situation? If you are a teacher, share your personal experiences with the class; if you are a student, discuss what you have read or seen about standardized testing for ESL/EFL. What are your thoughts on this sometimes controversial topic?

REFERENCES

Chen, G. (2008). The analysis and advice to the situation and policies of English teaching in China. *Foreign Language in China, 5*(2), 4–6.

Dong, Y. (2003). Are we ready for "an early start of foreign language learning": A survey of primary school English education in Guangdong province. *Modern Foreign Language, 26*(1), 39–47.

Inn-Chull, C. (2008). The impact of EFL testing on EFL education in Korea. *Language Testing, 25*(1), 39–62.

Jeon, M. (2012). English immersion and educational inequality in South Korea. *Journal of Multilingual and Multicultural Development, 33*(4), 395–408.

Jin, L., & Cortazzi, M. (2002). English language teaching in China: A bridge to the future. *Asia-Pacific Journal of Education, 22*(2), 53–64.

Liu, J., & Liu, Y. (2008). A survey of English teaching in elementary school in the rural area of western China. *New Curriculum Research, 125*, 151–153.

Liu, Q. (2009). English language teaching in rural areas and the strategies of improvement. *Journal of Huannan Normal University, 11*, 127–128.

Mihyon, J. (2012). English immersion and educational inequality in South Korea. *Journal of Multilingual and Multicultural Development, 33*(4), 395–408.

Park, J. (2009). English fever in South Korea: Its history and symptoms. *English Today, 25*(1), 50–57.

Seth, M. (2012). Education zeal, state control and citizenship in South Korea. *Citizenship Studies, 16*(1), 13–28.

Wu, Y. (2001). English language teaching in China: Trends and challenges. *TESOL Quarterly, 35*(1), 191–194.

Chapter 15

Technology-Transformed Language Learning

This chapter details various ways that technology has transformed ESL/EFL teaching modalities today. The **SAMR** (Substitution, Augmentation, Modification, Redefinition) and the **TPACK** (Technological Pedagogical and Content Knowledge) models are used to frame how technology has influenced education, with a special emphasis on knowledge, language activities, and effective technology activities. Last, this chapter provides examples of the technology being used today in the language classroom.

Technology and the Language Classroom

While the face-to-face language classroom is currently the most popular method for learning another language worldwide, technology is quickly catching up to the point that language learners feel they could learn a second language even without the access to a teacher or curriculum in a single physical space. Technology has transformed the classroom space into one that can include students from all over the world in one classroom, with no travel needed. There is still some resistance to the idea that language can be learned fully without the guidance of a physically present teacher, but as technology creates accessible situations where both formal and informal interactive communication can take place, what was resistance is turning into support. Table 15.1 illustrates some examples as to how technology has transformed the educational classroom of today, including the language classroom.

Table 15.1:   The Language Classrooms of Today

Traditional	Technology Based
Face-to-face classes where students meet their teacher physically on a regular basis, with minor contribution from technology-based pedagogy	Mixed-mode or hybrid classes, where students still study in a classroom setting with a teacher but the teacher provides a significant portion of the class materials online or the students complete activities and assessments using online materials.
	Fully online classes via online educational platforms (i.e., Blackboard®, Moodle®, or Canvas®) where students do not have any class time but complete all assignments, activities, and assessments online. Activities can be synchronous or asynchronous.
	Fully online websites that offer English materials free to any learner. These sites range from criminal (attempts to download malware to anyone who clicks on the material) to pedagogically sound sites that provide extensive materials and lessons.
	The flipped classroom, where students complete their readings, homework, and preparation prior to coming to the classroom. While technology is not necessary in this model, technology allows students to watch video lectures, read module materials, and access information before coming to class. Classroom time is then devoted to active learning and assessment of learning that has already taken place. (Hung, 2015)

Technology and the Language Teacher

The role of the educator today has inevitably changed because of technology, and language teachers are included in this group. Today's L2 teachers can utilize technologies both inside and outside of the classroom to enhance or transform the lessons and have unprecedented access to freely available online materials. Teachers can find complete lesson plans, texts, lectures, and interactive activities on the internet, some designed for any learner and some designed specifically for the language learner. While some materials are only available for a fee, most materials are freely shared, making the internet one of the most prevalent language curriculums available. This makes the internet a place of community for language teachers from around the world who can share materials and ideas. In a way, it changes the role of a teacher from an individual in the school classroom to one of many teachers whose ideas and materials are all a shared part of the classroom experience.

The language teacher also takes on a different role because of the interactive and communicative dimension of technology. Richards (2015) points out that traditional classrooms have limitations that can impede language learning including class size, time limitations, and curriculum and assessment requirements. Technology allows the teacher to bring more interactive and meaningful material into the classroom, such as videos via YouTube, and provides L2 learners with numerous sources of authentic material, including movies, songs, websites, blogs, and interactive games. With the popularity and prevalence of email, smart phones, and text messaging, students now have greater access to support. Some online classes even require students to have a smart phone so they can record themselves and send the file to the instructor. As students complete activities and assessments at home, if they feel they have misunderstood some aspect of the assignment and if their teacher says it is okay, they can email or text their teacher to correct themselves before they turn in the assignment. Or, if their language activity is an interactive, online test, the activity itself provides instant feedback, making the teacher's role one of recorder of information, rather than active participant.

CALL and Teacher Education

The goal of infusing **CALL** (Computer-Assisted Language Learning) into teacher education is to enable teachers to effectively bring technology into their future classrooms. It is no longer a question as to whether teachers will use technology in their curriculum, but how effectively they will use it; as a result, education in how to use current technologies is critical for all teachers (Kassen, Lavine, Murphy-Judy, & Peters, 2007; Kwang Hee, 2010). In fact, the importance of technology in teacher education programs is reflected in the current national standards for teachers by numerous international organizations, including the American Council on the Teaching of Foreign Language (ACTFL), TESOL, the National Board of Professional Teaching Standards (NBPTS), and the Teacher Education Accreditation Council (TEAC). In addition to increasing L2 teachers' confidence in using technology, CALL education positively affects pre- and in-service L2 teachers' attitude toward the use of CALL technology in the classroom (Kwang Hee, 2010). Therefore, as part of preparing to teach in the L2 classroom, it is important that teachers seek out educational opportunities to increase and extend their knowledge of and comfort with CALL technology.

Technology and the Language Student

Language learners also take on very different roles because of technological advances inside and outside of the classroom. While learning a language is still a cognitive process regardless of the methodology, technology certainly has made a difference in how that learning takes place. Inside the classroom, students are often expected to have a certain level of technological savvy, including the ability to use a keyboard on the computer; effectively use the internet; and complete assignments with a technology base, such as blogs, podcasts, or online discussions (Anne & Volker, 2007; Fidaoui, Bahous, & Bacha, 2010; Hashemi & Najafi, 2011; Jia, 2010; Meurant, 2010). Outside the classroom, L2 learners have access to free learning material, material that is interactive and provides instant feedback for language learning, or Web-based Language Learning (WBLL). While there are certainly differences in the quality of materials and differences in how that material is presented, in this online environment L2 students have more control over how they learn a language, when they can study, and where they access materials (see Loucky 2010 for an annotated list of text-based sites). This is a distinct broadening of the definition of language learning and of how and when learners acquire language.

The Effectiveness of Computer-Mediated Instruction

When looking at the research into CALL and **TELL** (technology-enhanced language learning), the question of how effective technology is at assisting L2 learners acquire language is overwhelmingly positive (Miyazoe & Anderson, 2010; Son, 2007; Wen-chi Vivian, Ling Ling, & Marek, 2011), with some studies reporting less than positive results when integrating technology into the language classroom (Lin, Lin, & Hsu, 2011; Matsumura & Hann, 2004). What studies do make clear is that more research is always needed to continually evaluate whether technology is delivering on its promise of enhancing instruction. According to Reynard (2003), "Current CMDE (Computer-mediated distance education) research tends to divide itself into two areas: technical (programming, software, and hardware) and pedagogical (how the teaching and learning will happen, i.e., the instructional design). What is most often missing, however, is an examination of the intent and application of the learning taking place and its significance to individual learning goals; that is, a critical look at the main purpose and the wider significance of the learning to personal and societal growth" (p. 126). The Technological Pedagogical Content Knowledge (TPACK) (see Figure 15.1) is a framework that attempts to do just that (www.tpack. org). It displays the knowledge that teachers need to use technology in the classroom effectively.

Figure 15.1:   Technological Pedagogical and Content Knowledge Framework (www.tpack. org)

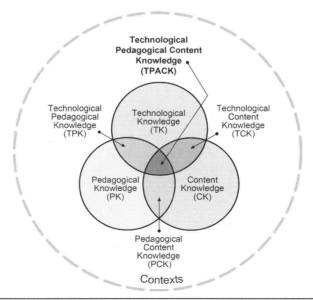

The TPACK framework emphasizes the interconnectedness of three types of knowledge—**Technology** (TK), **Pedagogy** (PK), **Content** (CK)—with a fourth kind of knowledge that develops when the various knowledges intersect, or **Technological Pedagogical Content Knowledge** (TPACK). (See www.tpack.org for more detail about this model.) What this figure illustrates is that when technology is introduced into the language classroom, L2 learners develop integrated knowledge through this intersection of content (language), pedagogy (teaching of language), and technology (computers) that is unique to each situation. This is consistent with what CALL experts in the field prioritize in terms of research focus for using technology in the language classroom—pedagogy and design of learning activities (Levy, Hubbard, Stockwell, & Colpaert, 2015).

TPACK Frame and Teaching the Language Skills

Teaching Reading

Chapter 9 showed that in an L2 Reading class students traditionally work with a piece of text under the guidance of the teacher. To refresh, reading is a cognitive process that happens when readers receive and interpret language in print, and comprehension takes place when the L2 reader successfully decodes and interprets the information contained in the text. The L2 reading class is often divided into pre-, during-, and post-reading activities that are centered on a piece of text that is at the appropriate level for the reading. Technology allows the teacher to enhance these pre-, during-, and post-reading activities, while keeping the focus on sound L2 reading skills. However, studies have shown that when L2 learners use technology and the strategies they have been taught when reading (e.g., looking up vocabulary word in dictionary or clicking on active links to deepen understanding) their overall reading comprehension improves, as does their ability to use more strategies (Akkakoson, 2013). Table 15.2 lists some of technological innovations that can be utilized in designing L2 reading activities with technology.

Teaching Writing

The goal of the writing instructor, as discussed in Chapter 10, is to provide a foundation for the language learner to understand linguistic principles and be able to use appropriate language for the assignment. Students need micro-writing skills, such as knowing sentence structure in English, and macro-skills, such as understanding acceptable forms of English for the assignment. Because technology has changed the way that learning takes place, it has also changed writing practices and pedagogy (Edwards-Groves, 2012). Teachers can use the pre-, during-, and post-writing model to teach the skills need for effective writing in the language. Table 15.3 provides some ideas for how technology can improve and enhance writing activities in the L2 classroom.

Table 15.2: Technology in Reading Activities

Content	Pedagogy	Technology
Understanding vocabulary within the text	Pre-reading	The teacher posts vocabulary words to the class website prior to a reading in class. Students look up and post their own definitions of the vocabulary before class and share those definitions in class before reading.
Clarifying content and understanding vocabulary within the text	During-reading	Students in a computer lab can use open-source screen readers such as Natural Readers® (www.naturalreaders.com) to listen to native speakers read the text after they have read the text once or twice. This can help to clarify words or pronunciation as they read.
Reflecting on the purpose of the text	Post-reading	Students post their ideas on the purpose of the text on a class blog. They read other students' opinions about the text and discuss the similarities and differences with each other.

Table 15.3: Technology in Writing Activities

Content	Pedagogy	Technology
Brainstorming ideas about the subject	Pre-writing	Students access Research Guides available online through university libraries (or free through online public libraries). Using the A–Z guides, students pick a general writing topic and then look up the sub-topics displayed through the online databases. They then use these to find three sources for their own writing.
Thinking about the purpose and audience for the writing	During-writing	Teachers set up a Google doc or Open Office document for pairs of students. Students can write freely and see what their partners are writing, allowing them to help each other stay focused on the topic and audience together.
Proofreading and editing for spelling and grammar	Post-writing	Instead of giving a grade on the first draft of a piece of writing, teachers use the written Comment Tool in Microsoft Word or oral Screencasting to give oral feedback to student on their writing [See Bitchener, Young, & Cameron (2005) and Edwards, Dujardin, & Williams (2012)] for more information on Screencasting in L2 writing.] Students must review and edit their work based on these comments before resubmitting to the teacher.

Teaching Speaking

Chapter 8 discussed how developing both accuracy and fluency is necessary in L2 speech. Communicative competence is built through speaking activities that target both accuracy and fluency in oral language. The introduction of interactive approaches to teaching speaking into classrooms (such as the use of Clickers®—audience response systems that allow students to instantly provide feedback, answer questions, and vote in response to questions teachers pose) changes the way L2 learners learn and the way teachers teach. In other words, technology can transform the methods we use to teach in the classroom and, therefore, the way students learn language skills such as speaking (Agbatogun, 2014). Table 15.4 looks at tasks for the classroom using pre-speaking, during-speaking, and post-speaking tasks, just as we have done with teaching of the language skills in other chapters.

Teaching Listening

Chapter 7 focused on the importance of teaching listening in conjunction with other L2 skills, such as speaking or writing. One pedagogical framework within the Listening classroom focuses on listener functions and listener responses, a helpful tool in designing listening activities. Additionally, listening activities can be classified according to purpose, such as listening for main ideas,

Table 15.4: Technology in Speaking Activities

Content	Pedagogy	Technology
Setting the context for the task	Pre-speaking	Before students give a speech in class, they look up 10 YouTube videos of EFL speeches (Fastrack English has many videos of speech contest winners on YouTube). Teachers ask students to note specific speech components, such as the opening, closing, tone, pronunciation, and content.
Focusing on fluency while speaking	During-speaking	Students are required to record themselves speaking on a designated topic for one minute using their smart phones, tablets, or computers. They listen to their own speeches, focusing on the use of fillers (such as *oh* and *um*), speed of the speech, and silences between words or sentences. They record again and share the recording with a classmate focusing on the same issues.
Listening and evaluating accuracy in speech	Post-speaking	Using the English Pronunciation App® (by KEPHAM on Google Play), students can speak into their technology devices and get instant feedback on their accuracy. They can also watch and listen to videos on vowels, consonants, tongue positions, and voice/unvoiced sounds.

details, or inference. Research into the use of technology in the L2 listening classroom (e.g., using podcasts) has demonstrated that technology can enhance listening comprehension in addition to listening strategies (Rahimi & Katal, 2012). The three stages of listening activities in Table 15.5 are organized around these principles within the framework of pre-, during-, and post-listening.

Cultural Issues for Language Learners and Technology

While technology can positively impact and enhance the L2 classroom in many cases, the language classroom can have some distinctive characteristics that impact the effectiveness of CALL. There are cultural, linguistic, and sociocultural issues that need to be considered when choosing the right technology for the classroom or when determining how that technology is best adapted to the environment. For example, Winke, Goertler, and Amuzie (2010) found that ESL learners of less commonly taught languages (such as Tagalog or Vietnamese) and ESL students who speak a language that does not use the Roman alphabet report less computer literacy than their Romance language–based counterparts who speak commonly taught languages (such as Spanish or German). When looking at participation in online discussions, Campbell (2007) found that East and Southeast Asian students may have difficulty joining in online classroom discussions, often because of cultural prohibitions related to challenging authority or debating a topic in a

Table 15.5:   Technology in Listening Activities

Content	Pedagogy	Technology
Pre-setting the context of the listening	Pre-listening	Before students listen to a speech about transportation advances around the world, for example, the teacher sends them to Instagram® to search for transportation. Students pick 10 pictures and captions in order to learn the vocabulary about transportation and contextualize what they will be hearing with visuals.
Focusing on information transfer during the listening	During-listening	In a computer lab setting or through a teacher-recorded audio message, students create a Doodle Poll® while they listen to the teacher describe the aspects of the poll. The teacher orally explains the days, times, and text needed to create a free Doodle Poll. The students then must invite other students to participate in the poll. Teachers can then review the polls to determine student listening comprehension.
Integrating listening with writing	Post-listening	Teachers choose 5 current movies and send students to www.rottentomatoes.com. The students must watch the movie trailers and read some of the reviews of those movies. They then must write a synopsis of the movie and summarize a review based on the numerous reviews listed.

Figure 15.2:   Learner Proficiencies for Online Activities

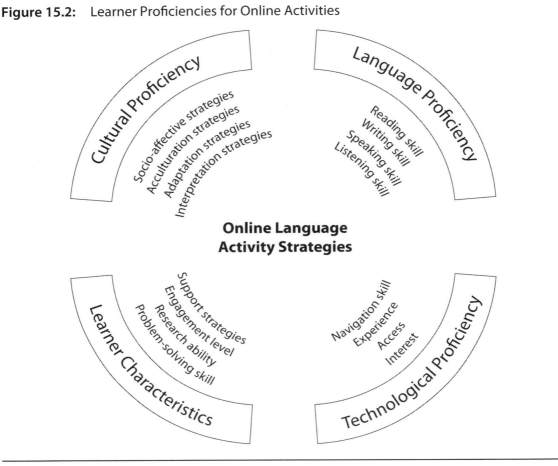

classroom setting. Loucky (2010), in his model for adapting online reading strategies for L2 learners, includes two aspects of success related to culture (background knowledge) and computer skill. Two further components in his model include language proficiency and content (text topic and difficulty level). Figure 15.2 offers an adaptation of his model to include culture when looking at strategies student use and need when participating in online activities, such as interactive discussions.

Use of Social Media

Social media, including platforms like Facebook®, Instagram®, Kik®, and Wikipedia®, which allow users to create and share content or to participate in social networking, are powerful tools for the L2 classroom. They create opportunities for language learners to authentically engage with other speakers worldwide in English and practice language in a stress-free environment. At the same time, there are serious security, content, and even political concerns with these websites, as some countries filter and block websites that they deem inappropriate. ESL/EFL teachers need to be aware of the policies of the countries in which they teach and also be aware that international students in their classrooms may have little understanding and knowledge of social media and other websites that might be used for education. For that reason, including common sense social media or internet use strategies in the L2 classroom can be very valuable for ESL and EFL students. These sessions can be focused on security (e.g., avoiding malware and viruses), safety (e.g., avoiding inappropriate or inaccurate content), and personal protection (e.g., not posting pictures or personal information). One website with free materials for teachers is www.commonsensemedia.org/educators. It provides free, research-based materials for K–12 students that could be easily adapted for use with adults in the ESL or EFL classroom. If language teachers plan to use technology, particularly social media or internet-based materials, in the classroom, they should initially ensure that learners understand how important safety, security, and privacy are when using these tools.

Other Technologies and the Language Classroom

CALL and its accompanying internet-based technologies have had a major impact on the diversity of activities that occur inside and outside the ESL/EFL classroom since the 1960s (Warschauer & Healey, 1998). It has changed the way L2 learners write (Edwards-Groves, 2012; Warschauer, 2002), read (Liu, Chen, & Chang, 2010; Zidat & Djoudi, 2010), speak (Carr, 2000; Dekhinet, 2008) and listen (Anne & Volker, 2007).

To discuss the way technology has impacted ESL/EFL activities and classrooms, the SAMR (Substitution, Augmentation, Modification, Redefinition) Model, as created by Rubin R. Puentedura (2010) (see his blog at www.hippasus.com/rrpweblog/) will be used. This model details how technology is used to redefine learning tasks, starting with simpler changes that enhance educational tasks, such as substitution and augmentation, moving toward complex transformation of learning through modifications and redefinition of tasks (Hockly, 2013). See Table 15.6 for how ESL/EFL tasks can be re-designed using technology for various purposes.

Substitution Models

Here technology acts as a tool **substitute**, with no functional change. These models are not attempting to alter the modality of the lesson or significantly alter how the student uses a language skill. Instead, the substitution technology tool enables the teacher and students to present and practice a language skill in a traditional way while taking advantage of a new technology to make it more convenient. Table 15.7 details some examples of routine tools that language instructors and students use which enhance how a skill is delivered but not how it is practiced.

Table 15.6:   SAMR Model

SAMR	Means That	the ESL/EFL Teacher...	the ESL/EFL Students...
Substitution	technology acts as a tool substitute, with no functional change.	wants students to complete a reading, so it can be emailed to them in an attached file rather than printing it for class.	read the text in exactly the same way but use a technological device to make that happen.
Augmentation	technology acts as a direct tool substitute, with functional improvement.	puts the grammar test online, rather than asking students to take class time to complete it.	are able to test get immediate feedback on the test, rather than waiting for the teacher to grade it.
Modification	technology allows for significant task redesign.	creates an audio file on the computer so students can listen and respond to questions related to the information.	can listen to the file again and again to complete the task, rather than listen in class just one time to a person speaking.
Redefinition	technology allows for the creation of new tasks previously inconceivable.	asks the students to record their voices via software that gives them feedback on the correct tone, emphasis, and pronunciation.	receive immediate feedback on their pronunciation, demonstrated visually to enhance their ability to refine it.

Table 15.7:   Traditional vs. Substitution Technology-Based Activities

Traditional	Technology Based
Reading a piece of text in a book, newspaper or magazine	Reading a piece of text in an online book, through a downloaded PDF or through email
Listening to the teacher read a piece of text in order to complete a cloze activity in the classroom	Listening to a song via the computer in order to complete a cloze activity in the classroom
Speaking to a classmate in order to practice a dialogue	Speaking into a microphone attached to the computer in order to record and practice a dialogue
Writing an essay in the classroom with pencil and paper	Writing an essay on the computer in class using the keyboard

Augmentation Models

Here technology acts as a direct tool substitute, with **augmentation** or functional improvement. These types of technology-based tasks differ from substitution tasks in that the technology actually adds a further component of functionality to the task. There is no significant difference in the depth of the learning but more of how the task can be designed and used. See Table 15.8 for some sample tasks.

Modification Models

Here technology allows for significant task re-design, or **modification**. These learning tasks have been modified in such a way with technology that the task itself is actually transformed in some significant way. One particular area of ESL/EFL where technology has modified, or transformed, the way certain tasks are accomplished is in the area of assessment. From assessment in the classroom to internationally recognized standardized tests, technology has transformed how evaluation is accomplished in the language classroom. For example, language students can receive immediate feedback on their tasks and correct their errors immediately, transforming the process of error correction and feedback. Table 15.9 details just a few of the ways in which technological advances have transformed how teachers assess L2 learner progress in the language.

Table 15.8:   Traditional vs. Augmentation Technology-Based Activities

Traditional	Technology Based
The teacher uses a blackboard or whiteboard to present new grammar content.	The teacher uses a SmartBoard to present new grammar content to students, using the interactive features to have students check online for examples.
Students read a book and use a dictionary to assist with new vocabulary.	Students read a digital book, which allows them to look up new vocabulary as they read.
Students take notes in class with a paper and pencil.	Students take notes in class with a digital recording, which they can listen to over and over.
Students write an essay on paper and turn it into the teacher for feedback.	Students write an essay on the computer, send it via email to the entire class, and get feedback from everyone before turning it into the teacher.

Table 15.9: Traditional vs. Modification Technology-Based Assessment Activities

Task	Traditional Assessment	Technology-Based Assessment
Grammar tasks	On a paper-based test, students complete multiple choice grammar tasks. The test is turned in and graded by the teacher, and then the student eventually receives feedback on the test.	On a computer-based test, students click on the answer for grammar questions. When they are done with the test, students receive immediate feedback on their test score.
Reading tasks	On a paper-based test, students read a text and complete open-ended questions about the text. The test is turned in and graded by the teacher, and then the student eventually receives feedback on the test.	A language teacher designates a time to test students; students then must read the text and answer within 3 minutes, using the appropriate social context and language.
Writing tasks	On a paper-based test, students read a prompt and write a response. The test is turned in and graded by the teacher, and then the student eventually receives feedback on the test.	On a standardized test, students use the computer to write in a response to a reading. They submit their responses via the computer. The tests are graded by a computer-based grading system and by people as a backup.
Listening tasks	Students listen to the teacher read a piece of text, and they write exactly what they hear. The tests are turned in and graded by the teacher, and then the students receive feedback on the test.	Students in an EFL class in Bangladesh listen to Martin Luther King, Jr.'s *I Have a Dream* speech via YouTube and then respond to questions about what they hear and how it relates to them.
Speaking tasks	The teacher interviews students, giving them open-ended questions. Students must answer appropriately. The teacher uses a rubric to score the session and gives feedback to students after the test.	Using the software included in the supplementary media provided by speaking textbooks, L2 students record their speech samples. Then, based on those recordings, the software provides individualized feedback as to how close pronunciation is to native-speaker pronunciation.
Integrated tasks	On a reading-writing test, students must read a piece of text and then write a response using material gleaned from the text. The students turn in their essays to be graded and returned at a later date.	In a testing situation, language students read a text on the computer and then listen to a lecture related to the reading. Using both listening/reading skills, students combine the information from both sections and answer questions.

Table 15.10:   Redefinition Technology-Based Activities

Language Skill	Technology	Technology Based
Listening	radio/TV/ internet/ smart phones	L2 learners around the world can listen to English songs on the radio, watch English-based programs on TV, and listen to millions of podcasts through the internet or on their smart phones.
Reading	internet/ smart phones	Students can use an online corpus (e.g., the British National Corpus www.natcorp.ox.ac.uk/corpus/index.xml), which is an interactive listing of the most common occurrences of a particular feature or combination of features in English texts. L2 learners can research English phrases, prepositions, or collocations in their readings. This can be a valuable tool for both the teacher and the student in determining widely used English language features in reading texts (Chen, Huang, Chang, & Liou, 2015).
Writing	internet	L2 learners can write for an international audience, sharing their writing through blogs or online sharing sites like wikipedia.
Speaking	VoIP (Voice over Internet Protocol)	Using Skype®, L2 learners can communicate directly with a native English speaker, having an interactive, communicative experience with the native speaker, regardless of where they live.

Redefinition Models

Here technology allows for the creation of new tasks previously inconceivable, or **redefined** ones. This is where language learning through technology gets interesting. With redefined learning tasks, L2 learners use technology in a way that fully transforms access to information, how that information is used, how they learn that information, and how they process and retain that information. In some cases, the traditional role of the human teacher is completely redefined, or even made irrelevant to the educational process. Another aspect of redefinition involves access. With the advent of technology from radio to the internet, language learners from around the world have unprecedented access to the English language in ways that were never imagined. Table 15.10 details a few technologies that have transformed the way L2 learners learn, use, and acquire language.

Distance Learning and the L2 Classroom

In addition to enhancing and transforming language learning activities, technology has completely altered the L2 classroom itself. **Distance education** involves learning with physical distance between the learner and the instructor and no regular or direct contact between the two in the classroom "space." Distance learning has been around for many years in various iterations. Distance education flows with the development of technology, adapting and taking advantage of the latest technology to attract new learners.

The advent of the computer and internet access, though, has taken distance learning to a new level of accessibility and volume. Today, online learning is talked about rather than distance learning. There have been significant changes not only to how materials are delivered but also to the focus of that education. What began as primarily a mode for vocational courses has become an increasing trend for public education (such as Alaska's Learning Network and the Florida Virtual School, both of which are fully online K–12 schools in the United States) and terminal higher education degrees (such as Great Britain's Open University and the U.S.'s University of Phoenix). Along the way, there has been much discussion and research devoted to determining if an online education is of the same quality and standard as a more traditional classroom-based learning environment. In a comparative bibliography of 355 studies of distance education programs, Russell (2001) found that while there can be differences in quality and interactivity depending on the course, overall there is no significant difference in the quality of education when comparing similar classroom and online learning environments. In the L2 classroom of today, there are even fewer restrictions on what an L2 learner can do inside and outside the classroom to enhance language acquisition. The availability of the English language through websites, social media, and online networking provides even greater opportunities for meaningful and authentic language use than those in traditional classroom setting (Richards, 2015).

When discussing distance or online learning and the ESL/EFL classroom, it is important to consider what the acceptable methodologies of language teaching are at the present time (Toffoli & Sockett, 2015). When the model for language education was focused on reading, writing, and grammar translation (see Chapter 1), these language skills were the focus of the methodology used in the classroom and distance language learning through written correspondence was considered acceptable. Students were sent readings and lessons through the mail, and they were to read, translate, and complete activities that were then mailed in to the teacher for review. With the advent of radio and TV, and certainly with the transition to a more communicative model in the language classroom (see Chapter 2), more oral-based language lessons were not only possible through the new medium but also current with the teaching philosophy for language at the time. For example, in contrast to the earlier correspondence courses, in televised language courses, students were expected to do more listening than reading, and lessons were focused on accent and pronunciation, rather than reading and writing.

The Future of Technology in the Language Classroom

Certainly, technology impacts how we learn and live. Language learning is forever changed because of technological advances, and conceptually, teachers look at how language is learned in a different way. Because technology will continue to advance, the L2 classroom will continue to evolve with it. With the advent of new ways of learning, such as with the freely available Kahn Academy and with accessibility to technology increasing daily (see http://one.laptop.org/), if L2 educators do not stay ahead of technology, technology can leave them behind. We are not advocating for embracing all types of technology at all times, as the classroom educator needs to carefully evaluate what technology is appropriate, accessible, and effective for the students. L2 students of today, though, embrace TELL, and because it improves their technological skills, increases their language skill, and assists with their career goals, it is the future of the language classroom.

This chapter discussed distance learning and its impact on the language classroom. It used the SAMR Model to delineate ways to enhance the language classroom using technology, including how CALL and TELL have impacted how L2 is learned. Technology has changed the way that teachers teach, and students learn. Readers were introduced to the TPACK concept, which focuses on how knowledge differs in a technology-mediated classroom.

Summarizing Statements

1. Distance learning has a long history in education, and the advent of the computer and internet have had great influence on the language classroom of today.

2. The SAMR Model of how technology is integrated into learning provides a solid foundation for discussing the varying levels of TELL in the L2 classroom.

3. Because of technological advances, many L2 learners must develop more integrated skills to succeed in the classroom of today, including technological, language, and learning skills (the TPACK concept).

4. Technological advances inside and outside the L2 classroom encourage learners to develop the integrated skills of technological knowledge, pedagogical knowledge, and content knowledge (TPACK) to boost the language learning process.

5. L2 teachers must keep in mind that there are cultural considerations, and sometimes drawbacks, when introducing technology into the classroom. Careful consideration must be made as to the pedagogical value of any technology used.

REFLECTION AND APPLICATION

1. Table 15.6 introduces the SAMR Model and what roles the L2 teacher and ESL student take in a classroom when using various technology-enhanced activities. Think about how the role of the teacher has changed over the years due to technological advances. List five or six ways that technology has changed the teacher role in the ESL/EFL class of today. Do you like these changes, or do you feel that the role of teacher has changed too much over the years?

2. Technology has had a significant impact on current L2 activities and assessments. Tables 15.2–15.5 detail some ways that activities and assessments have changed with advancing technology. For each language skill (reading, writing, listening, speaking), list one ESL/EFL activity and/or one assessment technique that uses technology to enhance how it is accomplished. Share these activities/assessments with the class.

3. In what ways has technology changed your own work as a student and/or a teacher? Reflect on the role technology plays in the current classroom and how it has impacted what a language teacher does. What impact has technology had on the ESL/EFL classroom, both positive and negative?

REFERENCES

Agbatogun, A. O. (2014). Developing learners' second language communicative competence through active learning: Clickers or communicative approach? *Journal of Educational Technology & Society, 17*(2), 257–269.

Akkakoson, S. (2013). The relationship between strategic reading instruction, student learning of L2-based reading strategies and L2 reading achievement. *Journal of Research in Reading, 36*(4), 422–450.

Anne, O., & Volker, H. (2007). Integrating CALL into the classroom: The role of podcasting in an ESL listening strategies course. *Recall, 19*(2), 162–180.

Bitchener, J., Young, S., & Cameron, D. (2005). The effect of different types of corrective feedback on ESL student writing. *Journal of Second Language Writing, 14,* 191–205.

Campbell, N. (2007). Bringing ESL students out of their shells: Enhancing participation through online discussion. *Business Communication Quarterly, 70*(1), 37–43.

Carr, S. (2000). A professor goes online to teach pronunciation. *Chronicle of Higher Education, 46*(43), A44.

Chen, M., Huang, S., Chang, J., & Liou, H. (2015). Developing a corpus-based paraphrase tool to improve EFL learners' writing skills. *Computer Assisted Language Learning, 28*(1), 22–40.

Dekhinet, R. (2008). Online enhanced corrective feedback for ESL learners in higher education. *Computer Assisted Language Learning, 21*(5), 409–425.

Edwards, K., Dujardin, A., & Williams, N. (2012). Screencast feedback for essays on a distance learning MA in Professional Communication: An action research project. *Journal of Academic Writing, 2*(1), 95–126.

Edwards-Groves, C. (2012). Interactive creative technologies: Changing learning practices and pedagogies in the writing classroom. *Australian Journal of Language & Literacy, 35*(1), 99–113.

Fidaoui, D., Bahous, R., & Bacha, N. N. (2010). CALL in Lebanese elementary ESL writing classrooms. *Computer Assisted Language Learning, 23*(2), 151–168.

Hashemi, M., & Najafi, V. (2011). Using blogs in English language writing classes. *International Journal of Academic Research, 3*(4), 599–604.

Hockly, N. (2013). Mobile learning. *ELT Journal, 67*(1), 80–84.

Hung, H. (2015). Flipping the classroom for English language learners to foster active learning. *Computer Assisted Language Learning, 28*(1), 81–96.

Jia, L. (2010). Learning vocabulary via computer-assisted scaffolding for text processing. *Computer Assisted Language Learning, 23*(3), 253–275.

Kassen, M. A., Lavine, R. Z., Murphy-Judy, K., & Peters, M. (Eds.). (2007). *Preparing and developing technology-proficient L2 teachers: CALICO Monograph Series* (Vol. 6.). San Marcos, TX: Computer Assisted Language Institution Consortium (CALICO).

Kwang Hee, H. (2010). CALL teacher education as an impetus for L2 teachers in integrating technology. *Recall, 22*(1), 53–69.

Levy, M., Hubbard, P., Stockwell, G., & Colpaert, J. (2015). Research challenges in CALL. *Computer Assisted Language Learning, 28*(1), 1–6.

Lin, M., Lin, C., & Hsu, P. (2011). The unrealistic claims for the effects of classroom blogging on English as a second language students' writing performance. *British Journal of Educational Technology, 42*(6), E148–E151.

Liu, D., & Jiang, P. (2009). Using a corpus-based lexicogrammatical approach to grammar instruction in EFL and ESL contexts. *Modern Language Journal, 93*(1), 61–78.

Liu, P., Chen, C., & Chang, Y. (2010). Effects of a computer-assisted concept mapping learning strategy on EFL college students' English reading comprehension. *Computers & Education, 54*(2), 436–445.

Loucky, J. (2010). Constructing a roadmap to more systematic and successful online reading and vocabulary acquisition. *Literary & Linguistic Computing, 25*(2), 225–241.

Matsumura, S., & Hann, G. (2004). Computer anxiety and students' preferred feedback methods in EFL writing. *Modern Language Journal, 88*(3), 403–415.

Meurant, R. C. (2010). iPad tablet computing to foster Korean EFL digital literacy. *International Journal of U- & E-Service, Science & Technology, 3*(4), 49–62.

Miyazoe, T., & Anderson, T. (2010). Learning outcomes and students' perceptions of online writing: Simultaneous implementation of a forum, blog, and wiki in an EFL blended learning setting. *System, 38*(2), 185–199.

Puentedura, R. (2010). *SAMR and TPCK: Intro to advanced practice*. Retrieved from http://goo.gl/78UJn

Rahimi, M., & Katal, M. (2012). The role of metacognitive listening strategies awareness and podcast-use readiness in using podcasting for learning English as a foreign language. *Computers in Human Behavior, 28*(4), 1153–1161.

Reynard, R. (2003). Internet-based ESL for distance adult students—A framework for dynamic language learning. *Canadian Modern Language Review, 60*(2), 123–142.

Richards, J. C. (2015). The changing face of language learning: Learning beyond the classroom. *RELC Journal, 46*(1), 5–22.

Russell, T. (2001). *The no significant difference phenomenon as reported in 355 research reports, summaries, and papers: A comparative research annotated bibliography on technology for distance education*. Raleigh, NC: Office of Instructional Telecommunications.

Son, J. (2007). Learner experiences in web-based language learning. *Computer Assisted Language Learning, 20*(1), 21–36.

Toffoli, D., & Sockett, G. (2015). University teachers' perceptions of Online Informal Learning of English (OILE). *Computer Assisted Language Learning, 28*(1), 7–21.

Warschauer, M. (2002). Networking into academic discourse. *Journal of English for Academic Purposes, 1*(1), 45.

Warschauer, M., & Healey, D. (1998). Computers and language learning: An overview. *Language Teaching, 31*(02), 57–71.

Wen-chi Vivian, W., Ling Ling, Y., & Marek, M. (2011). Using online EFL interaction to increase confidence, motivation, and ability. *Journal of Educational Technology & Society, 14*(3), 118–129.

Winke, P., Goertler, S., & Amuzie, G. L. (2010). Commonly taught and less commonly taught language learners: Are they equally prepared for CALL and online language learning? *Computer Assisted Language Learning, 23*(3), 199–219.

Zidat, S., & Djoudi, M. (2010). Effects of an online learning on EFL university students' English reading comprehension. *International Review on Computers & Software, 5*(2), 186–192.

Final Notes on Integrating Curriculum Design with Teaching Activities

Chapter 1 introduced four likely scenarios an ESL or EFL teacher might encounter while working in the TESOL field. Let's see how those teachers have used the information presented in this book to meet those challenges unique to each scenario.

Four Scenarios in TESOL

Scenario 1: EFL in Turkey

After graduating from the university with a master's degree in TESOL, Emily has moved to Turkey to take the position of an EFL instructor in a university English language program. The English program is brand-new, so there is no formal curriculum in place. The director of the program has asked Emily to develop and design the English language curriculum for the entire program.

After reading this book, Emily created an entire EFL language course curriculum for her Turkish school. She began by utilizing a Likert-scale needs analysis she modeled after the information presented in Chapter 5, determining the needs of the students in the school and the needs of the teachers of those courses. In collaboration with the other teachers, Emily set the broad goals for the program, which included goals related to speaking, listening, reading, and writing as the program director wanted. Emily and the teachers then turned those into specific objectives that were inserted into the syllabi for varying levels of students introduced in Chapter 5. The EFL teachers in the school felt the skills based–syllabus model presented in Chapter 6 best fit the needs of their current student population.

The teachers then worked together as a team to come up with activities that would meet objectives on the syllabus. Emily used the models in Chapters 7 to 11 to ensure that the activities met the set objectives. Because Emily was working with both native Turkish teachers and native English–speaking teachers from various countries, she took advantage of their combined knowledge of culture as well as information from Chapter 12 on incorporating a cultural component in activities. Turkish culture and Australian, American, and British cultural information were represented in class activities and dialogues, from lifestyle differences to dialogue styles. Emily also made sure that there were various types of assessment for students, from informal to formal, based on the set objectives. While Emily knows the curriculum will change based on information gathered as she and her colleagues teach, she also feels that they created a well-rounded curriculum to get started.

Scenario 2: ESL in the United States

José is teaching English at a language school affiliated with a state college in the United States. His institution has received a technology grant to upgrade the language lab. José has been asked to review and revise the language school's existing curriculum to ensure that technology will be utilized consistently throughout the curriculum.

José really enjoyed his task, since he had a budget to order technology for his school. After consulting this book, he decided to use an open-ended needs analysis as presented in Chapter 5 to gather information from his students and fellow faculty members. This analysis revealed that both groups were frustrated by the lack of interactive programs on their computer systems, and students, in particular, wanted to be able to practice English on their own in the computer lab. José decided that he needed to redefine how they used technology as explained in Chapter 15 and asked a task force of teachers and students to review English language software that would be useful for class activities and for individual ESL practice. In the end, the committee selected two programs that fit their needs. They decided to institute a needs analysis survey every year so students and teachers could share their up-to-date knowledge of programs to include in the lab.

Scenario 3: ESOL in the United States

Lindsey is a lead teacher for ESOL at her middle school. The school is adapting new ESOL standards required by the state. Lindsey's responsibility is to create a new syllabus for the ESOL classes offered to English learners as well as choose the accompanying textbook and supplementary materials. She also has to update every lesson plan integrating the new standards.

Lindsey knew she could not accomplish this task alone, so she pulled in English Language Arts and ESOL teachers from every grade for input. She passed out copies of the new standards and the syllabi examples from Chapter 6 so they could agree on which type of syllabus would work best with the new ESOL standards and also be appropriate for different grade levels. The teachers decided they wanted to use the same syllabus format for all grades, as required by the state, and felt that eclectic syllabi provided the best model as they could incorporate both knowledge and skill objectives into the syllabi. Lindsey also focused on some of the reading activity suggestions from Chapter 9, as the new state ESOL standards have a strong focus in reading.

Teachers were particularly concerned that their ESOL students were not doing well on the annual state-mandated test in reading. Lindsey and the team of teachers incorporated both intensive and extensive reading activities from Chapter 9 into their syllabi, both of which met the new state standards and added a new dimension for ESOL students in reading. The teachers felt that choosing activities appropriate not only for ESOL students but also for their students in general would help them prepare for the next test. After reading about the importance of vocabulary development for ESOL students detailed in Chapter 9, the team of teachers also decided to add some visual and contextual elements to their vocabulary work to assist ESOL students who may be struggling. In the end, it was not as challenging as Lindsey feared, and the teachers felt they could support each other even further with the consistency across their curriculum.

Scenario 4: EFL in South Korea

At his South Korean university, Hoyoung has been asked to teach a Listening class for one of his colleagues who had to leave suddenly. He has never taught a Listening class before, and the class starts in two days. He not only has to prepare a lesson plan but also has to lead two teaching and assessment activities for that day.

Hoyoung felt that time was of the essence. With only a few days to prepare, he quickly turned to the syllabus models presented in Chapter 6. He decided he would create a syllabus based on skill development, since listening is a critical skill for the EFL students who get very little English language input outside the classroom. Using the information in Chapter 7, Hoyoung incorporated the general pre-listening, listening, and post-listening model to create a number of activities for those first few days. He felt that if he used this model and included evaluation for each activity, it would help him to determine the level of the students and identify areas where students needed more work. He also decided to incorporate a needs analysis (Chapter 5) that would help him identify topics of interest to the students. Since Chapter 7 gave him some guidelines on which listening materials were appropriate for which level, he would use the needs analysis and level information to find content that was both challenging and interesting.

The first day of class, Hoyoung passed out a paper and used an oral, open-ended series of questions that would both determine need and provide feedback on student levels. He also used a video that had various listening activities. Hoyoung collected those papers to increase his knowledge about the student level and interest in this type of activity. Using that first day to both teach and collect information about his students worked great, and he felt he could plan the rest of the class session in a more effective manner.

After reading this book, we hope that this integrated approach between curriculum and teaching in TESOL contexts has given you the confidence to rise up and meet any challenge you might have to face in your English language classroom. Whether you teach children in fourth grade, adults in a community college in the United States, or university-bound students in Japan, this book will guide you through the entire process, from identifying needs to creating activities and assessments. Our intention has been to provide you with a strong foundation in SLA, language curriculum design, and English language teaching principles. Now it's your turn to apply what you've learned here to your current or future English language classroom!

Appendix: The International Phonetic Alphabet

English Consonants

Symbol	Manner of Articulation	Examples
[p]	voiceless bilabial stop	pan, sip, apple
[b]	voiced bilabial stop	bat, ruby, about
[t]	voiceless alveolar stop	touch, lot, laptop
[d]	voiced alveolar stop	dip, sod, adult
[k]	voiceless velar stop	car, tack, acorn
[g]	voiced velar stop	go, log, agog
[ʔ]	voiceless glottal stop	button, curtain
[f]	voiceless labiodental fricative	fluff, rough, ruffian
[v]	voiced labiodental fricative	vest, love, clover
[θ]	voiceless interdental fricative	thin, bath, ether
[ð]	voiced interdental fricative	then, rhythm
[s]	voiceless alveolar fricative	snake, bass, decent
[z]	voiced alveolar fricative	zoo, roses
[ʃ]	voiceless palatal fricative	shell, action, ashes
[ʒ]	voiced palatal fricative	visual, rouge, closure
[h]	voiceless glottal fricative	have, hill, house
[tʃ]	voiceless palatal affricate	child, reach, statue
[dʒ]	voiced palatal affricate	original, ridge
[m]	voiced bilabial nasal	man, mom, lamp
[n]	voiced alveolar nasal	nasty, run, ant
[ŋ]	voiced velar nasal	hanger, ringing
[l]	voiced alveolar (lateral) liquid	love, hill, plate
[r]	voiced alveolar liquid	ring, floor, crow
[w]	voiced bilabial glide	wood, awash
[y]	voiced palatal glide	young, canyon
[ɾ]	voiced alveo-palatal flap	tutor, betting

A Description of the English Consonants

	Bilabial	Labiodental	Interdental	Alveolar	Palatal	Velar	Glottal
Stops	[p] [b]			[t] [d]		[k] [g]	[ʔ]
Fricatives		[f] [v]	[θ] [ð]	[s] [z]	[ʃ] [ʒ]		[h]
Affricates					[tʃ] [dʒ]		
Nasals	[m]			[n]		[ŋ]	
Liquids				[l] [r]			
Glides	[w]				[y]		
Flaps				[ɾ]			

English Vowels

Symbol	Articulation	Example
[i]	high front tense	beans, creek, piano
[ɪ]	high front lax	picture, business
[e]	mid front tense	remain, shade, eight
[ɛ]	mid front lax	dispense, internet
[æ]	low front lax	math, act
[u]	high back tense	loot, you
[ʊ]	high back lax	pudding, foot
[ə]	mid central lax (unstressed)	today, about
[ʌ]	mid central lax (stressed)	but, other, oven
[o]	mid back tense	below, thorough
[ɔ]	low back tense	knot, August
[a]	low central tense	pasta, father

Index